Perils of Centralization

In this provocative and wide-ranging book, Ken Kollman examines the histories of the U.S. government, the Catholic Church, General Motors, and the European Union as examples of federated systems that centralized power over time. He shows how their institutions became locked in to intensive power to the executive level. The problem with these and other federated systems is that they often cannot decentralize, even if it makes sense. The analysis leads Kollman to suggest some surprising changes in institutional design for these four cases and for federated institutions everywhere.

Ken Kollman is Frederick G. L. Huetwell Professor, professor of political science, and director of the International Institute at the University of Michigan. He has written numerous books and articles on political parties, political organizations, and elections. His research and written works have been recognized with multiple awards and have contributed in diverse fields such as computational social science, comparative and American politics, European Union studies, and comparative political parties and elections. He is principal investigator of the Constituency-Level Elections Archive, the largest repository of election results data in the world.

Cambridge Studies in Comparative Politics

General Editor

Margaret Levi   University of Washington, Seattle

Assistant General Editors

Kathleen Thelen   Massachusetts Institute of Technology
Erik Wibbels   Duke University

Associate Editors

Robert H. Bates   Harvard University
Gary Cox   Stanford University
Stephen Hanson   The College of William and Mary
Torben Iversen   Harvard University
Stathis Kalyvas   Yale University
Peter Lange   Duke University
Helen Milner   Princeton University
Frances Rosenbluth   Yale University
Susan Stokes   Yale University

Other Books in the Series

Ben W. Ansell, *From the Ballot to the Blackboard: The Redistributive Political Economy of Education*
David Austen-Smith, Jeffry A. Frieden, Miriam A. Golden, Karl Ove Moene, and Adam Przeworski, eds., *Selected Works of Michael Wallerstein: The Political Economy of Inequality, Unions, and Social Democracy*
Andy Baker, *The Market and the Masses in Latin America: Policy Reform and Consumption in Liberalizing Economies*
Lisa Baldez, *Why Women Protest: Women's Movements in Chile*
Stefano Bartolini, *The Political Mobilization of the European Left, 1860–1980: The Class Cleavage*

(*continued after the index*)

Perils of Centralization

Lessons from Church, State, and Corporation

KEN KOLLMAN

University of Michigan

CAMBRIDGE
UNIVERSITY PRESS

CAMBRIDGE
UNIVERSITY PRESS

32 Avenue of the Americas, New York, NY 10013-2473, USA

Cambridge University Press is part of the University of Cambridge.

It furthers the University's mission by disseminating knowledge in the pursuit of
education, learning, and research at the highest international levels of excellence.

www.cambridge.org
Information on this title: www.cambridge.org/9781107616943

First published 2013

Printed in the United States of America

A catalog record for this publication is available from the British Library.

Library of Congress Cataloging in Publication data
Kollman, Ken, 1966–
Perils of centralization: lessons from church, state, and corporation/ Ken Kollman,
University of Michigan, Ann Arbor.
    pages cm
Includes bibliographical references and index.
ISBN 978-1-107-04252-0 (hardback) – ISBN 978-1-107-61694-3 (paperback)
    1. Decentralization in government – Case studies.   2. Decentralization in management – Case
studies.   3. Executive power – Case studies.   4. Decentralization in government – United
States.   5. Decentralization in government – European Union countries.   6. Federal
government – United States.   7. Federal government – European Union countries.   8. General
Motors Corporation – Management – History.   9. Catholic Church – Government – History.
I. Title.
JS113.K65   2013
320.4'049–dc23   2013013921

ISBN 978-1-107-04252-0 Hardback
ISBN 978-1-107-61694-3 Paperback

This book is dedicated to the memories of Pat Dowd, Ann Rieskamp, and Marie Ritchie

Contents

Acknowledgments

I owe debts to many people and institutions for providing help, time, space, and financial support during the period of writing and preparing this book. I am grateful to the Center for Advanced Study in the Behavioral Sciences at Stanford for its generous fellowship. The wonderful colleagues at the center during my time there helped set this project on course. Thanks to them for sitting through my initial attempts to describe this project in several seminars and presentations. In particular, Mike Tomz, Jonathan Rodden, Nancy Burns, Gillian Hadfield, Bob Mnookin, Jack Rakove, and Hayagreeva Rao helped when discussing the content. Daily volleyball games helped blow off steam, and fellow players Robert Bork, Laura Ruetsche, Bengt Sandin, Scott Schwenter, and Gordon Belot were a joy to play the game with. Beyond the folks at the center at Stanford, others were present at Stanford or our paths crossed in other ways during that year: Barry Weingast, Jon Bendor, David Brady, Mariano Tommasi, Robert Inman, Simon Jackman, Ken Scheve, Ken Schultz, Jonathan Wand, Alberto Diaz-Cayeros, Erik Wibbels, and Pradeep Chhibber.

Various units at the University of Michigan, as always throughout my career, provided resources of multiple kinds to sustain me toward completion: the Center for Political Studies, the Department of Political Science, the International Institute, the Rackham School of Graduate Studies, the Center for European Studies and the European Union Center, the Undergraduate Research Opportunity Program (UROP), and the Program in Organizational Studies. The Center for Local, State, and Urban Policy (CLOSUP) at the Gerald R. Ford School of Public Policy provided early funding for research on this topic, for which I am grateful.

Of utmost importance at Michigan are the colleagues who support me, compel me to improve, and push me in new directions. Liz Gerber, Jenna Bednar, John Jackson, Jim Morrow, Skip Lupia, Jon Miller, Nancy Burns, Brian Min, Bob Axelrod, Arlene Saxonhouse, Scott Page, Jim Hines, Bill Clark, Anna

Grzymala-Busse, Greg Dowd, Andy Markovits, Ted Brader, Lisa Disch, Al Stam, Kenneth McElwain, Allen Hicken, Pauline Jones Luong, Andrew Kerner, Robert Mickey, Daniel Halberstam, Michael Heaney, George Tsebelis, Chuck Shipan, Mariah Zeisberg, Pam Brandwein, and Mark Tessler have all listened and reacted to my ideas on the topic. In particular, the ideas of Bednar and Halberstam have shaped my thoughts. Page and Jackson, in distinct ways, have deeply influenced the way I think about social science. Chuck Myers listened often to my ideas on this book and offered useful comments. Pat Lord was helpful in multiple ways toward the end of the process.

The amazing graduate students at Michigan deserve my thanks for multiple reasons. Many of them helped as research assistants on the project: Deniz Erkman, San-Jung Han, Patrick O'Mahen, David Cottrell, Dan Magleby, Ben Goldman, and Mariely Lopez-Santana. Others also were useful to bounce ideas off of: Carolina de Miguel, Janna Bray, Jennifer Miller-Gonzalez, Charles Doriean, Andrew Feher, Tim Ryan, Richard Anderson, Molly Reynolds, and Jessuina Teran. I also had wonderful undergraduate research assistants helping with the project: Sarah Neumann, Hannah Bozian, Phil Schermer, Emma Rew, Phil Clark, Sarah Danserau, Peter Gutsche, Zachary Goldsmith, Nick Marcus, and Josh DeYoung.

Throughout this project I gave talks or led seminars at the following institutions, and I thank those who attended the sessions and those who invited me: University of California, Santa Cruz (UCSC); University of California, Los Angeles (UCLA); University of California, San Diego (UCSD); University of California, Davis (UCD); Stanford University; Yale University; and University of Michigan (various units).

I thank the following people for detailed conversations: John O'Malley, about Vatican II; Gary Chamberland, about canon law; and Marina Whitman, about General Motors.

The people at Cambridge University Press were supportive and have been patient, especially Lew Bateman and Shaun Vigil, as well as Abidha Sulaiman at Newgen, who managed the project through production. I appreciate the support of Margaret Levi and her good advice and feedback on the manuscript.

My family is the bedrock and they deserve all due credit for patience and tolerance. My thanks go to Colleen, Kathleen, Patrick, Paul, and Anne, but also to Dr. Paul, Fr. Paul, Carita, Anne Marie, Ron, and Ed. Some devoted friends have always been supportive to an extent they are likely not aware – Bruce and Scotti, Pete and Sandy, Herb and Sara, Al and Mary, and Paul and Cecelia. Paul Gargaro, in particular, read the entire manuscript and made numerous suggestions for improvements. I owe him a pasta dinner with Tuscan-style "gravy" and vino.

Thanks to all of these wonderful people for not asking too many questions about which book I am currently working on. It got tedious repeating the same answer for many years.

I

Introduction

In this book I examine the histories of the U.S. government, the Roman Catholic Church, General Motors Corporation (GM), and the European Union (EU) as examples of the evolution of large, lumbering institutions. The book focuses on how each of these political, religious, and commercial systems – all federated in some form or at some point in their histories – centralized authority away from subunits. Amid the many differences in these four institutional cases, I have found similarities in their trajectories and – most importantly for the purposes of this book – similar mechanisms that drove and sustained their centralized authority. The last case examined, the EU, remains somewhat different than the others because it has not yet changed the institutional nature of its executive authority and has not locked into centralization in the same manner as the others. For the remaining three cases, decentralization is difficult or impossible to achieve. The lessons of centralization to be gleaned from this analysis will likely be of most value to those with a stake in the EU's continued evolution. Monumental issues in governance between subunits and the central unit remain unresolved in the EU. Comparable issues have largely been settled in the other three examples examined in this book.

It is fair to ask why I would compare these gigantic, complicated entities and to wonder whether any substantial conclusions can be drawn from such comparisons. Some might question my intellectual credentials or personal sanity in devoting my time to such research. Furthermore, it is unlikely that there are many scholars who sit awake at night, pondering the governance connections between four such disparate institutions. Some scholars care about general questions of governance in federated institutions, whereas others focus on the broader questions of organizational and institutional design. In attempting to tie such concerns together and draw compelling conclusions, I am entering uncharted social science territory. My purpose here is to provide novel insight into comparative governance, including not only governance of nation-states, but also of organizations and sprawling units like global churches, international political systems, universities, corporations, and consortiums of all types.

It goes without saying that these four are canonical institutions, and regardless of whether or not they are worth comparing, they are certainly worth analyzing and making the effort to draw novel conclusions about them. For example, do they represent other federated institutions? This question, and my attempts to answer it, reoccur as subtext throughout the book and are addressed directly in Chapter 7. I am cautious about making strong, general claims that extend to institutions beyond the four analyzed here, even though I believe that the lessons here apply to other federated institutions. I often state conclusions in the abstract, but I do not show evidence from data to support claims of generality. That will have to be another research project.

The burden of this book is to make a convincing case that despite obvious differences between these distinct institutions, there are striking similarities in the evolution of their centralized governance. Comparison offers perspective on what is unique and what may in fact be common in these specific cases. I maintain a bird's eye view to point out similarities in their trajectories, to strip away detail, and focus on the moving tectonic plates reshaping the nature of governing authority over time.

As for credentials, I can claim academic expertise on the government of the United States and the European Union, having published a textbook and research monographs on U.S. government, and written academic journal articles on both U.S. and EU politics. I have also taught both subjects for many years. For the other two cases, my credentials do not come through my publications. Admittedly, most (although not all) of my knowledge of Church history and of General Motors comes from secondary sources. I do have personal familiarity with the Catholic Church, having grown up Catholic. I attended Catholic elementary and high schools, am the brother of a Catholic priest, pay close attention to the ongoing conflicts over Church governance, and continue to practice my faith. Over the past seven years, I have become a voracious reader of Church history, diving deeply into the controversies over potential and realized organizational changes related to authority in the Church. I have read primary Church documents, including large sections of canon law and documents from the two Vatican Councils, and have interviewed canon lawyers and priests. To learn about the General Motors Corporation, I have also done extensive reading, immersing myself in its history. I cannot, however, claim any personal connection to this industrial giant. I became fascinated by GM's trajectory and by the personalities involved, and read accounts of the carmaker's inner workings from a variety of perspectives. I listened to firsthand accounts from a retired executive and examined data on its governing boards.

The original idea for this book came from observing Canada's and India's relatively successful decentralization efforts during the past few decades. When I say "successful," I do not mean these countries are thriving; rather, subunits within each country have gained real authority over their internal affairs relative to the central governments. I learned about these countries' decentralization schemes when University of California (UC) Berkeley Professor Pradeep Chhibber and I were in the process of writing the book, *The Formation of National Party Systems*, on political parties and elections.[1] Numerous authors writing about federalism – and about governance in general – have asserted that the predominant tendency for large countries, large organizations, and international institutions is toward centralization of power.[2] Even casual observers of the U.S. federation, the German, Australian, and Latin American federations, the European Union, universities, large corporations, and nonprofit organizations often draw the same conclusion. There is a tendency for government and bureaucracy, as well as management, to grow in size and influence. True decentralization is hard to achieve, and the deck is stacked toward centralization. How, I wondered, could Canada and India escape the centralization trap?

Canada's and India's experiences with federalism were different than those in the United States. Perhaps decentralization in Canada and India is owing to the fact that each is a parliamentary democracy where executives are responsible to their respective parliaments. The parliaments, of course, are populated with representatives from local geographic areas. The parliaments themselves, through their elected governments, could decide to decentralize governance and return authority back to the provinces (Canada) and states (India). A representative body filled with people who might be interested in checking central power could collectively decide whether to centralize or decentralize authority. The check on central power, therefore, is a built-in function of the representative institutions.

This led me to explore the idea that the nature of governance in the central unit could be important in determining the success or failure of decentralization efforts. Locked-in centralization, perhaps, could be the predominant tendency when the central authority has a "separation of powers" character to it. It may be relevant that executive and legislative powers in Canada and India are fused together, and that decentralization is much harder to achieve when the central authority has a powerful presidency authorized to act independently of a parliament. In such a case, the president is an agent of centralization largely unchecked by subunits, or at least checked less frequently because subunits are not directly represented in the executive body. In political terms, we might draw a distinction between separation-of-powers regimes and parliamentary regimes.

I was also drawn to pay attention to the manner in which political parties in Canada and India represent geographic subunits. In both the Canadian and

[1] Chhibber and Kollman (2004).
[2] For discussions on this topic, see Riker (1964), Bryce (1888), Etzioni (1965), Elazar (1972), Grodzins (1961), Mattli (1999), Shapiro (1995), Stepan (1999), Ziblatt (2006), Rector (2009), Bednar (2008), Higgs (1987 2004, and 2007), Wheare (1964), and Stepan (1999 and 2001). Tilly (1990) argues in a similar fashion to my arguments in this book.

Indian parliaments, regional political parties play important roles in the crafting of national governing coalitions – either as foils or as component parts – and this feature is distinctive from more nationalized party systems. As I argue throughout this book, partisan groupings affect the fluidity of centralization in the way their identities intersect with organizational hierarchies.

The notion that the structure of governance within the central unit is important in facilitating or hampering decentralization efforts may also be applied to institutions other than nation-states. We call it separation of powers in political terms, but it is not clear what to call it in organizational terms once we step out of the realm of politics and government. There is no similar encompassing term, although people occasionally mention the rise of managerial governance in organizations (professional managers) as a cause of centralization.[3] Thus, there may be parallels between the rise of professional managers causing centralization in organizations and the role of presidential systems causing centralization in political systems.

From a variety of disciplinary perspectives, the vantage points shift when analyzing the governance of organizations and corporations. The organizational theory literature from decades ago was helpful, but there has been little written in recent years on the causes of centralization.[4] Quite a few sociologists have written on corporate governance and strike similar themes.[5] I was surprised, however, by the lack of research in any related discipline (including political science) that compares experiences of different kinds of cases and draws general conclusions across a landscape that includes governments *and* organizations.[6] It is undoubtedly true that the typical organization is fundamentally different in many ways from the typical democratic nation-state government. For one thing, democracy or some form of popular consent may not be the core concept underlying an organization. Therefore, comparison between organizations and governments may not always be useful. Nevertheless, I pursued these comparisons because organizational leaders devote a lot of attention to governance issues, which indicates that they care about collective decision-making processes. Perhaps I could learn from studying the experiences of prominent, important organizations and similarly, perhaps organizational leaders could learn from a political scientist studying federated institutions.

[3] Mizruchi (1983), Bachrach and Lawler (1980).

[4] For exceptions, see Hannaway (1993), Panizza (1999), and Mileti, Timmer, and Gillespie (1982). See also Stiglitz and Sah (1991).

[5] See, for example, Mizruchi (1983); Becht, Bolton, and Roell (2002); and Colley et al. (2003). See also Admati, Pfleiderer, and Zechner (1994).

[6] Exceptions include the well-known work of Hirschman (1970), March and Simon (1993), and Simon (1960). See also Mahony and Thelen (2010), and Pierson (2004). A large literature in sociology considers institutions and organizations in general; see March and Simon (1993), Meyer and Rowen (1977), Mohr (1982), and Wilde (2007, 143, fn. 9). Rarely, however, are cases considered together across different genres of institutions. There is also the social choice literature on committee decision making and collective decision making in general that of course can apply to any human institution (see Austen-Smith and Banks 1999 and 2005 for an overview).

With this in mind, I began reading the histories of federated institutions across many domains (the International Red Cross and the Native-American federations, for example) and read bylaws, canon law, treaties, and constitutions. I studied the lists of who sat on which boards of such organizations. In the end, I focused this book on the biggest and most important examples because they afforded me the luxury of extensive secondary literature and a familiarity among readers, which enabled me to compare as well as describe. The literature on the Catholic Church is vast, and the centralization of power to the papacy is a major theme of its historical accounts. Many of the same themes from the study of political federations emerged from these Church histories. The literature on the EU is similarly large and is aided by the sensitivity of its scholars to questions of where authority lies and how it moves over time. The literature on GM is not as large, but it is helped by Robert Freeland's wonderful book, *Struggle for Control of the Modern Corporation*, and a number of other insightful publications.[7] I immediately saw connections between the experience of GM and these other cases.

My research revealed similarities in patterns of centralization across disparate kinds of institutions, and similarities in the battles that took place over governance. These battles pitted central authorities against subunit authorities, as well as executives against representational bodies within the central units. It became clear that these conflicts were intertwined. I took it as a challenge to discern the significance of the confluence of these struggles.

It is possible that someday soon I will return to the questions of more direct relevance to my home discipline of political science, namely the difference between parliamentary democracies and presidential democracies in their experiences with centralization and decentralization. For the moment, however, I feel the need to work through the most general issues of governance that affect organizations as well as nation-states. Thus, this book attempts to makes sense of a rather abstract set of problems using concrete historical examples: how vertical (between the central unit and subunits) and horizontal (between executives and representative bodies) battles for power relate to each other and how the outcomes of these battles matter for the nature of governing authority.

There are a variety of challenges that come with making claims about the historical trajectories of such massive organizations. For each case, there are experts who will either find the historical material provided here not necessary because they know it already or not enough to do justice to the topic. Church historians may find my treatment especially thin, or perhaps worse, not thin enough (some may conclude that much of the information on Church history is obvious). Or, there are social scientists who will wonder why they need to

---

[7] See Chapter 5 of this book for various citations on General Motors. Freeland's (2001) book was influential in my decision to include GM as a case because he captured aspects of GM that resonated with the other three cases and seemed to offer both a parallel and a useful point of comparison.

learn this detail to understand my main points. Like most authors, I struggled with how much detail to provide in this book. My struggles were compounded by an awareness that my readers will have varying degrees of knowledge about the four cases explored here.

This work is not intended as a pure history of these cases. In writing it, I trod the middle ground, seeking to avoid unnecessary details that merely filled in chronologies. Instead, I have included details from particular historical moments to demonstrate the mechanisms at work. Readers will have to look elsewhere for complete historical accounts. I sought to remain focused on the key moments of change in each case. My target reader is someone who is familiar with the basic histories of these cases, but who does not take offense at being reminded of the overall outlines, and a reader who might be intrigued by my inclusion of idiosyncratic details. I assumed the reader would have less knowledge about GM or the Catholic Church, simply because we tend not to learn about these cases as a matter of routine in our educational systems or in popular books, newspapers, and magazines. I imagined this target reader to be like me, a person who finds value in comparison across disparate cases and who is fascinated by historical trajectory. I assumed that he or she would be driven by the search for generalities and more abstract causal connections, and who believes that there are underlying patterns in social systems that can be discovered by deep learning of multiple specific contexts and careful application of social science concepts.

A note about the portions on the Church. The reader will detect that I am cynical of centralization to papal power within the Catholic Church. As mentioned, I am a practicing Catholic, with all that it implies about my religious beliefs. Moreover, beyond theological matters, contrary to the prevailing sentiment in academic circles and the centers of culture in Europe and North America, and in spite of devastating failures by Church authorities in recent years in not preventing child sexual abuse, I believe strongly in the reality of and potential for the Church being, on balance, a positive force in the world.

For Catholics who follow internal Church politics, it will not come as a surprise to learn of a practicing Catholic – especially an American Catholic – who is concerned about assertions of papal authority that have occurred during the past 140 years. For those who know little about the Catholic faith or about the organization of the Catholic Church, it may be surprising to learn of the skepticism that I have, and many other Catholics have, of papal authority. So, to set the record straight: I am comfortable with the notion that in the modern world the pope is the leader of the worldwide Church, and that he has executive authority. I am far less comfortable, however, with the notion that the pope alone is the final authority on theological matters, and can declare some of his statements as infallible. The pope is a human being who benefits, first, from deliberation and advice from others in a formal setting such as Church Councils and second, from formal, collectivized checks on his authority. Humans inevitably make mistakes and can make bad decisions. Reading a history of the papacy only underscores how popes can err systematically and govern in a manner that increases human suffering and sets the Church back from its professed mission. More than a few popes in past centuries have appalling records that match those of the cruelest of European monarchs. Recent decisions by popes, often contrary to the advice of fellow bishops and theologians, on birth control, the use of condoms to fight the AIDS epidemic, and the ordination of women, in my view, all confirm the human fallibility of the person in that position. Monarchy, albeit one that is not hereditary, but is elected for life, is the wrong governance model for a federated, global organization. A better system would have the pope answerable and reliant on approval from representatives in a collective body. Even more importantly, the Church should govern under a better model of federalism with representation by subunits in central decision making, where the representatives are not chosen by the pope but by some other process that resembles the early Church – that is, with input by local Church members.[8]

Let me now describe the basic story line for a hypothetical organization. Consider an organization with subunits and a central unit (headquarters). Within the central unit there is at least one collective body of people representing the subunits and perhaps other interests such as investors or a board of directors in a corporation. There is also an executive in the central unit.

The subunits, in principle, could be quite self-sufficient in the sense that they can do the basic work of the organization by themselves within their domain. If this organization were a business corporation, then each subunit is a company that can make and market its own products, has its own customer base and a set of suppliers. If the organization were a hospital group, then each subunit is a hospital that in theory could deliver health care on its own. If the organization were a union federation, then each subunit is a local union.

Together, the executive and representative bodies govern the entire organization. This can mean different things. Perhaps they co-govern in some fashion, such as both having to approve new policies or perhaps the representative body acts as an executive committee, an advisory committee, or a congress of sorts. The most important fact about the central unit in this organization from our point of view is that the executive position derives its authority not directly from the representative body within the subunit, but from some other source such as from a board of directors, shareholders, or voting members of the subunits. In other words, the executive does not answer directly to the representative body, but to some other source of authority.

This should sound familiar because it is a widely used institutional structure for governance both in organizations and governments. It serves as a loose description of the U.S. government, for instance, and also for many corporations, trade associations, lobbying groups, churches, unions, nonprofit organizations, and political parties. In short, this describes a federated separation-of-powers

---

[8] For a full-blown description of a more democratic model for the Church, see Swindler (1996).

system. It is federated, according to one definition of the term, because the subunits form the basis of the organization and could be self-sufficient if necessary. The subunits are bound together into one system for a variety of reasons, including economies of scale and efficiency, as well as protection. It can also be defined as a separation-of-powers system because the executive is not directly accountable solely to the representative body.

The first argument of this book contends that in such systems, the overwhelmingly dominant trajectory is toward centralization of power, not only toward the central unit, but also toward the executive. Thus, federated separation-of-powers systems trend toward executive centralization.

This argument may not seem new. After all, one can reflect on the history of well-known examples and intuitively believe it to be true. Consider trends in U.S. history, for example. Surely the U.S. government has centralized over time, and more specifically, the presidency has strengthened relative to Congress.[9] Or, one could also point to patterns in other organizations as examples. This pattern may aptly describe evolution in higher education administration. Furthermore, those of us steeped in modern social science will find in this argument an underlying notion that, when given the opportunity, ambitious people will seek to increase their power. Executives in a federated separation-of-powers system will seek more power and autonomy from subunits and subunit representatives. For political scientists, we recognize James Madison's *Federalist 10* and *Federalist 51*, and Michels's iron law of oligarchy.[10]

The second set of arguments of this book, however, relate to the processes of centralization. The overall trend in my cases is similar, and that is toward centralized executive authority. When we probe *how* such centralization occurs, we discover that the processes described are also similar and that they occur in a variety of diverse realms. They show up, I will argue in this book, in governments (the United States), corporations (General Motors), churches (the Roman Catholic Church), and international political unions (the European Union).

The mechanisms can be summarized by five processes that often happen in rough chronological order: assent, representative centralization, partisanship,

---

[9] See, for example, Scheiber (1980).

[10] Madison, Hamilton, and Jay [1787–88] (2003), Michels [1911] 1962. Madison and Hamilton in the Federalist Papers wrote about the importance of having certain kinds of political institutions constraining the behavior of ambitious, greedy people. Their outlook was mostly optimistic, believing that the right kind of institutions could channel that ambition and greed leading to a stable, productive republic. But underlying their arguments was the idea that individuals in positions of authority, left without checks on their power, will seek to aggrandize that authority and abuse it. Michels has the same underlying assumption, but his outlook is pessimistic. He wrote about social democratic parties in Europe and how, even though their philosophies promoted egalitarianism, voice for the masses, and democracy, their leaders ultimately behaved in autocratic, undemocratic ways. It was a natural process of steady power grabs by the leaders of these parties, and the result was a recognizable contradiction: social democratic parties publicly criticizing unequal power in society, but those parties having inside their organizations vastly unequal power concentrated among a few people.

executive centralization, and lock-in. I will define these terms more precisely in Chapter 2. For now, I offer the following, brief overview to provide a taste of the fundamental arguments.

Subunits *assent* to representative centralization with the idea that they will continue to have a voice in decisions over whether to centralize or decentralize policies, and if a policy is centralized, what the policy should be. *Representative centralization*, referring to the process of centralizing authority to the central representative body, brings about increasing partisanship within the organization with partisanship referring to policy conflicts at the central level. *Partisanship* in this context does not refer to political party attachment, but rather to the concept that people at different levels link their fates to the success of movements at the central level in favor of specific kinds of policies.

Inevitably problems or crises arise that are common to all or most subunits, leading to calls for strong leadership at the central level. In order to deal with a given crisis, the executive makes the case that it needs resources, bureaucratic capacity, and statutory authority to make unilateral decisions in some policy areas. The executive typically asserts authority to make unilateral decisions with explicit approval of a substantial portion of the subunits or their representatives, although this approval may be designated for a temporary period. Under *executive centralization*, however, the executive's resources and authority, although approved initially by subunits and their representatives, outlive the period of crisis. The results of the buildup of executive resources, therefore, live on.

The crucial switch leading to *lock-in* occurs in the nature of partisanship. During the period of executive-led centralization in the midst of crisis, partisanship changes from being oriented toward the actions within representative bodies at the central level to being oriented toward the success or failure of specific executives and their policies. Executive centralization becomes locked-in, or solidified, when partisanship spans the organization from the subunit level, through the representative institutions at the central level, and then to the executive at the central level. Thereafter, the fate of people within the subunits and within the non-executive parts of the center becomes linked to the success or failure of executive policies. Often, subunit leaders and representatives internalize the policy goals of the executive, which means that they come to want what the executive wants, or what their candidate or prospect for the executive wants. However, if for whatever reason they do not internalize the executive's policy goals, the executive can use its resources to reward people at all levels for cooperating with its policy programs and punish those who do not cooperate. The executive can quickly end any serious attempts to decentralize authority back to the subunits.[11]

---

[11] The arguments in this book about thresholds and lock-in (discussed more fully in Chapter 2) bear resemblance to insights gained from Schelling (1978) and more deeply analyzed in Lamberson and Page (2012) regarding tipping points.

For our hypothetical organization, we can compare the before and after. Before the process enters the latter stages, the subunits are largely autonomous, and the center is relatively weak. The executive only has resources that are approved regularly by subunit representatives. Any centralization is assented to by the subunits or their representatives (assent could mean a legitimate process that involves the subunits collectively), as well as any policies chosen under the centralization.

After the final process of executive centralization, not only is the organization highly centralized, it is also highly centralized to the executive. The executive within the central unit has considerable autonomy to make unilateral decisions without the approval of the subunits or subunit representatives. The executive continues to amass resources and autonomy, which feed on each other. The executive can use the resources to divide and conquer coalitions that threaten to remove the executive's autonomy or return authority back to the subunits.

I have proposed an argument about centralization – specifically, executive centralization – that on the surface seems straightforward, at least in terms of the overall trajectory of organizations and governments. However, as I become more specific in Chapter 2 and subsequent chapters about the process of centralization, the arguments become more complex. In the abstract, the key to centralization becoming locked-in is a process of change in the way people come to see their interests as linked to different parts of governing institutions. Leaders succeed in building the lasting power of their office by institutionalizing the linked fate of their own policy programs to the ambitions and goals of subunit leaders and those representing subunit interests. This, I will argue, is what presidents in the twentieth century did in the United States, what popes have done through the centuries, heads of General Motors have achieved over the years, and what the executive of the European Union was poised to do before being held back, thereby casting uncertainty over the future.

Let me be clear about what I am not arguing with regard to executive centralization. The argument is not that executives necessarily become all powerful within their systems, or that they always end up dominating the representative bodies and subunits in an imperious way. In certain cases this is true, but not always. The pope has assumed final executive, legislative, and judicial power within the Church. The president of the United States, however, is relatively weak within his own system compared to presidents in other countries; he still needs help and cooperation from other units to govern. Instead, the argument here is that the critical changes in these systems locking in executive centralization were the relative strengthening of executive authority compared to its previous levels combined with the resulting development of partisanship linked to executive performance.

In Chapter 2, we move to a more detailed examination of these ideas, and later chapters will probe our four specific cases to provide telling examples. When we examine the cases, we shall see that the precise form of executive centralization varies – where they end up in terms of day-to-day understanding of the legitimate exercise of authority – mostly owing to different external legal environments and internal legal standards. What they share, however, is executive centralization occurring during moments of crisis and contention over authority.

This book is intended for multiple audiences. For political scientists, constitutional scholars, and organizational theorists, here is the main message of the book. The combination of federated form and separation of powers leads to a strong tendency for institutions to become centralized over time; once executive centralization is achieved, decentralization becomes difficult, even if it is warranted. Alternatively, large, federated institutions that do not have separation-of-powers characteristics – where the executive is directly accountable to the representative body only – are more flexible and can decentralize when it is advantageous. To understand the different outcomes, pay attention to the intervening mechanism – partisanship. Partisanship among subunit leaders and representatives reacts to centralization and affects executive authority. In the case of non-separation of powers systems, or systems like the EU that teeters between different forms of governance, I speculate that partisanship can go two ways: it can be the raw ingredient enabling increases in executive authority and it can help limit executive authority if the partisanship within the representative institutions happens to build around sustaining subunit autonomy.[12] In the case of separation-of-powers systems, that partisanship will enable increases in executive authority. [13]

Now here is the broader message, including for those outside of academia. Most of us are wary of centralizing powers. My point in this book, however, is not the normative claim that centralization is always bad or has been bad in these four cases. In some contexts, decentralized authority is obviously bad, especially when local governments are oppressive and national standards better protect basic human rights.[14] Rather, my claim is that over-centralization is often irreversible and hard to avoid, even when leaders of centralized institutions or governments make a solid case that their system should decentralize. To the extent that I can offer advice for institutional design, it is not to avoid executive power completely, but rather to maintain strong institutions that include the representation of subunits that have direct authority over the executive.

In particular, organizations and governments can be more flexible in moving between centralization and decentralization if they have one or more of these

---

[12] One way to read this is that in non-separation of powers systems, the outcomes are path dependent owing to how partisanship changes within representative institutions as the system centralizes.

[13] For separation-of-powers systems, the key path-dependent feature (the decisive moment) occurs with the choice of institutional design at the Founding.

[14] Riker's (1964) classic book on federalism highlights the concern that too much decentralization in the U.S. federation allows for continuing oppression of minorities by state governments.

institutional features. They are listed in order of importance. The first is the best safeguard against locked-in centralization, followed by the second and third. One, an executive who is (or that is) directly responsible to a representative body that includes the representation of subunits. Two, a representative body that includes representation of subunits and has authority to make decisions over decentralization and devolution. Three, a representative body that includes partisan groupings organized around subunit interests.

For the specific cases analyzed in this book, my suggested institutional changes range from implausibly ambitious to conceivable, although they are in principle achievable without fundamental upheaval of the core institutional design. First, there should be serious consideration of repealing the Seventeenth Amendment to the U.S. Constitution and returning to the situation where senators are appointed by state governments. Second, the Catholic Church should move toward real collegiality where the College of Bishops co-governs with the pope without implied hierarchy between them, and the choosing of bishops ought to include substantive input from local priests and laity. Third, corporations that market a variety of products produced by relatively autonomous subunits should incorporate leaders of those subunits into their decision making committees at the highest levels. Fourth and finally, the EU should maintain and solidify a more parliamentary model of executive authority rather than a presidential model.

Any one of these recommendations may meet with skepticism because they are unlikely or they would be extremely unpopular, perhaps the one on the Seventeenth Amendment for both reasons. However, the recommendations follow from the combination of understanding the histories as described in later chapters, recognizing that there are common patterns among disparate cases, and from observing different outcomes when different institutions exist. The recommendations can only be made after comparison.

2

Trajectories in Federated Institutions

How should governing institutions be designed for large, sprawling systems, such as global companies or international organizations? How can governments and institutions facing global problems provide enough autonomy for smaller units to flourish while at the same time achieve economies of scale from coordination?[1] Federation offers a promising, and common, answer to such questions. An allegedly successful model for governance, federation can survive in form and it can lead to productivity, profitability, safety, stability, enrichment, or whatever we want from our institutions. Federation offers the opportunity to combine diversity and unity. It is the "politically correct" form of governance. Celebrate difference, individuality, voice, but also recognize and harness unity of purpose, oneness, and overlapping interests. What is not to like in principle about the idea of federation?[2]

The separation of power between an executive and a representative body serves as another common institutional feature among organizations and governments. Under this typical institutional form, the organization or government

---

[1] Some who propose normative theories of where authority should lie in a federation acknowledge the problems of accounting for the real dynamics. For instance, Oates (1972) describes a wonderfully elegant theory indicating which economic policies should be centralized and which should be devolved. But he throws his hands up when trying to explain changes in actual distributions of authority across levels of government. He mostly agrees with his political science contemporaries that there is no way to account systematically for which level of government controls which area of national policy. He (Oates, 1972, 182) quotes Rufus Davis: "What functions are vested in the general government and what left to the regions ... there is neither science nor theory in this process. It is not a mathematical division where high exactitude is possible. There is only the skill of translating precedent to local circumstance, and the draftsmanship to express the compromised purposes of the key bargainer in language to satisfy them" (Davis 1967, 10).

[2] See Cooley (2005) for a large-scale view of the differences between forms of governance over subunits, including federalism. See also Kim (2005), Spruyt (1994), and Lake (2009). See Shipan and Volden (2006, 2008) and Kollman, Miller, and Page (2000a) for some benefits of the experimental side of federalism.

will have shared decision-making authority between a council, parliament, congress, or central committee made up of representatives of various subunits, and an executive whose authority is derived independently of the representative body. The representative body can include members from various constituencies, who are often grouped by geographic origin. The representative body is not solely responsible for choosing the executive, and the executive is not solely accountable to the representative body, but also to such other groups as voters, investors, or outside evaluators. Perhaps, as is the case with the U.S. government, the executive and the representative bodies check each other and typically must assent to the passage of new laws. That is, both have a veto over new policies.[3]

How, then, do federation and separation of powers systems work together? The latter supposedly frees the executive from the petty entanglements of the particular subunit interests. The executive can act with consideration of the good of the whole and not have to ask repeatedly for subunit assent. Yet this book confronts one of the ubiquitous and ageless conundrums in governance of organizations and nation-states: how to vest just enough – no more or less than necessary – concentrated power in a leader or a sovereign to enforce unity, solve collective problems, and protect against inside and outside threats without leading to oppression. Federations often face this conundrum because they are put in place with the intention of preserving autonomy for subunits. In that autonomy, however, lurks the potential disorder that can create pressure to establish stronger centralized authority.

I am arguing in this book that the horizontal movement of authority within a central unit and the vertical movement of authority between the central unit and subunits are related. Vertical centralization to a central unit that includes a representative body that assures the subunits retain a voice in policy decisions is one thing. Horizontal centralization to an executive that can use delegated powers to mediate or even undercut the representation of the subunits in policy making is another. Representative bodies over time cede authority to the executive; representative bodies delegate, often in times of crisis. When the crisis has passed, attempts to rein in executives are undermined by those benefiting from the newfound executive authority. Executives, meanwhile, carve out space to create their own capacities for consolidating authority. The solidification of executive authority carries with it the simultaneous undermining of attempts to grant authority back to subunits.

In Chapter 1, we introduced the stages of centralization: assent, representative centralization, partisanship, executive centralization, and lock-in. Each of these will be discussed in more detail later in this chapter. I present these in chronological order because the ordering roughly captures the typical pattern (see Figure 2.1). It is misleading, however, to suggest that they happen tidily in sequence with clear boundaries, where one stage stops and another

---

[3] For a theory of politics built around a general version of these arguments about separation of powers, see Tsebelis (2002) and Tsebelis and Money (1997).

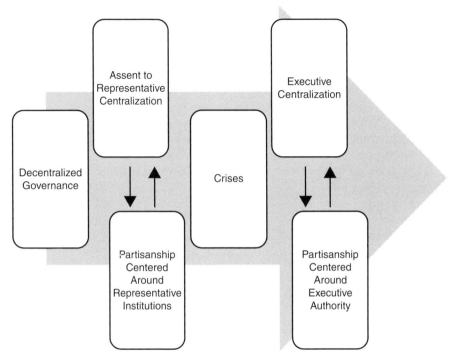

FIGURE 2.1 The common trajectory.

begins. Rather, all the stages can overlap in time. Centralization, for the cases in this book, begins with assent to representative centralization and for three of the cases, ends with locked-in executive centralization. Partisanship, which evolves in response to different forms of centralization, also helps the stages along, acting as the lubricant enabling the wheels to turn toward increased centralization.

Although the chronology makes for a standard narrative that assists our understanding, let me clarify: I am not proposing a kind of determinism. Albeit likely, centralization is not inevitable. Nor do I base my arguments on collective irrationality or false consciousness; people, either collectively or individually, must actively make decisions to centralize authority, and they usually do so willingly, although often uncertain of the consequences. Unlike human beings going through an aging process, institutions can reverse course, and certainly leaders can halt processes that might seem inevitable. Nevertheless, I conclude from this study that centralization is a natural process in large organizations and governments, like water rolling downhill. The *type* of centralization that occurs follows from the underlying structure, whether it is separation of powers or parliamentary in design. And the consequences for those assenting to executive authority in a separation of powers system are either (1) predicted but considered worth it for the short-term gains from strong executive action in the present or (2) are genuinely surprising and later regretted because they are difficult to reverse.

True decentralization after centralization, or even halting executive centralization, is like stopping the water. One needs to create special mechanisms that stop the process. It can be stopped and even reversed, but it takes active intervention. Left to their own devices without specific fixes to their structures, federated institutions with separation of powers will move toward strong executive authority at the central level.

Prominent examples to bolster these arguments are described in the next four chapters. Before moving to those chapters, it is incumbent upon me to attempt to clarify further the boundaries of concepts. Such clarity will be useful in later chapters and in drawing comparisons across cases. The concepts used as parts of the argument include federation, the meaning of centralization and decentralization, the various kinds of centralization, timescales in the evolution of these institutions, the meaning of assent to centralization, the meaning of partisanship, and the mechanisms of lock-in.

Federated Systems

The label of federation, or federalism, is typically reserved for systems with a de facto contractual relationship among the subunits and between subunits and a central unit. The subunits and the central unit have – in principle – mutual recognition of which issues will be the prerogative of the subunits, which issues will be the prerogative of the central unit, and which issues will require shared authority.[4]

In contrast, for the purposes of this study, I consider an institution to be federated if subunits exist that are capable of exercising autonomy in their own affairs, and if the subunits, willingly or unwillingly, submit to a central authority on at least some important policy issues.[5] This does not mean that they are necessarily granted this autonomy, and it does not require a codified, contract-like agreement protecting the subunits from central encroachment. In fact, one of the

---

[4] Rodden (2006, 32) emphasizes the central point from the modern literature on federalism: "Federalism implies contractual relations between central and subnational governments." There are, of course, a variety of definitions of federalism from the literature about nation-states. See Riker (1987, 13), Duchacek (1970), Hueglin and Fenna (2006), Gagnon (1993, 15), King and Preston (1982, 140–41), Sawer (1969, 179), Dahl (1984, 114), Burgess (1993, 8), Ostrom (1991, 17 and 252), Mousley (1940, 21), Linder (1994, 172), Smith (1995, 4), Elazar (1987, 5; 1969, xii), Rubin and Feeley (1994), Stepan (1999, 2001), Wheare (1964, 33), and Forsyth (1981).

[5] Starting with the basic idea that definitional boundaries are useful to a specific purpose, I concede that this definition blurs the boundaries between other concepts, such as empire, confederation, and fiscal federalism. It also means that I would include a corporation based on a franchise model as federated. I do not see the cost of being expansive in my definition, and in fact, the main benefit for my purpose – maintaining a conceptual category for our four cases such that we can trace their histories over time in the degree to which the subunits gain or lose authority relative the central unit – outweighs the cost in my view.

major things at stake in our four cases is that these agreements remain in flux throughout the life of any federated system. Highly centralized federated institutions have subunits that could have considerable autonomy but do not, and highly decentralized federated institutions have subunits with a great deal of discretion and authority to make policy decisions binding in their own domains.

Based on my definition, if a federated institution were to decentralize, the subunits would already be in place to run their own affairs. That is, they have more than one level of governance with a central unit and subunits; the subunits have considerable potential autonomy to make policy decisions in many realms. A possible feature for federated systems, but certainly not a requirement and something that often changes over time (as in our four cases), is that subunits would have a voice in decisions at the central level that would affect them and would steer the overall direction of the organization or government. Many large organizations and governments are federated in form. Corporations can be federated, as well as hospital groups, religious organizations, universities, trade associations, unions, international organizations, and of course, nation-states.

At certain moments in its history, for instance, GM did have representative subunits in central decision making. Division leaders were not only part of the central management team in some eras at GM, but the central units of GM were de facto limited in the degree to which they could interfere in the operations of the auto divisions. At various times, the participation of the auto divisions in central governance was deeply contested by investors and senior management. This forms a major part of our story about GM in Chapter 5. Federated institutions can range over time between poles of substantial decentralization and substantial centralization. At times, as in the case of GM, they can cease to be federated at all.

In comparison, some scholars believe that Great Britain is not formally federal because the Westminster Parliament has the sovereign legal authority to abolish subunit governments.[6] The United States, however, qualifies because, according to the U.S. Constitution, the national government cannot unilaterally abolish or amend the boundaries of any state. Two of our cases, the Church and GM, meanwhile, cannot be said today to qualify as federations by standard definitions. The Vatican can abolish a diocese or archdiocese at will; likewise, GM and its auto divisions. In previous eras, however, these two cases probably would have qualified as a federation in the standard definition.[7]

---

[6] For discussion on this point, see Burrows and Denton (1980).

[7] For many organizational theorists, especially those who focus on corporate governance, the relevant framework is not federation in either the standard sense or in my sense. Rather, it is not the potential for subunits to be autonomous, or the nature of representation of subunits in central decision making, but a principal-agent model with the central unit as principal and the subunits as agents. The interesting questions have to do with how completely the central unit, which has full legal authority over the subunits, can or should control what the subunits do. See Jaffee (2001), Robbins (1990), Daft (1992), or Pfeffer (1997). See also Colley, Doyle, Logan, and Stettinius (2003). Reading Shafritz and Ott (2001) provides a solid grounding in the trajectories of attention among organizational theorists.

But the Church today and GM for much of its history definitely qualify under my criteria for federation (so does Great Britain). Indeed, many non-state institutions qualify, including other religious federations in the United States such as the Southern Baptists, international labor federations, Indian federations, interest-group organizations like the National Association for the Advancement of Colored People (NAACP) or national environmental groups, international organizations, farm cooperatives, and trade associations.

A word about democracy: for two of our cases – the United States and the EU – democracy (or at least republicanism and popular sovereignty) is presumed to be the underlying principle of operation. Subunits have been constitutionally empowered to be included in the assignment of authority, and at various times, have had to decide collectively about schemes of representation. Within those subunits and across the entire system, the people are supposed to be the ultimate authority legitimizing governing power. For our other cases, the Church and GM, the central units have, for most of their histories, had ecclesiastical or legal authority to alter representational schemes without the approval of subunits or the people within those subunits. The amount of actual power the central units have had independent of the subunits has changed over time and remains open to debate. To the extent that democracy is about giving voice to more than a few, to many, or most of the people within an institution, such institutions as the Church and GM have ranged along a continuum of democratic governance throughout their histories.

Decentralization and Devolution

The distinction between decentralization and devolution is crucial to our story. It is key to understanding the limits on centralized federated systems once they lock-in. Decentralization occurs when subunits have legitimate authority to make policies within their realms, and those subunits collectively play a major role in approving decisions to centralize policy-making authority to a higher level. That is, subunits collectively do not have centralization foisted on them without their approval through some collective-choice process. Devolution occurs when subunits are granted authority by the center to make policies within their realms, but that authority can be taken back by the center without the subunits collectively approving the centralization. Decentralization runs deeper than devolution. Its reversal requires a legitimate decision-making process that includes the subunits. Devolution, however, is more easily and unilaterally reversible by central units.

Deciding whether to decentralize or devolve (or neither) is a constant agenda item, implicit or explicit, for federated systems. Leaders of these systems must determine who holds meta-authority and who holds policy-making power. In questions about federation or federalism, meta-authority means the power to establish the decision-making rules for resolving future centralization and decentralization questions.[8] When more power is vested over time in executives to make these decisions regarding the allocation of authority, executives gain the upper hand in this meta-authority and thus in interpreting when they can wield authority, enabling lock-in. Subunits themselves, often represented directly in the central unit in some fashion, can lose their voice in decisions over centralization and decentralization.

If the basic argument about the trajectory toward centralization is true, why have we observed so much decentralization in governments and organizations over the past few decades? I would argue that most of these changes are selective devolution and not true decentralization of the kind just described. When the president of the United States allowed states to loosen educational standards in 2012 as part of the No Child Left Behind policies, this was devolution that could be reversed unilaterally by the national government. If it were true decentralization, the subunits (state governments or representatives of those governments) would need to assent explicitly to recentralize. If it were devolution, the center could unilaterally take back the authority. Exceptions – that is, true decentralization – have generally occurred in non-separation of powers systems. Now that India has decentralized to its states in recent decades, it would take the approval of those subunits to recentralize. This, therefore, is true decentralization. I will name similar examples in Chapter 7.

Representative and Executive Centralization

Centralization can also be a tricky concept because it is related to the notion of authority. A standard definition from organization theory refers to centralization as "the degree to which the formal authority to make discretionary choices is concentrated in an individual, unit, or level," typically high up in the organization, permitting lower-level employees or units "minimum input into their work." [9] But what is the nature of the authority at stake here? Some economists have drawn a distinction between formal and real authority in organizations.[10] Formal, or de jure authority, refers to decision-making power legally granted by contract, statute, bylaws, or constitution. This includes the power to overrule subunit decisions. Real, or de facto authority, means decision making that actually leads to changes in behavior. It often is held by subunits because higher-up units cannot or do not monitor and enforce decisions because of the high costs of doing so. The insight here is that central units can have formal but not real authority, while subunits can have real but not formal authority, and this occurs because of the costs borne by the central unit in monitoring subunits. Central units may not even try to assert authority because it is not worth it, leading to de facto but not de jure authority by the subunits.

---

[8] This is related to the notion of "residual power." See Lake (2009).

[9] Robbins (1990, 106).

[10] See Aghion and Tirole (1997) and Mohr (1982).

According to the bylaws of most universities, for example, the provost has the ultimate authority to hire faculty. In reality, most universities' departments or deans make faculty hiring decisions, which are then rubber-stamped by the provost. The provost has delegated hiring authority to lower units. In large universities, the multiple demands on the provosts' time means they cannot make such decisions. This gives the subunits the real authority. It is common to conclude, therefore, that many large universities have decentralized faculty hiring processes to the college or departmental level, but only if this conclusion is based on the definition of real rather than formal authority.

One might wish to emphasize conformity and potential sanctions, and thus proffer an amended definition of centralization. For example, the central unit makes policy decisions binding on all lower-level subunits and those policy decisions lead to de facto compliance; when subunits do not comply, punishments are usually applied. This definition can be limiting. Others make the important point that one should not assume that centralization means policy is uniform across all subunits.[11] If the center has formal or real authority, it can mandate distinctive policies for different subunits, or even permit devolution. This implies a more general definition of centralized authority, where the central unit has discretion to decide what policies the subunits adopt. These can be uniform or varied across the subunits.[12]

Relying on these distinctions, we can say that our interest here is mostly with formal authority of a central unit relative to the subunits' abilities to make independent policy decisions. The location of authority within the central unit matters to our story. Is it lodged with a body representing the subunits or the population or membership as a whole, or with an executive accountable to some others besides the subunits or representational body, or both? The answers to that question vary over time for our four cases.

Representative centralization of varying degrees refers to something akin to notions of consent coming from the Enlightenment, especially the writings of Locke and Rousseau, who relied on ideas of democracy from the Greeks. The subunits are willingly granting authority to a collective body on two conditions: (1) that the subunits will be represented in decision-making processes and (2) that decisions of the collective body, once made, will be binding on the

---

[11] See Lockwood (2002) and Oates (1972). There is a large amount of literature taking a political economy approach to the study of federalism. See Besley and Coate (2003); Boadway and Shah (2009); Bolton and Farrell (1990); Cheema and Rondinelli (2007); Cremer and Palfrey (1996 and 1999); de Figueiredo and Weingast (2005); Gordon (1983); Inman (2008); Inman and Rubinfeld (1997); Koremenos, Lipson, and Snidal (2001); Myerson (2006); Oberholzer-Gee and Strumpf (2002); Ordeshook and Niou (1998); Qian and Weingast (1997); Rodden (2006); Roland and Qian (1998); Seabright (1996); Strumpf and Oberholzer-Gee (2002); Weingast (1995); Wibbels (2005A, 2005B, and 2006); and Wittman (1991).

[12] Treisman's (2007) discussion of the different kinds of political authority between subunits and central units is helpful in disentangling some of overlaps in definitions of authority. See also Cheema and Rondinelli (2007), Zald (1970), and Cooley (2005).

subunits. Decisions, at one extreme, could require unanimity, which implies that for every policy chosen, the subunits are required to assent repeatedly to centralized authority. This is a highly decentralized version of representation; other versions typically involve more workable decision-rules that require something less than unanimity but at least a majority – sometimes a supermajority – of subunits to agree to changes.

The representative approach often has an impact on the degree of centralization. Federations can remain decentralized to a large degree when subunit representatives, in an effort to protect the interests of their subunit, demand a role in deciding when and what policies should be centralized. In 1913, the American states for example, collectively agreed that the national government could set an income tax, thus permitting centralized direct taxation. Congress then moved to set the tax. These were two separate steps, and subunit leaders or representatives participated in both.

Furthermore, subunits, in agreeing to be bound by decisions of the collective body, have also agreed to the decision-rules leading to centralized policy choices. Unless the decision-rule requires unanimity among subunits, representatives understand that they and their subunits might lose in these collective decisions. However, the continued assent arises from the calculation that general gains from union outweigh the losses from being outvoted on specific policies.

Executive centralization has a different character. It involves a delegation of authority to a separate, executive unit. That executive unit could be an individual or a collective body. In the process of delegation, the input by subunits into policy making is not guaranteed, regularized, or formalized. Executives who want more authority and freedom to make quick decisions can ask for the assent of the representative body (or bodies) and may receive that assent in principle. Alternatively, executives can unilaterally assert these powers, gaining them if there is not enough collective opposition in their way. Either way, executive centralization is the process of the leaders of the central unit, who in principle can act on behalf of the entire federated system, carving more and more space for their own policy making and actions without the overt, routine approval of either the representative body in the center or the subunits. These executives may gain office with the approval of the other units, and usually gain additional institutional authority with the support of their partisans in the representative unit. But thereafter, many of their decisions are not subject to the approval of the other units, and they are not directly accountable to the representative body. This kind of centralization means growth in the day-to-day prerogatives by the central executive to enforce a centralized policy and impose costs on subunits.

Later chapters will provide numerous examples of this executive centralization. The degree to which the Pope has gradually worked to codify supreme executive, legislative, and judicial authority – thereby ensuring that any claims challenging centralization toward the papacy are illegitimate under canon law of the Church – offers a classic, although extreme, example of executive centralization. For long periods of Church history, not only were efforts to organize opposition to papal authority grounds for excommunication, but even discussion in support of such opposition warranted severe sanctions.

Time Scales and Moments

The arguments made in this book revolve around the common trajectories of institutions. The cases examined are very old institutions, making the use of time scales a challenge. One problem is that what seems like a trend on one time scale can appear to be a temporary drift or a correction from a temporary drift on another time scale. I address this problem explicitly in Chapter 4 when discussing the Church. For an institution more than 2,000 years old, identifying a trend requires demarcating a specific period of time for which controversies of central unit versus subunit authorities remain salient and politically connected. I claim that the time period from 1850 to the present represents an era in the Church for which overlapping generations of actors have engaged in continuing the controversies over papal power and Church governance, struggling with the meaning of concepts like collegiality.

Specifying "a moment" of potential or realized institutional change poses the challenge of nailing down the timing of those changes and detecting the changes themselves. What is a "moment"? The definitional boundaries here are admittedly loose; a moment can be quick or it can stretch on.[13] It is fundamentally related to the problems of detecting change and evaluating that change.

To explore the conceptual and empirical challenges here, consider the following simple example. The goal for coffee drinkers who like sugar in their cups is to create the perfectly sweetened drink. Suppose sugar was added one grain at a time to a single cup of coffee, in discreet time intervals with tastings in between. We can consider two relevant thresholds: the moment when the coffee becomes "sweet enough" and the moment when the coffee becomes "too sweet." It is virtually impossible to detect the change in taste from the addition of one grain of sugar to the next, and it may therefore be difficult to know when either of these thresholds is passed. Conceivably, if the coffee drinker was not paying close attention, the cup would become too sweet after the addition of too many grains. Now suppose the sugar was added in cubes. Depending on the number of grains in the cubes and the relationship between the thresholds, the second threshold might be passed unintentionally and the existing coffee ruined. A cube might be added to encompass both thresholds and jump from not sweet enough to too sweet, skipping the desired, intermediate gap between the first and second threshold. One would need to dilute the coffee or start anew.

---

[13] Sociologists and historians have wrestled with how to define moments of institutional change. See Sewell (2005), Pierson (2004), Clemens and Cook (1999), and also Wilde (2007, 2 and 143 [fn 9]). Key to Sewell's definition of an "historical event" is the notion that contemporaries recognize that institutional change will or might occur, and that such changes will be durable.

Federated institutions can be subject to both of these kinds of change, and over variable time scales. First, centralization can occur in small increments like grains of sugar in coffee. The steady accretion of authority toward executives and the building of bureaucratic and extractive capacities are hard to notice as they happen and seem natural and incremental until they go beyond the desired level and it might be too late to avoid lock-in. Or, centralization can occur quickly in large steps, punctuated by key moments in history. Centralization may be a good thing in principle up to and just beyond a certain ("first") threshold. But the second type of threshold, when the federation becomes irreversibly "too centralized," can be leapt over in a short period of time with an unanticipated end result for the institution. A given bout of centralization seems appropriate for the moment, but pushes the federation past a key point, or at least a point that enables the federation to reverse itself if circumstances warrant.[14]

In evaluating our cases, we need to keep in mind these two aspects – the variable time periods over which change can occur (gradual or sudden) and the thresholds that institutions can cross (appropriate level of centralization or too much centralization) – in considering the means of centralization in federated institutions. Timing and scale of change can be related, as the example of the sugar grains versus cubes indicates. The grains of sugar might be added gradually as executives build their legal and bureaucratic capacity to decide and enact policy in small steps. Or the sugar might be suddenly added as sugar cubes when crises arise and demand coordinated action. In the latter case especially, centralization by an executive can occur with the clear assent of the subunits and of the representative bodies within the central unit. Crises might require centralized authority because the subunit leaders recognize their limitations and their collective dilemmas. But that assent, which is often understood to be temporary until the crisis is over, may instead allow institutional changes that end up being permanent.[15]

Assent

Assent as used here means a collective agreement among the relevant actors – in this case, typically subunit leaders or subunit populations – on a set of institutional principles and can occur in a focal, founding moment, such as when the U.S. Constitution was ratified in the late eighteenth century. Assent often occurs, however, in other moments and can unfold gradually, such as when agreements are made to include new subunit members. This is evident when

---

[14] The relevant social science argumentation here is owing at least in part to Schelling (1978) who explored in detail the notions of "tipping points" where social institutions and situations drop into patterns that are difficult to reverse. Lamberson and Page (2012) probe the logical variations of tipping points.

[15] This echoes the argument of Higgs (1987) about U.S. governmental authority.

the European Union enlarges to bring in new member states or when national churches in the past decided whether to ally themselves with Rome. Assent also occurs in decisions to incorporate a set of policy areas that will be brought into the federated scheme of governance such as when the United States moved to allow the regulation of most commercial activity at the central level as opposed to the state level.[16] The moments requiring assent can be provoked when subunits threaten to leave the federated system, such as when the threat of southern succession loomed in the United States for several years in the late 1850s. Or moments when the central unit decides to reorganize, as in the many efforts of GM to refashion its organizational structure, which required buy-in from its division managers and unions. These moments do not always arise like storms, outside the control of the major actors involved; they can be brought on by the actors themselves. But actors do not always wish them to happen. Usually one group, reacting to problems arising among units or from outside of the system, pushes for these moments to occur, forces a settlement of major governance issues, and asks for assent.

Chronologically, assent to representative centralization is the first event or set of events in our overall story. We can think of many moments of assent occurring early as forming a federal bargain. Under a federal bargain, subunits are the key components. They will band together and cede some authority to a central unit, resulting in a codified process of settling disputes regarding authority among subunits and between subunits and the central unit. Leaders or representatives for a subunit have interests in preserving the autonomy of the subunit on matters of importance to it. They also have interests in improving the circumstances of the subunits, interests which they believe can be achieved through union with other subunits. Later, they may assent to executive centralization as crises emerge.

For our four cases, here are the moments (or eras) of potential assent to centralization of either kind – representative or executive – that will be highlighted in the following chapters.

The United States:

The Founding to 1840
The fight over the income tax
The New Deal era

---

[16] I recognize, of course, the important role that the federal courts, and specifically the Supreme Court, have played in defining the boundaries of central government authority on the regulation of commerce. Supreme Court decisions may or may not reflect a well-understood consensus among subunit leaders and representatives over such boundaries. Some court decisions regarding federalism have shocked or offended large portions of state leaders or the Congress, but over time, the courts cannot sustain positions on federalism that are at odds with prevailing sentiment among large majorities of Congress and state governments. Constitutional amendments or even statutory laws can undo legal precedents, and have on federalism matters (e.g., the income tax, as described in Chapter 3).

The Church:

> Vatican I Council
> Vatican II Council

GM:

> The air-cooled engine proposal
> Reacting to the Great Depression
> Reacting to World War II

The EU:

> The Treaty of Rome
> The Single European Act
> The Maastricht Treaty and negotiations over governance of Economic and
> Monetary Union (EMU)
> The Amsterdam treaty and continued negotiations over governance of
> EMU
> The eastern enlargement negotiations and the Lisbon Treaty

During moments of assent, there are usually groups that favor centralization and opposing groups that favor decentralization – maintaining the existing autonomy or, at a minimum, the voice of the subunits. Examples described in later chapters include the Federalists and anti-Federalists in the founding era of the United States, the papists and the conciliators in medieval Europe, the central management of GM and the automobile company managers in the 1920s and 1930s, and the federalists and the unionists among European leaders in the 1940s and 1950s. Not surprisingly, the centralizers are typically those who already have power in the central unit and those among the subunits that will likely have the most influence on central decision making. The decentralizers are those among the subunits who fear central encroachment into their affairs and fear domination of the central unit by opposing subunit interests. Since the 1970s, for example, the British government has continuously played a decentralizer's role based on its concerns over French and German domination of the EU.

During these moments, neither the centralizers nor the decentralizers can forge enough momentum to settle the governance issues without support from some on the other side. For now, we can briefly address the obvious question: Why do those in favor of decentralized governance sign on to institutional changes that might lead to centralization? I will offer answers to this question in the next four chapters. Specific historical episodes recounted across four very different cases will tell the tale as well as any summary. Nevertheless, here are some general answers.

One answer is that the people signing on to the federated system are not the same as those who end up facing the consequences when the central unit later interprets the federal bargain in its favor. Another answer is that for many federated systems, the units with the higher probability of "winning" in the future – those with the higher likelihood of having the central unit aligned with their interests – are able to sweeten the pot just enough for the units that ultimately lose to convince them to go along. This pot sweetening could be in the form of getting people to believe in the goodwill of the others. Or, it could simply be bribery, such as when the EU member states agreed to grant France generous agricultural subsidies in return for French agreement on centralized regulation of industry. Third, certain subunits may have less real choice in being part of a federated system than is implied. A centralized union is often more beneficial for subunits than operating alone: a union can provide leverage in disputes and by threatening to leave the union, subunits can weaken other members' positions.

So what does assent of the subunits mean? Or, put in historical terms, what did assent mean during specific moments in our four cases? Answers can vary when comparing such disparate cases. Assent could mean unanimity – all subunits must assent. The EU formally operates this way when altering treaties or admitting new members; every member state must assent to treaty changes. In practice, the smaller states, which can cause trouble in the process of gaining assent, get bought off when they object. Denmark and Ireland have by referendum defeated key treaty changes, only to have minor changes to the proposed treaties (supposedly in their favor) be approved in subsequent referenda.

With the exception of the EU, unanimity is rarely the formal or informal (but well understood by all) decision-rule for assent during these moments. The threshold is often defined – or commonly understood – to be more than a simple majority, but less than unanimous. One well-defined and codified example is the threshold of the nine states required to approve of the new U.S. Constitution before it took effect in 1789. Less well-defined is the "near-consensus" rules required of votes during the Second Vatican Council for approval of council documents. Similarly, there was the well-understood, "near-unanimous" support required of the automobile divisions in the early years of GM.

As is often the situation, certain key subunits are necessary for settlement to occur. The subunits are not treated as equal. In the case of the states during the struggles over the U.S. Constitution, it was clear to all that the largest states, especially New York and Virginia, had to sign on to the new document or it would not move forward. Most of the action during the moments in the EU occurs among the largest states – Germany, France, Britain, and to some extent now, Poland. They bargain among themselves and seek allies from the group of smaller states over the most important potential changes, like whether to allow new members or the structure of governing institutions.

Unfortunately for those interested in clean models of institutions, the meaning of assent is not always codified. The threshold for assent is not always interpreted in the same way by interested units in specific moments. To learn how federated institutions reach settlement and move past these moments, we not only need to identify these moments and separate them out from normal governing periods, but also recognize the events that led them to pass. There comes a time when there is a pervasive sense among people within the federated system that the moment of assent has passed and it is time to move forward. These are the moments we focus on in later chapters. When Canadian politicians understood that the crises regarding Quebec's independence were largely resolved by the mid-1990s through tense negotiations and institutional alterations, the moment passed and Canada moved on.

Pliable Concepts

As will become clear in the following chapters, promulgation of a pliable concept is necessary to gain assent. Not all issues of institutional import can be settled. The subunits instead collectively agree on a set of pliable concepts that are vague and postpone difficult interpretative questions. For a settlement to occur that does not lead to rupture, or is not imposed on one group (centralizers or decentralizers, or both) against their deepest wishes, there is typically a set of words or concepts agreed upon – sometimes literally voted on and signed – that are well understood by all groups in that moment. "Well understood," however, does not mean that each group has the same understanding, or the same predictions of how the future will play out. In fact, the opposite is the case. The concepts and words are left deliberately vague in order to smooth over remaining differences and get on with the business of running the federated institutions. The task of clearly defining authority is left for the future.[17]

Concepts analyzed in later chapters – such as subsidiarity (for the Church and the European Union), or collegiality for the Church, or the M-Form organizational design for GM – loom as vitally important; there are words used to describe prerogative, such as "necessary and proper" in the U.S. Constitution. These concepts and words are used by subunits among themselves and between subunits and the central unit within federated systems to make claims of authority and autonomy.[18] The words provide frameworks for where authority resides, for cooperation among units, and for decision-making procedures. These concepts and words leave room for interpretation and can later cause misunderstanding and contestation. The vagueness at the moment of assent is inevitable and necessary. On the matter of inevitability, nearly all words used to define the allocation of authority will be vague in their application to specific contexts; that is why we need lawyers and judges.

---

[17] Bednar (2008) provides a theory of the "robust" federation that relies on the notion that violations of the federal bargain are imperfectly monitored and imperfectly punished. The imperfections are crucial, according to Bednar, to ensure that the federal bargain is not too brittle, but instead remain in place through periods of conflict. My notion of a pliable concept is related to, and certainly consistent with, her notion of imperfect monitoring and imperfect punishment. See also Dahl (1986).

[18] On this point, see Conglianese and Nicolaidis (2001), and Halberstam (2001).

Yet words spoken or written, and concepts shared, can range in clarity and ease of application. Take, for example, the words in Article 4 of the U.S. Constitution: "This Constitution, and the Laws of the United States ... shall be the supreme Law of the Land." This can scarcely be read as indicating that state courts can override federal court rulings, or that state laws can contradict the Constitution. Since the early nineteenth century, it has been well established that the federal courts can legitimately override state courts, although, of course, specific rulings can be controversial. In contrast, the three-part combination of the commerce clause ("Congress shall have Power To regulate Commerce ... among the several states"), the supremacy clause ("supreme Law of the Land"), and the Tenth Amendment ("The powers not delegated to the United States by the Constitution, nor prohibited by it to the States, are reserved to the States respectively, or to the people") have led to numerous and continuing disputes over meaning and the proper allocation of authority in the U.S. federation. It has been noted that the Tenth Amendment "does not alter the distribution of powers between the national and state governments," and "is merely a truism ... This amendment was adopted to assuage fears."[19]

These concepts bring together – or maintain – a union led by individuals and subunits who must look to the future with confidence in their ability to guard their own prerogative and autonomy. There are, at the time of agreement, different beliefs among people in how real decision making will occur in the future. As the future plays out, some subunit leaders will have their expectations dashed – usually those who believed, when agreeing to become part of the federation, that their autonomy would be maintained. Someone – usually members of subunits with the preferences most different from the "average" of the subunits – will end up being wrong in predicting the future. For example, when the U.S. Constitution was established, some state leaders signed on after being assured that the national government would not become too powerful; the Bill of Rights would provide protection for individuals and states. Others signed on believing that the central government would protect the southern states from anti-slavery movements, and especially from the mercantilist northern states and their key economic priorities.

Another example is how the term federalism itself was being used in the 1990s during controversies over the ratification of the Maastricht and Amsterdam treaties in Europe. It meant different things in the different domestic political debates of countries: the British and Danes believed federalism meant centralizing authority to the European level and away from the member states, whereas Germans, believed it meant preserving member-state autonomy relative to the central unit in Brussels.[20]

---

[19] Peltason, 1986, 305.
[20] Dinan (2010, 92–93). See Safire (2000) for a discussion of the contradictory meanings of federalism.

Partisanship

In political systems, we can think of partisanship as loyalty to a political party, but in the context of this book, it has a more general meeting, namely the self-identification with a group seeking common policy goals. Subunit leaders within an organization can be partisans when they come to understand their goals as being similar to a subset of others who desire power and influence within the organization.

Something happens over the course of a period of representative centralization that shifts the nature of the federated system.[21] The decision-making representatives of the subunits at the central level – members of Congress or the European Parliament or Commission, bishops and cardinals, executives of auto divisions – gradually begin to have interests that become increasingly more complicated and include factors beyond the interests of their subunits. Indeed, subunit representatives at the central level develop partisanship that has meaning increasingly at the central level. Their interests in protecting the autonomy of the subunits and in advancing the well-being of the subunits become diluted by several things: their own ambitions to lead to the central unit, their desire to gain the approval of the leaders of the central unit and to link their fates to those central leaders, and their prospects for career advancement within their subunits. This is the first key switch in partisanship – when representatives of subunits begin to act less as supporters of subunits and more as independent agents in a game for control of the central unit.

The next level of change that occurs, however, is when the executive leaders of the central unit gain autonomy to make policy and extract resources without the regular assent of the representative body (or bodies). Their own partisans within the representative body often permit this to happen. The key to having centralization locked-in is found in the political connection between the executive leaders and the subunit representatives so that the careers of the latter depend on the success or failure of the former. The primary mechanism for executive authority becoming locked-in is not change in formal codes over authority, but rather, change in peoples' expectations about where authority lies. The mechanism is the linkage of peoples' frameworks for understanding governance with specific executive initiatives and ideologies. As authority centralizes to an executive, it comes to mean the shared interest in promoting someone from their group to capture control of the executive office in the central unit.[22] And the definition of "their group" has changed from being defined by subunit boundaries to being defined by agreement or disagreement

---

[21] For an important perspective on the relationship between political parties and federalism, see Filippov, Ordeshook, and Shvetsova (2004). Their overall argument concerns the importance of partisan loyalties in keeping federations together and productive. See also Katz and Mair (1994), Muller (1993), and Lipset and Rokkan (1967).

[22] See Samuels (2002) and Samuels and Shugart (2010) for analyses of presidentialized political parties.

with central-unit policy goals as linked to executive action. Naturally, members of the U.S. Congress are partisans when they link their fates to a party label and to the fortunes of a presidential candidate.[23] Business executives can also be partisans when they tie their fates to the successes of other executives who share their goals, whether they are policy goals within their corporation or their ambitions for control over the corporation, or both. This is the essence of the final stage of partisanship.

Partisanship as I use it here, and as will be evident in our cases, is ultimately about how one thinks of oneself relative to authority.[24] It also relates to the way in which individuals are affected by governing bodies at various levels of government. It both responds to institutional change and enables its continued evolution. The change in partisanship often happens gradually through repeated behaviors and interactions, and after paying attention to where authority lies.

Lock-In

Movements within, across, or among subunits that might seek to reverse the executive centralization or the overall centralization to the central unit will face serious obstacles. The executive centralization essentially changes the character of the federation by creating built-in incentives by those at the top of the central unit to avoid decision-making processes that incorporate the voices of subunit leaders or representatives who genuinely care about subunit autonomy or interest. Executives maintain a governing style that focuses on preserving power and if necessary, placating representatives who do not so much represent the subunits as they do the interests of groups devoted to control the central unit.

Earlier I described moments of change, and in using the word *threshold* in this book, I refer to changes occurring that are widely recognized (usually at the time, but definitely after the fact) as being in the direction toward centralization. Some portion of those thresholds will lead to locked-in centralization. How can we recognize this special kind of threshold? There are two ways that are related and intertwine observationally. First, we observe that attempts by the subunits to decentralize are thwarted. We will see this most directly in two of our cases: the U.S. government and the Church. Second, we observe the presence of signature elements (tools) of executive authority that preempt or scuttle moves toward decentralization. We will see these elements in three of our cases (all except the EU) that have passed the threshold leading to lock-in.

What are these tools of executive authority? Once authority is centralized to the central unit and ultimately toward the executive, the executive can thwart

---

[23] Campbell (1997).

[24] See Cox (1987) for an influential account of how partisanship changes in response to increasing governmental authority. See also Caramani (2004), Ware (1996), and Chhibber and Kollman (2004).

efforts to undo the autonomy of that office in four specific ways. First – and most important in causing lock-in – the executive strengthens executive-centered groups (such as political parties or interest groups within the federated system) that link the fate of subunit representatives to the fate of the executive, which is based on the level of the executive's success. Second, the executive uses resources to divide and conquer the subunits that might otherwise oppose the executive. Third, the executive builds the bureaucratic capacity to become the obvious place for policy making and implementation. Bureaucratic structures persist, and when they can be wielded by the executive to extract and dispense resources, that gives the executive the upper hand in authority relations. The subunits themselves come to rely on the executive-led bureaucracies for their sustenance and information. Fourth, the executive plays a huge role in interpreting the vague concepts of assent that were previously discussed; this occurs either at the moment of their conception or, more likely, later when the concepts come under scrutiny.

To see the powerful effect of this fourth way of locking-in executive authority, consider the following alternative (fictional) history of the founding of the U.S. republic. Suppose there had been a strong president already in place prior to the Constitutional Convention, and George Washington was named the president of the new U.S. government in 1781. (In reality, he took office in 1789 *after* the Constitution was ratified.) Further, Washington wielded the power well, but firmly, to that point. Suppose there was concern among many about presidential power and the convention was called to address, among other things, concerns that the presidency was not what the state delegates wanted.

Then suppose Washington was invited to the Constitutional Convention to discuss the details of the new Constitution, and was granted extraordinary influence within that convention over the selection of presidential powers. Perhaps he could veto any passages proposed for the new Constitution that involved presidential powers relative to Congress, the courts, or the states. It is not hard to imagine that Washington probably would have sought to prevent any changes to reduce his power and in fact, would have attempted to solidify his presidential power as much as possible, making it subject to little constraint by Congress, the courts, or the states. Additionally, he would have insisted on having sway over any processes in the future that would interpret the law regarding presidential power. Most importantly from our perspective, he would have insisted that in times of crisis (defined by him), he would possess extraordinary powers to compel the states to contribute to his schemes for protecting the country or improving the country's situation.

This fictional scenario is predicated on the commonsense idea that when executives are involved in deciding how much authority the executive should have, it should be no surprise that they push for – or if possible, insist on – supremacy over subunits and over representative bodies within the central unit. An abstract version of this mind game is not too far from what eventually occurred in at least three of our four federated cases, as we will see in the following chapters. In the United States, the presidency has evolved to the point that he now plays a predominant role in shaping the interpretation of presidential power. The pope has retained complete supremacy over the Church by making sure that at key moments of threat to his authority, he has been able to veto proposals for sharing authority with bishops. And General Motors departed from a decentralized model of governance because its executive took advantage of ambiguity in his legitimate authority to control the subunits, and did so by making sure he controlled the interpretation of what was legitimate and what was not. This early moment in GM profoundly shaped its history as a corporation. The European Union is on the brink of a threshold whereby the executive could, under one future scenario, become not only supreme, but the interpreter of *how* supreme and over what areas of policy.

We are now ready to move on to our four cases. As made necessary by the nature of these cases, a few of the concepts detailed in this chapter have flexible boundaries. What counts as a moment, for instance, or what is the evidence for assent by subunit leaders? One may argue with specific categorizations in what follows, but taken as a whole, the trajectories of three of our cases have striking similarities. The fourth (the EU) sits at a crossroads. Metaphorically, its descent on a downhill slope toward executive centralization – the same path taken by the other three cases – would be easy to follow. Remaining near the summit, however, with its measure of decentralization and moderate representational centralization, will require conscious effort to fight gravity.

3

Nation-State

Until the early twentieth century, the national government was not much of a presence in the lives of most Americans. State governments had predominant authority over the internal affairs of their states. They regulated businesses, schools, police forces, byways, relief for the poor, zoning, and liquor sales. With the exceptions of national government intrusion into canal and harbor construction, the running of postal services and customs houses, and occasional drafts for wars – and wars themselves, with Native Americans (i.e., Indians) and Civil War opponents – national and state law, as well as revenues collected by Washington, D.C., sharply limited the role of the national government. Above all, it was expected that government in general be limited, and even if national government intruded, state government was where public policy decisions were made that most affected peoples' lives.[1]

A description of this time period – until about 1930 – is revealing. First, consider the incentives of the politically ambitious. In this past era, politicians ultimately strove to be mayors, state legislators, and governors. A stint as a member of the U.S. House of Representatives was often temporary and regarded as less desirable.[2] Ambitious politicians who wanted important jobs typically sought positions in state government, whereas joining the U.S. Congress was akin to a grand tour of Europe – an interesting sojourn and time away to gain perspective. Often, as a member of the ruling party in state government, one had to take

[1] McKay (2001, 13) summarizes the situation well: "While it is easy to infer that continuing national control over defense, internal order, social welfare, and important aspects of citizenship disqualified the EU from nation-state status, the historical experiences of other decentralized federations suggests otherwise. Until 1812, the defence of the US was mainly in the hands of state-controlled militias. No national policy authority existed in the US until the creation of the Federal Bureau of Investigation in the 1920s. States were the key providers of transfer payments to the needy until the 1930s ..."
[2] See Polsby (1968) for the seminal article contrasting congressional careers before and after the mid-twentieth century.

his turn in Washington. It helped the state governments to have representation in Washington, to stay informed, and especially, to fight against national policies that could harm the state. Occasionally, a native son would ascend to a position of real power in Washington, D.C. – perhaps even president – and that could be beneficial to the people in the home state. Capturing the chairmanship of a key committee could pay dividends for a state. In sum, the purpose of being in Congress was to look toward one's home state as the beneficiary.

In addition, consider the committees of state legislatures in the nineteenth and first part of the twentieth centuries. State houses and senates typically had committees with titles such as "Militia," "Veterans Affairs," "Military Affairs," "Public Defense," and "Immigration." Even as late as the 1930s, a look at the committee titles among the state legislatures reveals that state leaders considered it their responsibility to cover the full range of activities that were also the typical responsibilities of nation-states at the time. The committee titles reflect a widespread understanding of states in the nineteenth century as quasi-sovereign units.[3]

U.S. federalism does not look like this anymore. The bulk of the action now takes place in Washington, D.C. A huge proportion of Americans receive life-sustaining cash assistance and medical insurance directly from the national government. A large majority of their tax dollars go there, too. The state governments now rely heavily on the national government for grants, transfers, and subsidies. They have to conform to standards set in Washington, D.C. for their police departments, roads, schools, and medical clinics. The structure of their tax systems mirrors that of the national government. On many matters – for instance, in education and medical policies over the last dozen years – the national government is the maestro and the states are members of an orchestra, coordinating with the maestro's baton so as to be in sync and get paid for contributing to the overall effort. Today, the economic health of a given state or region is directly affected by decisions taking place in Washington: from military contracts and the building of military bases to the awarding of earmarks to local universities; from small business grants and loans to the building of roads and the making of lakes, rivers, and waterways; from the declaration of nationally protected wetlands and national parks, forests, and preserves to the national regulations that affect nearly every aspect of work, play, and living in one's home.

In today's political environment, state legislators typically consider their time at the state capital as the minor leagues compared to the major leagues in Washington, D.C. They bide their time waiting for members of the U.S.

---

[3] I conducted an analysis of committee names in state legislatures in state government handbooks, selecting random years at ten-year intervals for dozens of states. The pattern described here and in a subsequent paragraph is unmistakable and irrefutable. I gained access to the most extensive list of books on Rhode Island and New York (see the *Rhode Island Manual* and the *New York Assembly*) and I also had access to sporadic state manuals for many other states. See also *Book of the States* (various years).

Congress to retire or for the opportune moment to challenge an incumbent member of Congress. The ultimate goal is most often Washington, not only because of the spotlight, but also because what happens in Washington deeply affects the home state. If one wants to improve circumstances for the state, where better to be than in Washington, D.C. to capture federal money or shape regulation affecting one's local companies?

As for state legislatures, committee names reflect the authoritative responsibilities of states. Today there are committees on, among other things, education, finance, corrections, elections, transportation, and labor. By the 1970s, states no longer had committees in charge of the militia, public defense, or veterans affairs. Neither do states today (with rare exceptions) consider immigration to be within their purview. Besides adding to its own agenda enormous areas of responsibility such as social security, medical and financial assistance, and technical research, the national government by the mid-twentieth century had removed wide swaths of policy responsibility from the states' agendas.

This before-and-after depiction might seem exaggerated or too starkly rendered. It surely leaves out important countervailing features and diminishes the value of a comparative viewpoint with other countries. In comparison with many other countries around the world, even many federations, the United States remains a robustly federated country, with shared power across levels of government and protected status of the states. The states retain key authority over important matters. They have much autonomy to tax and spend relative to their peer regional governments in other countries. State governments are directly elected and protected from national government intrusion on many matters. Governors cannot be sacked by the national government, for instance, and there are substantial hurdles before the national government can step in to override the authority of governors and state legislatures, even on matters of public order. On most matters involving money, the national government cannot act without the approval of representatives elected by citizens of the states. Therefore, when political scientists closely examine the degree of centralization across the world's democratic countries, they rate the United States as highly decentralized.[4]

Yet, if we compare over time – the United States before, say, 1910 and after 1955 – the contrast is unmistakable. The previous description of two eras, although missing nuance, is largely true. To live in the United States in the nineteenth century and then in the late twentieth or early twenty-first century would entail being transported to a country unrecognizable for more than just the technological wonders. The authority of the national government would astound, maybe trouble, this time traveller. Even the size of state governments changed.

---

[4] Hooghe, Marks, and Schakel (2010) provide a convincing and useful systematic measurement of the degrees of centralization across democratic countries.

Take, for instance, the governor of 1925: he could expect a few congressional dollars for highways, agricultural extension work, and vocational education ... Otherwise he expected little, and worried less about the bickering on Pennsylvania Avenue ... His successor in 1940 inhabited a different world. While purely intrastate matters continued to dominate the governor's time, national policy intimately affected the economic health of his state and his own political future. Like it or not he usually played along with the New Deal ... Partly because of federal activism, the American state of 1940 spent more, taxed more, and provided much more than it had two decades before.[5]

A comparison of most countries from the nineteenth and twentieth centuries, some might retort, would lead to the same conclusion about the remarkable power of their national governments now as opposed to the past. The point is apt, but as discussed in more detail in Chapter 7, there is variety in whether and when the trajectory toward larger government became monotonic (one-directional) among explicitly federal countries. Also, some countries are more locked-in to executive centralization than others.

The overall trend toward centralization in the United States has been pronounced and palpable, despite some fits and starts along the way; moments of centralization – such as during the Civil War, for example – were partially reversed in later decades. One can quibble over the details of particular moments, decades, or governmental actions and court decisions, but the real story is well known and accepted, based on two centuries' worth of examples. U.S. federalism has experienced mostly steady movement from state-based authority to dominance and substantial control from Washington, D.C. It has occurred sometimes as slow accretion, and sometimes in punctuated bursts, toward executive centralization.

Historical Overview

A typical rendition of changing authority in the U.S. federation would break history into periods.[6]

Pre-Civil War: decentralized, with states predominant

Civil War: brief period of centralization

Late Nineteenth Century: return to decentralization, with small moves toward national regulation

Progressive Era: increasing regulation, defense buildup culminating in national income tax, but states remain predominant

New Deal Era: dramatic rise of national power, strengthening of national regulatory agencies and Washington becoming responsible for relief from economic distress

Post-New Deal and World War II: enormous financial and regulatory influence of the national government over the states; if anything, the national government has only increased its influence over the states since the 1950s.

---

[5] Patterson (1969, 198).
[6] See Scheiber (1980, 681) for this same listing of eras.

This list reflects an historical tableau in broad strokes. The Founders created a true federation, but one with vaguely defined powers for the national government. Prior to the Civil War (up to 1860), the national government was weak. State governments were also weak to the extent that people paid attention to their government and governments took actions affecting people's lives. The Civil War briefly centralized authority away from the states and toward the national governments of the Union and the Confederacy in order to wage total war. After the war, economic and social policies largely returned to state control, again to the extent that such control existed at any level.

In the late nineteenth century, a process of creating an administrative state at the national level began, with regulatory commissions and statutory changes establishing uniform commercial rules across the entire country. This continued slowly through the Progressive Era, and then the size and reach of the national government enhanced dramatically with the New Deal (1930s), in which scores of new regulatory bodies, social security and welfare systems, and agencies were created for the purpose of coordinating and subsidizing relief programs jointly run by states and the national government.[7] U.S. international predominance after World War II added to these new domestic institutions a huge set of defense agencies with enormous budgets, largesse to construct military bases and research facilities, and the ability to award defense contracts to local areas around the country.

By the late 1950s, the political economy of every part of the United States – including transportation, research, and higher education – was affected by actions of the national government. The 1960s and 1970s saw increased attention to alleviating poverty through nationally led programs that made the states dependent on federal-to-state transfers. In the late twentieth century, there was some slowing down of centralization and even resistance, with some policy areas devolving toward the states deliberately. In the first part the twenty-first century, a confirmation of the centralized nature of the federation occurred amid concerns over security from terrorism and losing economic steam relative to foreign competitors, with states deeply reliant on national government funding for police, education, medical care, transportation, and research.

There are various perspectives on this trajectory, some complementary and some at odds. It could be that the centralization was an inexorable process, inevitable because it was built into the institutional fabric of the country at the Founding. The Constitution was too vague about limits on national power, and a leviathan national government took advantage when possible.[8] Some might focus attention on how changing technologies made centralization inexorable, and that new transportation and communication technologies increasingly

---

[7] Skowronek (1982) offers a widely heralded account of the building of the U.S. bureaucratic state.
[8] The work of neofunctionalists comes close to this view (see Keohane 1984). See also Lakoff (1994), Miller (1992), Moe (2005), Rakove (1997, chapter 7), Rubin and Feeley (1994), Shapiro (1995), Tilly (1990), Tullock (1994), White (2000), Wood (1969), Higgs (1987), Derthick (1999), Elazar (1972), Riker (1964, 1987), and of course, Brutus (1787–88).

made both problems and potential solutions to those problems national in scope. As a variant of these perspectives, clearly centralization was punctuated by specific moments, such as the Civil War and the New Deal, and was not so gradual or inexorable.[9]

Another vantage point is that the current situation is a sort of saturation; centralization is largely complete – the states are no longer meaningful political entities with autonomy.[10] Alternatively, one might concede a measure of centralization, but argue that decentralized U.S. federalism is alive and well, with the states and the central unit being balanced in a relatively healthy way.[11] Finally, scholars of law point out how the federal courts have been the necessary players in protecting the states and preserving whatever federal balance exists.[12]

All of these perspectives are helpful, although some are more descriptively or historically accurate than others. To argue, as some do, that the states today are hardly meaningful politically goes too far. But to claim that the national government, in fact, is constrained and weak without the implicit approval of state representatives misses the many ways by which the national government – especially the executive branch – can act unilaterally or divide and conquer state leaders. It uses its enormous financial, regulatory, and legal capacities to overpower states when there is a conflict over authority.[13] The courts occasionally check national authority, but only in specific policy areas.

Any explanation for the shift toward centralization in the United States must include the notion of momentum, of spasms at crucial moments that occurred because of institutional changes building on what happened previously, and then after those spasms, the centralization solidified gradually thereafter.[14] We

---

[9] See, for example, Higgs (1987), Scheiber (1980), Chhibber and Kollman (1998 and 2004), Higgens-Evenson (2003), and Bryce (1888).

[10] Rubin and Feeley (1994) provide a strong version of this point of view. See also Higgs (2007).

[11] See Eskridge and Ferejohn (1994), Bednar, Eskridge, and Ferejohn (2001), Ferejohn and Weingast (1997), Kramer (1994), Teaford (2002), Beer (1993), Burns and Gamm (2000), Ostrom (1991), and Weingast (1995).

[12] See Bednar (2008), Eskridge and Ferejohn (1994), and Bednar, Eskridge, and Ferejohn (2001).

[13] See Baack and Ray (1985b), Donahue (1997), Riker (1987), and Higgs (1987, 2004, 2007).

[14] Higgs (1987) has a theory of why "the ratchet" toward big government. By this he means the encroachment of government on the economy. His basic argument is that crises create spaces for government to increase its involvement, to pass laws, to create the bureaucracy, to develop the legal theories and political ideologies that justify the interventions, and especially, the interest groups that become dependent on government also become skilled defenders of rent-seeking. His argument is related to mine, except for two important differences: he starts from a normative position that markets should be free and subject to little government regulation, and he is focused on government intervention on the economy from any level (although his examples are from the national government – Progressives, the New Deal, and the Great Society programs). In contrast, I take no normative position about the desirability of "big government" versus "small government," and my focus is on the relative authority of the national government versus state governments. However, I share with Higgs the interpretation of U.S. history as a ratcheting of national political power that ticks markedly upward during and immediately following crises.

will devote much of our attention to three crucial moments in this history: the Founding, the establishment of the income tax, and the New Deal. There are other time periods meriting discussion, although these three – and especially the last – ratcheted the U.S. federation profoundly. The basic arguments made here are four fold. First, the Founding laid the institutional basis for both representative and executive centralization because the system it created combined separation of powers and federalism. Second, most of the centralization in the nineteenth century (with the short exception of the Civil War) and through the Progressive Era was of the representative variety. Third, the New Deal blended the two types of centralization with the executive type becoming the most consequential and lasting, which led to locked-in national centralization. Fourth, national government authority – predominant over the states – is largely locked-in with little or no possibility of true decentralization toward more state autonomy any time soon.

Throughout all of the eras, the mechanisms identified in Chapter 2 were crucial. My arguments about the mechanisms hinge on several points; it helped that the Constitution was vague about centralization. State leaders and their representatives by and large assented to representative centralization and to most – but not all – instances of executive centralization. Evidence from all three of these crucial time periods is straightforward on establishing assent by subunits. Moreover, the nature of political parties and partisanship changed over time as both cause and consequence of the centralizing changes that occurred in governance. Most generally, the parties – and people's identifications with the parties – became nationalized and then focused on the executive.

The two types of centralization happened largely in chronological order in the United States, although there was overlap. Representative centralization was the more steady and gradual, and was manifest through substantial buy-in from the states and from Congress when members of Congress were acting as representatives of the states' interests. The executive track was less steady, and even had reversals. But the 1930s and 1940s comprised a threshold era, when the executive in the national government amassed the resources and solidified executive-led political parties to such degrees that overall centralization to the national government became locked-in. Of special importance was the evolving nature of political parties into executive-led nationalized institutions – and the seizing of opportunities by presidents to turn powers that were justified as temporary in times of crisis into permanent authority over certain kinds of policies. The combinations mattered: representative and executive centralization occurring in combination with changing nature of partisanship.

Representative Centralization – Founding and the Nineteenth Century

Representative centralization involves the assent of subunit leaders at two stages: first, at the creation of or change into new institutional forms permitting centralized decision making (what we might call a change in authority relations); and second, when policies are chosen through a collective choice process involving the representatives of the subunits in a representative body. The Founding and the income tax battle offer two clean examples of the first stage – a moment of creation assented to by the subunits. Later, I also discuss how some aspects of the New Deal were also instances of representative centralization, although more of the latter type; policies chosen rather than authority relations fundamentally changed.

The original Founding period when the Constitution was written and ratified was a radical act of centralization, if seen in relative terms to what preceded that period. Regardless of how that era compares to later historical moments in the overall degree of federal power, the creation of a new regime under the Constitution was undoubtedly an enormous transfer of authority from state to national government with the eventual assent of all thirteen states.

Why did the states agree to such a centralizing document as the U.S. Constitution? There are four interrelated reasons.[15] First, state leaders (by which I mean state legislatures or governors – the notables who ran the states) feared the European powers, and thus understood a strong central government, including a relatively strong presidency, as necessary to maintain military power that protects the states and U.S. economic interests.

Second, state leaders feared internal division and potential war within the North American continent. There were various threats to internal peace as perceived by the state leaders, including rebellion by dissident population groups, war and sabotage waged by Native American tribes, and conflicts among the states over territory, claims on foreign lands, and money. Among the greatest threats to peace were ambiguous state boundaries and definitions of ownership of western lands.[16] By granting the national government authority to define and enforce state boundaries and claims on western lands, the states would avoid war with each other.

Third, state leaders were weary and wary of fierce competition among the states for foreign trade. Centralization of trade policy and trade negotiation authority enabled them to devise a united, collusive trade bloc against larger economies in Europe.

And fourth, some states saw advantages to a stronger union, and compromised. Leaders of the smaller states and leaders of the larger states, for example, agreed to compromise on questions of representation. The smaller states envisioned having a centralized power – the national government – to protect them against being bullied by the larger states, and leaders of the larger states envisioned being predominant within the national government. These groups of states were willing to join together as long as the representative scheme was

---

[15] See Rakove (1997) for an excellent overview of the entire Founding process. See also Ellis (2008) and Wood (1969) for entertaining accounts. See also Elster (1995).

[16] This is an underappreciated point about the Founding, but is made clear by the pioneering work of Onuf (1983), Onuf and Matson (1990), and Onuf and Onuf (1994).

not too out of line with their long-term interests. The small states agreed to have a small voice in the central government in return for drawing clear boundaries of autonomy that the larger states could not encroach upon. The larger states reluctantly agreed to share some real power with the smaller states represented in the Senate in return for substantial power in the House of Representatives and in choosing the presidency. On a different matter (not size of state, but type of economy) the states with substantial slave economies received assurances in the Constitution itself against national-level encroachment. Whereas most state leaders recognized these threats and problems and saw centralization as the appropriate solution, it was not a foregone conclusion that they would approve something as centralizing as the Constitution.

These four reasons, when considered together, form a core account of the Founding. They make it understandable how a coalition of centralizers was able to win over some – and ultimately defeat others – who feared centralization more than they feared these threats and problems. Nevertheless, an anti-Federalist, were he alive today, might utter a version of the adage that history is written by the winners.[17] The standard historical account makes it sound as if the centralizing Constitution had to happen for these reasons and that the federalists were brilliant theorists whereas the anti-federalists were selfish protectors of privilege within their home-state domains.[18]

In fact, although the coalition that wrote and approved the Constitution included people with different views about how the "federalism" of the U.S. republic should and would unfold, they also agreed on a decentralized country, by and large. There was a shared concern to preserve the sovereignty of the states against central encroachment. Even the centralizers among Founders, with a few exceptions, generally held the view that the states would retain their powers and the national government would remain weak.[19] If so, they believed, people would have the advantages of living in small republics free from the dangers of being small and vulnerable.[20]

The Constitution itself was an attempt to make more concrete the concept of a federal bargain. The states were the component parts of the political system, and held residual powers. Yet they not only had obligations to the union; they also agreed to abide by decisions made by the central governing units. On the centralized side of the ledger, the Constitution put the following words into

[17] A careful reading of Brutus and other anti-Federalist authors shows how skeptical they were, in a reasonable way, of Federalist assurances that the national government would protect state interests against national power.

[18] See, for example, Ellis (2008).

[19] The *Federalist Papers* are filled with assurances that the states would retain their "vitality."

[20] The term "Congress," for instance, was used to describe the legislative body of the national government instead of "Parliament" because the former was used in Europe in that era (and still today) to refer to a meeting of the sovereign states of Europe, whereas the latter meant a body with its own sovereign authority to decide on behalf of the entire country (Donahue 1997, 18). The terminology signifies an understanding that the federation would be highly decentralized, with mostly reserved powers with constituent, sovereign units: the states.

the lexicon of (U.S.) governance: necessary and proper, the commerce clause, and the supremacy clause. The centralizers and decentralizers agreed later to include the Tenth Amendment, which supposedly protected the states from national encroachment. The collection of passages in the Constitution was ultimately vague about federalism, and, according to some, contradictory. Its words did not settle how federalism would play out (how could any words?) and gave both centralizers and decentralizers hope that their visions for the future of the union would be fulfilled. Even if vagueness kicked the proverbial can down the road for later generations to settle, it helped preserve the federal bargain.[21]

Vagueness about the powers of the president made matters complicated as well. The Constitution proscribed the president's powers, some of which were clear and others hard to interpret. Certainly, powers to veto legislation and the pardon were relatively straightforward. As the lead diplomat for the country, the president's role was also clear. But he was to "take Care that the Laws be faithfully executed" and was to be "Commander in Chief" of the armed forces, "when [the armed forces were] called into the actual Service of the United States." Both the "take Care" clause and the role of commander in chief left much room for interpretation, which presidents later exploited to their advantage. As with the language about national powers relative to the states, the language about the president was vague enough that Founders representing various interests could sign on with optimism that in the future, their interpretation would win out.[22]

These words enabled the assent of the states that was necessary for the union to occur and the federal bargain to continue. This assent was also based on an understanding that Congress was to be the predominant branch in the national government, and moreover, that the Senate, being composed of representatives of the state governments, would give the states a direct voice in national policy. No one state could veto national policy, but a collection of states could. The president, meanwhile, was a figure ostensibly removed from and above day-to-day politics, overseeing a small number of bureaus, and involved in decision making when national interests were at stake.[23] In the early years of the Republic, leaders in the states and leaders of the major parties in Congress were agreed on these elements.

Not surprisingly, however, there was division over the appropriate powers of the central government to compel the states on matters not explicitly identified in the Constitution. A tendency toward a regional split hampered coalition formation. The Founding Era and subsequent decades saw the Southern states as decentralizers and the Northern states as centralizers. Southern states in the

---

[21] Bednar's (2008) innovative book describes the usefulness of vague concepts in federations and how they smooth over problems, putting disputes into courtrooms as opposed to battlefields.

[22] See Rakove (1997), Peltason (1987), and Riker (1964).

[23] See Howell (2003) and Skowronek (1997).

first part of the nineteenth century were primarily interested in maintaining decentralization for two reasons. First, they feared onerous policy changes at the national level that would threaten their autonomy to maintain their slave economies. Second, they feared that centralization would, because of the numerical advantages of manufacturing and banking states, lead to more trade barriers (i.e., higher tariffs) that would hurt Southern planters. Northern states wished for more centralization because they wanted these tariffs and because they stood to gain from national government investment in infrastructure in the relatively undeveloped, new Midwestern states. The investment meant money to forge canals, build roads, new postal routes, forts to fight Native Americans, and pay surveyors to plan cities.

From then on after the Founding, representative centralization took the form of Congressional lawmaking (usually with presidential approval in the form of a signature on a law) that asserted authority to nationalize a given policy area. The Congress asserted the authority to level taxes on all citizens or compel them to contribute to the armed forces, or to force uniformity over all the states on selected matters such as providing routes for postal carriers in the early years to mandating worker safety regulations in recent times. After all, just about any lawmaking act by the national government is a centralizing act. Generally, as the national government makes laws, it centralizes. Over time it will accumulate laws. Even when the national government makes a law devolving authority to the states – for example, the welfare reforms in 1996 and 1997 – it is using its well-established authority to decide whether to devolve. Representative centralization can also occur when the state governments themselves are involved in the form of constitutional amendment procedures that strengthen Congress, as the income tax example will highlight.

With the exception of some moments in the presidencies of Jackson, Lincoln, and Theodore (Teddy) Roosevelt (discussed later in this chapter), centralization in the nineteenth and early twentieth centuries was mostly led by congressional efforts. One can mark a period of representative centralization after the Founding until the 1930s. In the earliest periods, three policy areas in particular attracted congressional attention and led to centralizing schemes: Western expansion, banking, and economic development. Federal court decisions friendly to an expansive interpretation of the commerce clause bolstered congressional efforts. For the middle part the nineteenth century, representative centralization was initially driven by fears and then the reality of division between North and South, and then aided further by the tragedy of the Civil War. Both the issues of slavery and tariffs drove the regional splits. Then finally, in the Progressive Era, Congress began to regulate the effects of new technologies of transportation and communication and sought to redress gross imbalances of wealth and industrial power, culminating in the passage of the income tax amendment.

Presidents were not the prime movers behind centralization through the nineteenth century. For instance, Congress passed the Missouri Compromise before the Civil War, rescinded it with the Kansas-Nebraska act, and then passed reconstruction acts post-Civil War with limited presidential input or hostility. Both the Missouri Compromise and the reconstruction acts passed with substantial margins, and all three legislative actions were proposed and led by congressional leaders. President James Monroe did not intrude into the congressional debates over the Missouri Compromise and although he signed the law, he questioned its constitutionality. President Franklin Pierce played a small but timely role in the passage of the Kansas-Nebraska act when he prodded Democrats to go along with it and suggested a few key phrases in the amendment. Senator Stephen Douglas – not Pierce – was the driver of the legislation.[24] President Andrew Johnson vetoed the major reconstruction acts, which were subsequently and overwhelmingly passed in override votes. Johnson's actions on reconstruction, including dragging his feet in implementation, led to impeachment and near removal from office.

In these centralizing moves, Congress and the states held the executive in check and retained the balance of the ongoing decision-making authority. Even as the national government began to regulate commerce using executive agencies in the 1880s and through the Progressive Era into the 1910s, these agencies were given limited autonomy from congressional control.[25] The first regulatory commissions for railroads, and then later for electronic communication, marked the beginnings of a change toward an active administrative state, and these were the stirrings of a more permanent executive centralization. But Congress and the courts held the line for a long time against strong assertions of autonomous presidential and executive power. Only through considerable efforts late in the Progressive Era by agency leaders to develop industrial and social constituencies was legislation rewritten to protect regulators from day-to-day Congressional pressure. The transition occurred later when, for the first time, the national government built parts of a bureaucracy with some independence from Congress and enough expertise to develop political constituencies that could take on powerful senators.[26]

Representative Centralization – Income Tax

Congress and the states maintained their major roles in approving centralized actions well into the twentieth century. In perhaps the most consequential act of representative centralization after the Founding, Congress passed – and then nearly all the states approved – the federal income tax. This culminated

[24] For accounts of this era and these presidents, see Howe (2007), Ammon (1990), and Potter and Fehrenbacher (1976).
[25] Skowronek (1982), Sylla (2000), and Carpenter (2001).
[26] Carpenter's (2001) important book describes the persistence of bureaucratic leaders during the Progressive Era in building their own constituencies apart from congressional support. See also Vietor (2000).

in the 1913 constitutional amendment. Like earlier moments of representative centralization, the federal income tax battle was led by leaders in Congress, with presidents more or less on the sidelines. The legislation's structure preserved for Congress the authority to set the details of the tax itself.

The income tax fight is worth expounding on as it highlights the two sides of representative centralization: the approval by the states and their representatives of the basic institutional change toward centralized authority, and the subsequent policy making in the aftermath by the Congress. It also offers a contrast with executive centralization, especially of the kind occurring in the 1930s.

An 1894 income-tax law was struck down by the U.S. Supreme Court in a series of decisions, known in summary as the *Pollock v. Farmers' Loan and Trust Co.* (1895). The Court ruled that the law violated the Constitution's prohibition on Congress's authority to tax persons directly without being proportioned among the states. The Court had no problem with state income taxes, which had been variously imposed since the Civil War; however, the Court was specifically concerned with congressional authority to tax people directly.

The 1894 vote on the law in Congress had been sectional. By and large, representatives from Southern and Western states voted in favor of the law while those from the North, especially from the wealthiest Northeastern states, voted against it.[27] The vote was widely seen as an attempt by the less-wealthy states to replace the burdensome tariff with an income tax, shifting the tax burden to the Northeast, and hopefully passing additional legislation that would enable the federal government to spend money on internal improvements in the poorer parts of the country. Important to our later story about political parties is that the early 1890s voting on the income tax pitted region against region and state against state.

Supporters of such a tax among Democrats and reform Republicans stayed the course. In 1909, the Congress almost passed an income-tax law that was narrowly tailored by its proponents in the hope that it would survive court scrutiny. That proposed law had enough opponents to defeat it, especially from the industrial Northeast. As part of an attempt to thwart the income-tax momentum, Northeastern, conservative Republican senators, led by Nelson Aldrich of Rhode Island, proposed a constitutional amendment permitting an income tax. It was part of a deal they struck with President Taft at the time. Proposing the amendment was a popular move for the party as a whole but one that "stand-pat" (i.e., conservative) Republicans hoped would ultimately defeat the income tax movement because they thought the amendment would be killed by the states. It is worth noting that Taft had publicly supported the income tax as a presidential candidate in 1907, but was not much involved in the Congressional action. Neither he nor members of Congress – both those in

---

[27] This is clear from the data analysis in Baack and Ray (1985a). See also Sylla (2000).

favor and opposed – considered the amendment to be a change resulting in a more powerful presidency or executive branch.[28]

The income-tax amendment was overwhelmingly passed by Congress in 1909. Supporters held the commonsense view that it could only help the cause, and in a situation not uncommon in legislative politics, many opponents actually voted for the tax. Opponents supported it with the belief that by passing the amendment – which they thought would never pass the states – they were forestalling statutory efforts to write an income-tax law that would pass constitutional muster. One irony is that Aldrich wrote the amendment, but he opposed corporate and personal income taxes; by all indications, he was instrumental in making Rhode Island one of the six states that ultimately did not pass the amendment.[29]

Most knowledgeable observers at the time believed that these stand-patters would be vindicated; that the income tax amendment would ultimately fail. Only twelve states were needed to block the amendment, and even though many states immediately passed it within the first year, the momentum among the states stalled. As late as spring 1911, it looked as though the amendment would be defeated. The *New York Times* in March 1911 ran several in-depth articles that predicted defeat for the amendment.[30] Six states had outright rejected it up to that time, and the *Times* mentioned four other states that were definitely leaning against it. It seemed certain that at least twelve states would fail to approve the amendment, thus killing it. Most of the remaining states that were leaning against or had voted against it were from the Northeast.

The turnaround came in spring 1911 when the key state – New York, which had rejected the amendment twice in the previous two years – reversed course and approved it in July 1911, to the surprise of many.[31] Other holdout states, many in the Northeast, approved it over the next twenty-one months. Overall, forty-two states approved, and among the six that did not, at least one chamber of the state legislature passed the amendment.

Why the switch occurred and why the ultimate passage of the amendment included support from many of the Northeastern states has been the subject of debate among historians. Some credit the rise of progressivism in the states, others claim that the Northeastern and upper-Midwestern states were bought off with money for naval bases and veterans benefits. And some argue, plausibly, that the income tax projected to pass would be quite moderate and hardly redistributive; it therefore won the support of enough Republican moderates.

[28] This history of the fight over the income tax is told, in various levels of detail, in Ratner (1942), Stanley (1993), (1985), Cataldo and Savage (2001), Comstock (1929), Joseph (2004), Waltman (1985), Weisman (2002), Witte (1985), and Baack and Ray (1985a). For the role of Taft, see especially Ratner (1942).

[29] See Stanley (1993) and Ratner (1942) for details on Aldrich's role. See also Conable and Singleton (1989).

[30] *The New York Times* reporting is summarized in Baack and Ray (1985a) and also Stanley (1993).

[31] Stanley (1993) analyzes the state-level New York vote in detail.

The Republican moderates were likely persuaded that the tax would only fall on the wealthiest citizens, and would not have the overall effect of redistributing wealth to other states.[32]

Of relevance to our analysis is the question of why those concerned about national versus state power became persuaded to go along with the amendment. The issue boils down to what these people were predicting about the future powers of the national government. There is, first of all, the interesting question of how people like Aldrich and his colleagues who opposed the amendment could have guessed so wrong about the future of the amendment. They miscalculated badly. But a lot was changing at that time, including insurgent progressives in 1912 led by Theodore Roosevelt who were mobilizing former Republicans against the old party guard and the brand of conservatism they represented. Aldrich could not have foreseen this in 1909. Second, and far more puzzling, was the fact that many of those who were sympathetic in general to American decentralization ended up supporting the amendment for ideological reasons without foreseeing the spigot the amendment would open.

In fact, the conflict over the income tax was infused with questions about national-state power from the very beginning. Proponents of the tax tried to argue that its subject was not really federalism, but rather the raising of revenues in a fair way based on people's ability to pay. But during the culmination of the 1894 Congressional debate on the bill that eventually became the original income tax (the Wilson Tariff), those arguing against its passage complained that such a tax would be sectional. They contended that it would redistribute from the Northeast to the South and West, and that it would trample on states' rights.[33] When the Supreme Court struck down the law as unconstitutional in 1895, Justice Brewer stated that it was an attack on states' "vitality."

During the latter stage of the Progressive Era, when various governors led by Charles Hughes of New York came out against the amendment, opponents decried the possibility that an income-tax law by Congress would enable the national government to tax income from state and municipal bonds, and that this would open the door wide to national imposition on the states. This was a major hurdle for proponents to overcome. There was intense opposition from state leaders concerned that income derived from interest on state bonds would be taxed by the national government. It was widely thought then (and even

[32] For the argument that it was the rise in the states of the Democrats and the progressive Republicans that turned the tide, see Buenker (1985). For the argument that it was in fact a triumph of "centrism," that it was an easy way for moderates in the Northeast to claim to their left-leaning constituents that they supported the income tax while they could claim to their right-leaning constituents that the income tax was not going to be progressive, and that it would have little allocatable significance, see Stanley (1993). For an argument that explains the switch by arguing that the Northeastern states were bought off by the rest of the states with funding for naval shipyards and veterans' pensions, see Baack and Ray (1985a).

[33] Ratner (1942) has numerous quotations and detailed summaries of the writings and speeches of politicians during the income tax fight, and these altogether are straightforwardly interpreted in this manner.

today) that a national tax on income from state and local bonds would exceed permissible national powers, but the matter had not yet been settled. Leaders from New York and New Jersey in 1910–13 were especially worried because of the large numbers of people in their states working in banking and finance. (Law and current legal interpretation hold that such incomes are not taxable by the national government.)

Agreement on the income tax – if we can, in the abstract, consider the overwhelming support for the amendment to signal an agreement on its merits –reflected one of three major concerns about national power. First, the money newly spent by the national government was starting to benefit the states enough to justify the taxes, even if the taxes crept up.[34] This mindset was probably increasing in frequency as progressives gained power within the Republican Party and the Democrats surged in the state legislatures. Both Democrats and progressives were comfortable with an active, larger national government. Second, the overall goal of redistribution across income classes had gained enough support even within the wealthier states (i.e., state leaders saw the internal redistribution within their states as worthwhile). This mindset begs the question of why the states did not just conduct their own income-tax schemes, and instead supported a national scheme. Third, there was a confidence that the national government would use the taxes in much the same way it had used other streams of income from tariffs: to fund a limited government with limited reach into the prerogatives of the states.

This last mindset seems naïve in retrospect, but available evidence suggests it was widespread. Supporters of the amendment made various arguments that in the end swayed quite a few governors and nearly all the state legislatures. John Franklin Fort, governor of New Jersey, wrote a letter to the Senate leadership in 1910, expressing his confidence in the representatives in Congress to protect the sovereignty of the states: "As to the claim that the Federal Government might injure the States, as such, by taxing state bonds under an income tax … The Congress is representative of the States and elected by the citizenship thereof, and the remedy is in the hands of the people of the States by not returning such Congressmen."[35] Fort's confidence in the link between the interests

---

[34] A stronger version of this: "Congress, through its use of discretionary power in allocating federal expenditures among states, appears to have played a critical role in forging the coalition that passed the income-tax amendment. By capturing the support of states like Maine, Massachusetts, and New York supporters of the amendment had the votes necessary to risk taking a constitutional amendment to the states" (Baack and Ray 1985a, 624). Their conclusion fails to account for the well-documented attitude among the people who wrote the amendment that they did so in order to ultimately *defeat* the move toward the income tax (Ratner 1942). That does not mean that other proponents might not have captured the idea and did what Baack and Ray contend. But the timing is off here, in that Baack and Ray posit that proponents began ten years earlier to target benefits to win over states, well before the amendment was proposed. It asks much of the prescient powers of members of Congress to target benefits beginning around 1902 for an amendment that was eventually passed by Congress in 1909.

[35] Fort (1910).

of state governments and members of Congress is noteworthy, and from our perspective today, naïve even for his time. (Although as he wrote, senators in many states were still appointed by state legislators.)

He went on:

> [N]o Congress could be elected that would lay any tax with a view of destroying the power or integrity of the States. If this be not true, the relation of our States to the Republic is surely of much less importance than many of us have hitherto supposed ... Under a republican form of government the people rule, and they can be safely trusted to see that their representatives make no unjust exactions in the way of taxation or in the curtailing of the rights of the State or otherwise.[36]

Elihu Root, former secretary of war and secretary of state, writing in his position as a senator from New York in 1910, stated confidently,

> This amendment will be no new grant of power. The Congress already has the power to impose taxes on incomes from whatever source derived ... but the taxes so imposed must be apportioned among the States ... It appears therefore that no danger to the powers or instrumentalities of the State is to be apprehended from the adoption of the amendment.[37]

These words from Root in a letter to the *New York Times* reflect a reasonable legal interpretation of the amendment's likely affects, but they were proven demonstrably false in short order. New income taxes passed by Congress following the amendment would become the main source of revenue for a national government fighting two major world wars, and, more importantly, become a primary regulator and stimulator of the economy, as well as a major agent of redistribution across the country's social groups.

Taking their statements at face value, both Root and Fort were poor predictors of the future. They badly miscalculated the effects of the amendment. Fort saw the world much as an anti-Federalist, but favored this particular centralizing act. Fort understood that the amendment had deep implications for U.S. federalism and that at its core, it was about federal power. Although he recognized that an "unleashed" national government could be injurious to the states, he remained optimistic that Congress, with representatives from the states, would protect against this possibility.[38]

Thus, the states overwhelmingly approved the income-tax amendment, with the understanding that Congress, comprised of representatives from the states, would choose tax policies and decide how to spend the tax revenues. The states assented to centralization, but the catch was that they would have a voice in what decisions were made by the central unit. This is a classic instance of representative centralization, and in some ways, the last hurrah before a dramatic rise in executive centralization.

[36] Fort (1910).
[37] Root (1910).
[38] Fort (1910).

Representative Centralization and Partisanship

We have so far only lightly touched on the role of political parties in the story. Parties, both as coalitions of regional and state interests and coalitions of cross-geographic economic interests, were absolutely crucial to the representative centralization that occurred. There was a complicated symbiosis between the development of national political parties and the process of sustaining momentum toward Congressional power relative to the states. Even though the states and regions differed and bitterly contested policies, groups of them could agree whether proposed centralized policies would be beneficial or harmful.

The form parties took immediately following the Founding facilitated the establishment of coalitions of local interests organized around legislative efforts either to pursue centralizing policies or to prevent them from occurring. The divisions over central versus state power were not solely regional, and in fact, became the basis for the development of political parties after the Founding. The Federalists and the Democratic Republicans (or Jeffersonians) – the world's first mass, national political parties – contested the elections from 1794 onward, and both crossed regional boundaries. In truth, these parties, such as they were at this time, were extremely decentralized as organizations, weak centrally and locally, and oriented more toward coordinating candidate and voters' behaviors at the local level than in making national policies. They were mostly local political organizations, each with a common cause and each weakly linked across county and state boundaries.[39] Members of a given party shared common labels and information. They formed with the intention of helping each other with strategies for defeating opponents, but did little else. Evidence has shown that over time, these parties were able to establish a measure of discipline and organize legislative action within Congress in ways familiar to us today. However, the presidents or presidential candidates themselves were not involved in organizing party action either electorally or legislatively,[40] and party leadership in the Congress was not equipped for coordinating action across the country or within the legislatures.

Nevertheless, the parties had clear connections to the groupings that massed on the two sides in the fight over the Constitution, with the Federalists coming out of the centralizers and the Jeffersonians coming out of the decentralizers. If the coalition in favor of centralization held power through the Founding and through the first three presidential administrations (until 1800), it was because of a shared conception among most that the federation would retain a measure of balance. Within the coalition were those who expressed threatening views that the others disparaged and worried about. Gouverneur Morris, a prominent Federalist, represented the extreme centralizers: "We must have it in view eventually to lessen and destroy the state limits and authorities."[41] This

---

[39] See Chambers (1974), Main (1973), Dinkins (1977), Charles (1956), and Fischer (1974).
[40] Aldrich (1995).
[41] Donahue (1997, 21).

was not in any way the view of the vast majority of members of his party, the Federalists. Both major parties agreed to preserve substantial state authority.[42]

There were many minor parties active at the state level through the nineteenth century.[43] Major parties within the states were threatened not only by their major opponents, but also by the state-level parties. Nevertheless, the major parties held the vast majority of seats in Congress. Throughout the nineteenth and early twentieth centuries, among the two major parties – the Whigs and Democrats, and then the Republicans and Democrats – one generally favored centralization more than the other depending on the salient issues of the day. The South was the strongest Democratic region. Generally, the Democrats emphasized states' rights and were opposed to increasing congressional power based largely on fears among Southern Democratic leaders that their states' slave-based political economies would be threatened by federal encroachment. They worried that policies adopted and approved by Northerners would forge change in the slave and feudal economic system, thereby placing it at a disadvantage relative to other regional economies.[44]

State-level parties organized up through the parties in Congress and were instrumental in pushing for centralization to fight the Civil War and then decentralization after the war and the Reconstruction era. Republican unity in the 1860s and early 1870s, for example, enabled the harnessing of resources to fight the rebellion and to maintain peace afterward. The Democratic unity, and ability of the Democrats to join forces with more moderate wings of the Republicans, softened and then killed Reconstruction, and enabled the income tax and New Deal legislation to pass.

Although the bursts of representative centralization were sometimes brought about by partisan coalitions and sometimes by bipartisan coalitions, the trajectory of the parties mirrored the trajectory of congressional power (and as we will discuss later, presidential power) relative to the states. The focus of attention after the Civil War, for instance, went from national politics back to winning control of state governments and electing their favorite representatives to Congress, and every four years helping with presidential elections. The U.S. parties remained highly decentralized and state based until the late nineteenth century.[45]

---

[42] As an aside, if by this Morris was expressing the hope that eventually the national government would have virtually complete dominance over the states, some would claim today that his hopes were fulfilled a century-and-a-half later. The states have not been destroyed, but the current degree of dominance by the national government, while it unfolded in fits and starts for more than 150 years, is hard to square with the conceptions of state sovereignty agreed to at the Founding.

[43] See Chhibber and Kollman (2004), Link (1959), and Rosenstone, Lazarus, and Behr (1994).

[44] For wonderful histories of the parties in these eras, see Gienapp (1987) and Holt (1999). See also Howe (2007) for the Federalist era, McCormick (1975) and Potter and Fehrenbacher (1976) for accounts of the antebellum period, and Foner (2002) for an account of the postwar period.

[45] Aldrich (1995), Bibby (1998), Brady (1988), and Schlesinger (1991).

As the economy industrialized by the 1880s, there were strengthening calls among Democrats and Republicans, and a number of minor parties, for national-level solutions to economic problems. Previously much of the political action in the country occurred within the states, and therefore policy-making coalitions arose within state-level political parties. Gradually during the forty years between the 1880s and the 1920s, small, regional political parties faded away and the only path to a seat in Congress was increasingly through one of the major parties. The national parties operated through the workings of Congress in the late nineteenth and early twentieth centuries, and they increasingly dominated state-level electoral politics. Local politicians became identified by their party affiliations and linked to national political programs as carried through Congress. The ambitions of these local politicians were fulfilled partially, and increasingly, through the success of national political parties in accomplishing legislative goals.[46]

By the 1930s, the U.S. political party had changed from a set of state-level party organizations that met every four years into a relatively permanent national organization oriented around national policy programs and, importantly, electing presidents and passing their policy programs into law.[47]

Executive Centralization – Nineteenth Century

Representative centralization occurred apace throughout the nineteenth and early twentieth centuries, facilitated by political parties and, in turn, facilitating the nationalization of parties. Executive centralization, meanwhile, occurred in spurts in the nineteenth century, but generally did not remain in place until the 1930s. Moments during the presidencies of Jackson, Lincoln, and Theodore Roosevelt brought about surges of presidential power and autonomy, but these either did not become sustained institutionally or were superceded by later surges of congressional authority. Only with the development of the administrative state headed by a relatively insulated presidency, solidified in the 1930s, did executive centralization firmly surpass representative centralization.

Executive centralization in the U.S. context occurs when presidents are granted autonomy to make policy decisions. Sometimes they have made unilateral decisions over centralization – although this can be checked by the Congress or the federal courts – but more often, they are able to make unilateral policy decisions after a policy has been centralized to the executive by Congress. As for the latter, it is not correct that Congress is always eclipsed or absent in the process of intensifying executive centralization. The president

---

[46] For extensive evidence to support these claims about the changes, see Chhibber and Kollman (1998, 2004). See also Brady (1988) and Kleppner (1987). Key (1949) chronicles these changes in the American South. Muller (1993) and Shefter (1994) provide broader evidence linking authority and party organization.

[47] Schattschneider (1960), Brady (1985, 1988), Burnham (1970), Chhibber and Kollman (2004), Claggett, Flanigan, and Zingale (1984), Kawato (1987), and Aldrich (1995).

can gain these powers when Congress approves executive centralization for reasons having to do with the national political goals of the president (usually for short-term reasons), but on a continuing basis, the president exercises those powers without congressional oversight or regular assent. And this is a matter of degree as well. To the extent that members of Congress put much more weight on presidential national policy goals, and do so at the expense of state autonomy, they are complicit in executive centralization.[48]

There was a measure of executive centralization early on, especially in military and foreign policies. Several bold moves took place in the late eighteenth century and then in the nineteenth century, but with the exception of one moment in foreign and military affairs, they were not lasting in their institutional effects. For all but this one, the moments of executive centralization were severely tempered and sometimes even reversed. Congress and the states, acting in opposition to presidents, reasserted themselves.

Determining the important powers of the president to conduct foreign policy and wage war proved to be the exception. A large degree of executive centralization occurred when Congress quickly passed legislation by 1795 that, according to a later Supreme Court ruling, made the president the "sole and exclusive judge" of whether a situation requires a military response.[49] This Congressional legislation delegated to the president the sole power to represent the country in foreign affairs. These steps, affirmed by the Court, dramatically strengthened the hand of the president not only during wartime, but also in the initiation of wars. The laws essentially handed to the presidency decision-making power over war making that holders of that office continue to use to the present day.[50] What is important to see is that these laws provide the president with key legal justifications for compelling the states to contribute to war efforts. Presidents used these justifications multiple times in the nineteenth century, most notably during the War of 1812 and the Civil War, and also during Native American resettlement and the Mexican-American War.

In the Founding period, it was believed, even by the Federalist writers, that Congress would play a central role in decisions over military policy. After all, even though the president was commander in chief and chief diplomat, only Congress could declare war, and constitutional voting rules effectively said that two-thirds of the representatives of state governments (the Senate) needed to approve treaties with foreign governments. Why, then, did members of

---

[48] It is interesting to compare such a process under a presidential system as opposed to a parliamentary system. As Cox (1987) describes in the case of Britain, partisanship formed around common goals achieved in the legislature. Likewise for nineteenth-century American parties, but then by the mid-twentieth century, the process was that partisanship was increasingly linked to presidential action and proposed action by presidential candidates. See also Brady (1988) and especially Samuels and Shugart (2010) for a comparative perspective.

[49] The relevant case is U.S. Supreme Court, *Martin v. Mott* (1827), which interpreted the 1795 legislation as granting the president broad powers for calling forth the militia.

[50] See Neudstadt (1980).

Congress, including senators representing their state governments, hand over foreign-policy authority to the president in 1795? The answer relates to the apparent advantages – seen even by decentralizers – in having military decisions made with dispatch and by a single individual empowered to compel the states to contribute soldiers, money, material, and use of their infrastructure to a common military goal. They did not, of course, use the language of contemporary social science, but state leaders understood clearly the collective action (free-rider) problems and coordination problems facing the states as they confronted threats from the great European powers, pirates, and Native Americans. It was advantageous to empower and pay for central authority to compel states to go along with national military strategies.

As for the temporary nineteenth-century instances of executive centralization, the nullification crisis in the 1830s, the Indian Wars in the same era, and the Civil War in the 1860s are of special significance. These crises were seen as threats to the union, resolved by the strong hands of presidents who redefined and stretched their legal powers as understood at the time. In each case, however, the presidents afterward were held in check to a much greater degree than later presidents.

Andrew Jackson played a strong hand in both the nullification crisis and the Indian Wars during his presidency. When the South Carolina government acted to nullify federal trade laws within its boundaries, Jackson threatened military action and the arrest of state leaders, and emphatically declared such acts to be contrary to the Constitution and potentially treasonous. When state leaders balked at sending troops for Native American battles and relocation, and expressed strong opposition to allowing federal troops inside their states, Jackson acted against the wishes of state leaders who saw themselves as protecting their integrity. Jackson had the majority support of Congress for these actions, but state leaders understood the precedents being set. The state leaders who were directly affected – most importantly, those in South Carolina in the nullification case – eventually backed down because they were sure to lose in any military or political struggle against Jackson. The consequences were felt immediately within political circles around the country; Jackson had established a precedent for federal supremacy, emphatically closed the door on nullification, and headed off a major threat of secessionism.

Jackson set many other precedents for presidential power, such as using the veto to shape legislation rather than merely to thwart laws he considered unconstitutional.[51] The Jackson presidency was not, however, a period of pure executive centralization. He actually wanted to strengthen the presidency in order to avoid a stronger Congress relative to the states. Jackson believed the president was the only one who represented the entire country and that the president ought to be granted more powers over Congress than his predecessors. Jackson saw Congress as getting in the way of effective, democratic

---

[51] See Remini (1988) for details on Jackson's presidency.

governance. He also saw the federal bureaucracy, small as it was, as a potential barrier to democratic governance because it had until then stayed in place across presidencies. He instituted the spoils system whereby presidents coming into office could replace federal employees with his own loyalists.

Jackson was a strong proponent of overall federal decentralization. He was really a Jeffersonian – one who believed that state autonomy ought to be protected. His actions against South Carolina were exceptional; he also fought the national bank because he believed it overreached legitimate national power. He believed that one of his roles as president was to protect the states from an overreaching national Congress, and that the president would preserve federalism. In many of his actions, he prevented Congress from passing centralizing laws and he undercut implementation through his control of the national bureaucracy.

Thus, Jackson's legacy is complicated in terms of federalism. In assessing Jackson's presidency, one is hard pressed to conclude that the national government had become permanently stronger relative to the states under his watch. Jackson enhanced the powers of the presidency, and he established the illegitimacy of nullification, but otherwise, a mostly Jeffersonian, decentralized U.S. federation remained, and Jackson can be credited with its preservation. If anything summarizes his presidency, it would be that Jackson prevented the strong representative centralization for which many of his contemporaries were pushing.

Based on his conduct during the Civil War, the same can be said for Abraham Lincoln's legacy. There is little question that Lincoln and his Republican Party dramatically centralized authority in the early 1860s. When the Southern states declared secession, Congress – led by Lincoln and his supporters – enacted laws that gave broad powers to the national government to assess the states for money and troops to fight the rebellion. Lincoln interpreted those laws and implemented them in ways consistent with the views of George W. Bush in the 2000s and Barack Obama in the 2010s: Congress gave broad powers to the executive branch, essentially delegating crucial details about the means of enforcement and the actual numbers involved (i.e., money and soldiers, and what was legal in fighting the enemy). The executive could act as a lawmaker and policymaker, not merely an executor of the laws.

Lincoln's wartime actions remain controversial. Several of the national government's actions were of "dubious legality," but were effective in forcing the states to cough up troops.[52] Key examples occurred in 1862. With the war going badly for the Union in July of that year, Lincoln himself called for 300,000 new troops for the cause, and paid bounties directly to men who signed up. When that was not enough, Congress that same month passed a law authorizing the president to call state militias into service for up to nine months. The law gave the president the authority to "make all necessary rules

---

[52] McPherson (1988, 492).

and regulations ... to provide for enrolling the militia and otherwise putting this act into execution."[53] Then on August 2, the War Department, relying on this language, declared that the states needed to send an additional 300,000 on top of the previous amount. When reaction was resistance and riots in some areas, the army sent troops into four states to enforce the draft, and then in September, Lincoln issued his infamous proclamation suspending the writ of habeas corpus and declaring martial law in areas where people were discouraging men from enlisting or being drafted. The War Department then implemented these harsh decrees by deputizing marshals to arrest and imprison, by historians' count, several hundred persons, all without trial. The various actions in 1862 were without a doubt "an enormous expansion of federal power at the expense of the states."[54]

Lincoln's actions, however, did not lead to a durably strong presidency and weakened states. After the war, and especially after Reconstruction, the national government retrenched, largely because of the efforts by state leaders and their representatives to ensure the dismantlement of the army and the bureaucracies supporting the army. More broadly, the states once again became the primary centers of people's political lives, and the state-level political parties returned to their prominence in controlling congressional and senatorial delegations and electors for the presidential contest. The national government shrank in size between 1865—79 by various measures, including its number of employees, budget, and new laws that asserted dominance over the states. Jackson and Lincoln led the federation past several thresholds but the system nevertheless turned back toward decentralization.

Executive Centralization – Progressive Era and New Deal

The presidency of Teddy Roosevelt (TR) held similarities to Jackson and presages some of the political battles that later presidents (e.g., Woodrow Wilson and Jimmy Carter) would wage against their own parties. TR intended to strengthen the presidency because he believed, like Jackson, that the president alone represented the American people as a whole and that Congress was a bastion of special interests typically acting in ways harmful to the country. He wasted no opportunity to appeal to the broader public to criticize Congress, but importantly, his presidency occurred during a time of exceptionally strong, disciplined parties in Congress. And doubly frustrating to him was that as a Republican president, he faced a strong Republican-led Congress that often refused to go along with his programs, and thwarted him when they could. To TR's endless annoyance, they lived up to his image of Congress, exercising myriad ways to bottle-up proposals that, in his view, would have improved life in the United States for most citizens.

---

[53] McPherson (1988, 492).
[54] McPherson (1988, 492).

TR's overall effort to change the presidency had little lasting effect, save one relatively minor exception. He used legal powers in innovative ways, bringing suit against forty-four companies in his first year in office, a novel use of the Justice Department.[55]

The most crucial and lasting moment of executive centralization, of course, occurred during the New Deal era through the changes brought about by TR's distant cousin, Franklin Delano Roosevelt (FDR). The New Deal itself was a series of government actions with both representative and executive centralizing consequences. It unfolded over two waves of policy changes. The first, in 1933, was mostly for the benefit of large farms and big businesses and banks, and was oriented toward stabilization. Its purpose was to raise prices for farmers and businesses, enabling them to repay loans to banks, and the benefits overall would then trickle down to the population. The second, in 1935–36, was more relief oriented, and included benefits for small farmers and small businesses, and also social security (broadly defined) for the population.[56] Both of these waves of new policy exhibit representative and executive centralization. It is useful for our purpose to divide the parts of the New Deal into these two types of centralization.

The specific, legislated decisions by Congress to allocate resources across the country to different groups and regions were acts of representative centralization. These decisions involved ordinary politics – horse-trading, logrolling, partisan favoritism – among members of Congress acting both as representatives of their states and members of party teams seeking to gain or retain control of Congress. Importantly, while at first state governments expressed hesitation in supporting federal programs, many of these policies were ultimately supported (albeit reluctantly) by most state leaders.[57] The 1930s Depression immediately hit all the states hard, and there were suggestions that national action be taken right away. In 1931–32, a group of governors – most famously Huey Long – let it be known that they did not want federal intrusion and guarded state autonomy vigorously. When President Hoover finally offered money for the states in July 1932, he did so in a clumsy way, making $300 million available in loans, but deducted from future highway grants. This infuriated state leaders and many governors did not bother to apply for the money. On top of this, state fiscal policies tended to be highly regressive in the 1930s, and became more so during the Depression. Business groups bent on keeping state and local taxes and spending low dominated state politics in this era. Throughout the 1930s, some Democratic governors expressed hostility to the New Deal. When campaigning they complained that it was either socialistic or an intrusion on states'

---

[55] For an entertaining account of T. R.'s presidency, see Morris (2001).

[56] See Rauch (1963) for a useful history. See also Couch and Shugart (1998), Rosen (1992), and Finegold and Skocpol (1995).

[57] For the detailed information in this paragraph and the next on the states, I rely mostly on Patterson (1969) and Cohen (1984).

rights. One Democratic governor, David Sholtz of Florida, said in 1935, "We are all beginning to look to Uncle Sam to be Santa Claus. I think the toughest problem that we as governors have is to stay away from it if we can."[58] Governor Albert Ritchie of Maryland in the early 1930s proposed a House of Governors to govern alongside Congress, to safeguard states' rights.[59]

The majority of governors, however, benefited from the overall popularity of the Democrats, FDR, and the New Deal; in the end, most state governments went along. They recognized their limited capacity. State bureaucracies at the time were mostly weak, disorganized, and decentralized without the ability to raise resources. Not a single state had a "centralized unemployment relief commission, and none provided state funds for relief."[60] Instead, local governments organized relief, but clearly they did not have much capacity to deal with the scope of the problems. Enough state leaders recognized by 1933 that the states themselves did not have the capacity to deal with the Depression; it became clear that the economic gloom was a national problem. The crux of FDR's election victory in 1932 and the most potent of his arguments in favor of his programs was this: if it was going to be solved by government at all – a controversial notion, to be sure – it was to be the national government.

Some of the most famous acts as part of the New Deal were instances of representative centralization. The initial creation of the Federal Emergency Relief Administration in 1933 made grants directly to the states from congressional legislation. The Social Security Bill of 1935 "was introduced and completely enacted by Congress."[61] It divided responsibilities between the national government and the states. Age-old pensions were the completely federal part of it; the states were, with subsidy from the federal government, to pay unemployment and disability benefits. The Wealth Tax Act in August 1935 made the federal tax system much more progressive. Democrats were responding to calls by Huey Long and others for very radical, socialistic reforms. The Wagner-Connery Labor Relations Act greatly strengthened unions' bargaining power with employers. This act was not initiated by FDR, and not advocated

---

[58] Patterson (1969, 194).

[59] Although I recognize the extremely low probability that this would ever be considered, I believe a house of governors is not a bad idea and should be discussed seriously. It is interesting to compare how it differs from state government representation prior to the Seventeenth Amendment. When state legislatures chose members to the U.S. Senate, the implicit understanding was that the people of the states – through their typically bicameral legislatures – were indirectly represented in the upper chambers of the national government, but through the legislative portion of their state governments. A house of governors would simply substitute the executive portion of their state governments as the source of the representation, and be a more direct form of representation, because the idea would be, not that the governors would appoint someone, but rather that the governors themselves would sit on the representative body. This institutional form would directly tie state representation to national government decision making, an intriguing possibility.

[60] Patterson (1969, 41).

[61] Rauch (1963, 161).

in advance by him. Nevertheless, he supported it after its passage, signing it in July 1935. Finally, various agricultural bills and the Fair Labor Relations Act (FLRA) of 1938, which prohibited child labor and other forms of labor abuse, emerged as congressional initiatives. They had percolated in Congress for many years and passed with FDR's signature, although he was not the driving force behind these landmark pieces of legislation.

What is in common among these actions is the degree of buy-in from people in the states and in Congress who were fundamentally concerned with the accretion of national power. They saw in these enactments their future voice in shaping the nature of implementation and their ability to cull national power. To see how Congress retained some strength at this time in relation to FDR, consider the creation of the Federal Emergency Relief Administration (FERA) and its relationship to the Social Security Act. FDR's administration, especially in the person of Harry Hopkins as head of FERA, oversaw discretionary grants given to states. Although these kinds of grants would seem to be appreciated by the states, the fact that Hopkins lorded over their administration meant that state leaders felt like they needed to focus their energies on pleasing a single man. In fact, Hopkins dealt harshly and somewhat arbitrarily with different states over the administration of relief. Hopkins, to his credit, wanted to separate the administration of relief from politics and avoid state and local pressure on FERA. But in his behavior – which was brusque, domineering, and vindictive in cases – he zealously prosecuted corruption cases and put several state leaders in jail. He engendered a great deal of animosity among state leaders and members of Congress, and this animosity spilled over to evaluations of the entire set of FERA policies.[62]

Unhappiness with FERA was an important reason why Congress replaced these policies with the Social Security Act. Thus, when a new round of relief measures was passed in 1935, of which Social Security was part, Congress insisted on matching grants – the federal government and the states would share costs on projects. The matching grants were given according to formulas and the states' qualified projects. If they qualified, it was essentially federal money to subsidize state-level initiated projects. Because of the nature of the decisions over grants (mostly by formula), this took away from the executive branch much of its discretion and much of the ability to use grants for political or other arbitrary purposes. Congress, in this instance, successfully legislated policy that moved from executive centralization back into the realm of representative centralization. In this era, "[t]ies between congressional delegations and political organizations back home were strong."[63]

Members of Congress succeeded in reining in FDR's team because the actions of the White House and New Dealers had unified Congress and state leaders against the executive branch, and the original policy setup was based

---

[62] Patterson (1969, 54 and 62).
[63] Wallis (1991, 520).

on a model of representative centralization. In 1938 Congress continued to
bare its teeth, dealing FDR a number of legislative blows. Through a coalition
of conservative Democrats and Republicans, for example, Congress lowered
taxes against FDR's advice and will. FDR, substantially weakened in that year
politically, did not sign the bill but let it become law.

Although representative centralization occurred with lasting consequences in
the 1930s, it was the executive centralization that fundamentally altered authority relations within U.S. government in the long run. This was the lasting, institutional legacy of the New Deal that solidified the new character of U.S. federalism.
The policies of the New Deal passed by Congress and pushed by FDR forever
changed how Americans saw the responsibility of their national government to
improve their lives. FDR seized opportunities that did not seem, at the time, to
grant any more power to the executive than the previously mentioned policies.
However, many of his actions tilted authority substantially in the president's
favor, especially in domestic policy matters that had previously been the prerogative of Congress. The legacies of FDR's moves are more in the substantial
increases in presidential power that became evident after his time in office.

In the early years of the Depression – much like the Founding Era – even
decentralizers recognized the need for a concerted action. And true to the common pattern after the Founding, executive centralization resulted from presidents seizing opportunities to make the power last far longer than intended by
the Congress. Power accumulated for one purpose during an emergency and
intended by decision makers at the time to be temporary was used for another
purpose later in a different area of policy.[64] FDR relied on specific language in
laws approved by Congress to act unilaterally and build presidential power.
One of FDR's actions during his first 100 days in office used a war power won
during World War I by President Wilson – the Trading with the Enemy Act of
1917 – to deal with the banking crisis, a domestic situation and not one having to do with foreign policy. FDR declared in a proclamation on Monday,
March 6, 1933, that he was suspending all transactions in the Federal Reserve,
and all financial transactions made by banks, credit unions, and building and
loan associations until March 9. He then relied on a clause in the Emergency
Banking Act (1933) that "granted the president authority to take whatever
steps he deemed necessary in regard to gold, silver, and foreign exchange."[65]
FDR used this pretext to stop the export of all gold, silver, and U.S. currency.
He called leading bankers to meet with him to alter the regulatory system on
financial transactions, bypassing Congress. His purposes in all of these early
actions were to stop the spiraling downward of U.S. banks by stemming runs
on asset holdings, and to signal the arrival of a new regime on banking regulation. He succeeded temporarily and brought the various interests together to
help him plan the next steps in fighting the causes of the Depression.

[64] See Rauch (1963, 60) for a discussion of this. See also Cohen (1984).
[65] Rauch (1963, 64).

Although much of FDR's early actions were based on his expansive interpretation of earlier legislation, this was not always the case. Congress increasingly became complicit in expanding presidential authority. Actions by Congress to enhance presidential power had the effect of permitting the president deliberately to bypass Congress and state governments in an ongoing manner. This came about most clearly when Congress gave executive branch bureaucrats tremendous control over the location and amounts of federal grants. The National Industrial Recovery Act, passed and signed in June 1933, included an amendment that said in summary, the "president might limit, prohibit, or make conditions governing imports when the new law caused rises in prices which invited foreign goods into the American market."[66] The Thomas Amendment of the Agricultural Adjustment Bill, gave the president the authority to inflate or alter the currency in a manner he saw fit. This was a compromise among those representing indebted farmers who wanted really cheap money, and those who feared runaway inflation. Both assumed (correctly) that FDR would strike a balance that was not disastrous for either side.

Hassle with the states led FDR and his New Deal strategists to try to accomplish their goals with new agencies. His administration created the National Emergency Council (NEC) to coordinate all the New Deal agencies. The NEC appointed a liaison in each state – a state coordinator for the NEC. This did not help much, as these agency officials were deeply resented in the states, and many state leaders expressed that they did not have much use for them and tried to ignore them.

The New Deal programs that were intended to allow federal agencies to avoid political battles at lower levels gave executive branch bureaucrats leeway to bypass Congress as well. After all, members of Congress were wrapped up in those local disputes. Often the problem was at the state level. The Public Works Administration dealt directly with localities, not the states. The states were bypassed altogether, and naturally this made many governors angry.[67] The program was run by Harold Ickes, who was impatient with state political infighting (this pattern would reoccur in the 1960s with Great Society Programs). The Works Progress Administration (WPA) set up in 1935 was run by the federal government and established federal jobs in the states. No matching money by the states was necessary. At the time, other than some complaints from conservative governors against "socialism," not many governors objected to this because it did not ask anything financially from the states. Because there was no state cost sharing, the WPA bureaucrats could claim to want to stay above intrastate and interstate policies, although they could succeed only to a point.

---

[66] This quote is from Rauch (1963, 80) and summarizes the law. It is also interesting to note that in the debates over the income tax bill in 1913, it was proposed and discussed in the House Ways and Means Committee whether the president should have the authority to adjust income tax rates based on fiscal needs (Buenker 1985, 361). It is startling that this was even raised as a possibility. Such a change would have been the granting of huge taxing authority to the president.

[67] See Patterson (1969) and Teaford (2002).

There was tremendous strain between WPA officials, White House advisors, and state officials over who controlled the awarding of jobs. Endless squabbling among advisors, members of Congress, state government officials, and party leaders hampered effective decision making. Did it help in the allocation of jobs if the governor was loyal to FDR and the New Deal? Did it matter if people getting the jobs favored Democrats? What if the governor hated the New Deal and FDR? Did his state get jobs? The intra-party, intrastate competition for jobs frustrated FDR and Hopkins, and led to tremendous strain between the so-called New Dealers and state parties. At times Hopkins threw up his hands and let Republicans organize local jobs instead of trying to settle matters among squabbling Democrats.[68]

FDR's frustration with Congress and dealing with politics at lower levels led to bold moves that often backfired when Congress struck back at FDR, sometimes on issues that had little to do with the handing out of resources and jobs. Reaction to his attempt to pack the Supreme Court in 1937, for example, was decidedly negative, even among his closest supporters in Congress. They overwhelming rejected the attempt on the idea that it set a precedent for presidential encroachment on judicial power. In the midst of this controversy, FDR urged Congress to approve the creation of a bureaucracy that would report solely to him and could be reorganized for the president's purposes. The idea was that this new bureaucracy would serve his needs by giving advice and coordinating the other cabinet departments around the president's programs. Congress was cautious and turned him down twice – once in 1937 and again in 1938. FDR, responding to the considerable concern over increasing presidential powers, denied (unconvincingly) that the changes would enhance the powers of the office:

I realize that it will be said that I am recommending the increase of the powers of the presidency. This is not true. The Presidency as established in the Constitution of the United States has all the powers that are required ... What I am placing before you is the request not for more power, but for the tools of management and the authority to distribute the work so that the President can effectively discharge those powers which the Constitution now places upon him.[69]

Critics, especially conservatives in both parties, accused him of wanting to become a dictator, or a permanent executive, with no checks on decision-making power and an executive-branch bureaucracy not accountable to Congress. In the end, FDR had to prod Congress to allow minimal moves to establish an executive office bureaucracy and had to supplement and organize it using a variety of executive orders to achieve the results he wanted. Through sheer determination, he created a White House-based bureaucracy. Formation of this bureaucracy has rightly been heralded as one of his signature acts transforming the presidency. Now the president had at his disposal bureaucratic resources to receive advice, gather information, pressure potential political allies within

[68] Patterson (1969).
[69] Rauch (1963, 286–87).

Congress and the bureaucracy, prepare budgets, and organize to maintain office (i.e., win reelection) through campaigning.

In comparing the assent over the income tax and the assent over the New Deal, the key difference lies in the gap between the expectations of those assenting to the centralization over who would make policy decisions in the future and the reality as it unfolded. A comparison of those expectations reflects the coalitions bringing about the changes. The coalitions to bring about the income tax and certain elements of the New Deal, such as those dealing with workers' rights and conditions, were not executive led. They were initiatives by legislators and party leaders from the states. The parts of the New Deal granting enhanced authority to the president were proposed by one man, and then brought about by people who had to make a decision about their political fortunes in relation to this one man.

FDR set in motion changes in the national government that enabled the president and bureaucratic leaders to make important policy decisions without continuing input from congressional representatives. These changes were approved by Congress with little commentary among the supporters (as opposed to the critics) on what this meant in the long term for the power of the presidency.

FDR's precedents led to subsequent presidents continuing to build up bureaucratic resources and prestige. Each of the presidents since FDR has used the Executive Office of the President (EOP), but on a steadily increasing scale over time. The EOP today consists of 2,500 people and a budget of $400 million, with about 500 people working directly for the president as White House staff. These staff members provide the president with enormous resources to wield his authority.

Presidential scholars have tended to focus on the ways in which presidents can use unilateral powers to bypass the other branches.[70] Since the turning point of the New Deal, the powers of the presidency have continued to grow, including powers to act unilaterally. In virtually stepwise progression, presidents since FDR have asserted and then acted on new authority to determine foreign and trade policy, make domestic policy decisions, set the agenda on the national government's budget, influence the interpretation of the federal bargain, and divide and conquer coalitions that advocate decentralization.

Increasing use of executive orders, executive agreements, and signing statements are held up as evidence of increasing presidential authority independent of Congress.[71] Likewise, the larger role of administrative law in determining the details of regulations of commercial activity and judicial proceedings has given the executive branch substantial autonomous legislative authority. A good deal of attention has been on the actions of George W. Bush and Barack Obama in

[70] See, for example, Howell (2003) and Posner and Vermeule (2011). See also Cohen (1984).

[71] Howell (2003) documents the secular trends in unilateral presidential policy making. Arnold (1998) analyzes the Hoover Commission (in 1947 under Truman, headed by Hoover), and found that it was more concerned with expanding the institutional powers of the presidency than with administrative reform. This only follows the long-standing trend.

their assertion of legal powers to detain suspects and enemy combatants and to monitor the behavior and private speech of people without legislative or court approval. Undoubtedly, presidents since FDR, including G. W. Bush, have moved the dial in the direction of more allowable unilateral presidential action. They have pushed these boundaries and typically won against their partisan enemies and Congressional opponents.

The growth of executive authority in the United States has often occurred as subtle, short-term change, but the changes accumulate and their long-term impact becomes unmistakable.[72] The change is in how the president has come to sit atop the partisan coalition nationwide, pursuing programs spanning and affecting the entire country. It is not merely that he can act without Congress, but rather, that he can lead political action that includes Congress and the states. The difference is subtle but important. It is not just unilateral powers, but the assumed and agreed-to leadership role in orchestrating across partisan groups at all levels of government – horizontally with Congress and vertically with the state governments. We will return to this partisanship shortly.

In returning to the New Deal, it may seem as if the controversies over FDR's actions were unfolding as contests of will between Congress and the president, or between the states and the national government. However, it is important to keep in mind that Congress usually approved the institutional changes. So after FDR's assertions of presidential prerogative and institution building, the immediate question arises: why would Congress or the states not act to rein in later presidents when they had the chance? This is the crucial piece of the puzzle regarding executive centralization in the United States and elsewhere. Why did the changes stick in place?

There have been some limited attempts to rein in presidents. The War Powers Resolution (1973), for instance, was seen as a dramatic curtailing of presidential autonomy to use U.S. troops abroad. It did not, however, realize its intended effect and has hardly constrained subsequent presidents who have complied with the letter but not the spirit of the law. Similarly, Congress passed laws trying to force George W. Bush's hand in how he dealt with terrorism suspects. It has had an effect at the margin, but even Barack Obama largely continued along the same path as G. W. Bush on these policies. The congressional attempts have not mattered much in curtailing presidential power.

The answer to the question of why the changes in presidential authority and overall centralization have stuck in place has to do, once again, with the massive resources available to the national government (led by the executive) and the corresponding changing nature of partisanship and party politics. On the resources side, the New Deal created a set of national policies that linked the political fate of politicians at every level of U.S. democracy to the success or failure of a president's program. There is, of course, the development of

---

[72] Teaford (2002) makes the important point that over the course of the twentieth century, governors have become increasingly powerful relative to state legislatures.

bureaucracies in the executive branch, including the White House itself, that have gained considerable autonomy from Congress to make distributive and redistributive decisions through executive orders, executive agreements, and administrative law.[73] There is also the capacity of the president to set agendas on budgets, defense spending, and domestic policy in order to undercut attempts by state leaders to form coalitions and try to decentralize.

Although we have contrasted the income tax fight with the New Deal policy changes, the two are connected in important ways. Other changes in the Progressive Era in federal regulation (continued in the New Deal) mattered as well. Federal money and federal regulations affecting commercial activity across the country were crucial. The income tax centralization made the New Deal centralization possible. It was not merely that the income tax provided the money for the New Deal to work – this is undoubtedly true – but also that the money the national government could now raise was substantial enough by the late 1940s to overwhelm any amount of resources the states could provide their own local areas. The largesse from Washington, D.C. to local areas that began under representative centralization (before and during the New Deal) linked the fate of state-level parties to the fate of domestic national policy programs. Under FDR and in the years following his administration, presidents and presidential candidates led these national policy programs.

By the 1950s, the massive budget of the national government – along with the capacity of the national government to spend money on and regulate conduct within the states – has altered the orientation of people toward their governments. It has also altered how state governments operate individually and collectively. State governments incorporate federal grants, regulations, and policies into the fabric of their policy making, taking what Washington is doing as the starting point and then reacting. States build around federal policy,

---

[73] White (2000) argues that starting in the 1920s, the federal courts came to terms with the idea that agencies will do a lot of governing because the need for expertise is so great. The orthodox legal arguments in the late nineteenth century by the courts were that Congress was not allowed to delegate lawmaking authority to another branch "unless that unit was clearly an agent of the legislature" (White 2000, 97). But that changed by the 1920s as the courts, and others, legally accepted the authority wielded by the Interstate Commerce Commission (created in 1887) and other agencies. Over time, it was widely accepted that agencies would have to have lawmaking power because of the need for expertise. Modern society demanded such autonomy by the agencies. This became the legal justification for administrative law. White notes that the Administrative Procedures Act (APA) from 1946 was really just a legal justification for procedures already in place in many agencies, and hardly a real revolutionary statute. White also profiles James Landis, head of the Securities and Exchange Commission and Dean of the Harvard Law School. Landis wrote a book in 1938, *The Administrative Process*, which defended agencies and agency discretion. It did say those agencies must operate under the supremacy of law (meaning that they were checked by the courts and the legislature), but that because the agencies will be staffed with experts, the facts of the world and the scientific expertise (and their objectivity) will result in even more important checks on their discretion. So they will be checked by their objective approaches to data, but in order to do this (resulting in wise decisions), they need discretion and autonomy (White 2000, 115).

rather than the other way around. Collectively, the states end up following mostly in lockstep with federal policies, either because they are required to by Congressional statute or because of the huge amounts of money at stake. The federal government regularly threatens to withhold money from the states if they fail to comply with federal standards regarding education, transportation, and law enforcement. States more or less have to comply or else replace the funding some other way. The amounts from the federal government are so large that even stalwarts end up giving way in the end. For example, in 2011 and 2012, Republican state governments (mostly conservative governors) sought to turn back federal government money for health care and education initiatives, but in the end, this did not stick. There was enough of an outcry from people in their own states – including fellow Republicans – claiming that turning away federal money was unwise, that the recalcitrant state governments relented. The states always end up accepting federal money when offered.

Executive-Led Partisanship

As for political parties and their effects, they were reshaped to foster and react to the politics of Congress and in the states, and thereby shifted from being protective of subunit autonomy to needing to be in on the action at the national level. Presidential power continued to be built and held in place after the New Deal Era by the glue of partisanship that revolved around presidential policy initiatives. It began earlier with stronger congressional parties, but these parties were badly split and the regional conflicts, especially North and South, hampered Democrats in unifying their goals. For a time, Southern senators and members of Congress continued to play the role of protecting autonomy around issues of race. This role, however, did not survive the 1970s with intense federal encroachment into states' management of elections, hiring practices, public works contracting, and education. The end result of processes begun in the 1930s – when FDR's coalition bridged the ideological and regional gaps on the Democratic side and in doing so, unified Republicans against those policies – was a situation that, by the 1980s, saw both parties fully nationalized and members of House and Senate no longer defenders of state prerogative.

The U.S. parties were nationalizing in the decades prior to the New Deal, but they changed even more in the 1930s. A major legacy of the New Deal that solidified the gains made by the presidency through the 1930s was the culmination of changes in the U.S. political parties, away from state-based, decentralized, regional coalitions, to president-centered, national coalitions oriented toward passing national policies that touched every region. After FDR's New Deal, national parties in every region of the United States were oriented ideologically in relation to what was happening in Washington. This was a direct consequence of representative and executive centralization. In the former, it was in policies that made it the national government's responsibility to bring prosperity to all areas of the country. But it was the latter that took it one step further, making the orientation about the president or the presidential candidates, not simply what Congress was doing.[74] Presidents, both by leading legislative initiatives and through unilateral executive action, became the very heart of national power and were ultimately held responsible for the well-being of every person in the country. Congressional authority, meanwhile, came less from being the locus of national power than from being reactive to presidential action. Congressional campaigning for office, for instance, became more focused than ever before on reacting to actions of presidents and national parties led by those presidents. Voters, likewise, increasingly came to expect their congressional representatives (and even their state-level elected officials) to orient themselves relative to the president and his party.[75]

The partisan changes have fundamentally affected the capacity of president-led coalitions to influence the interpretation of the federal bargain. A commensurate change in the past fifty years has been the politicization and increasing partisanship of the federal judiciary, which often proscribes the limits of national authority. Federal judges have always been nominated by presidents and then approved by the Senate. But a widely observed trend has been the increasing degree to which presidential appointments have been made with the intention of shaping the ideological composition of the courts. Court decisions, especially on the Supreme Court, correspond to the partisanship of the judges as measured by the presidents who appointed them.[76] Matters of national versus state power are no exception, and have taken on substantial partisan and ideological casts in recent decades. The federal district and circuit courts across the country line up either for or against the overall policies of the president-led party coalition, including questions of federalism, depending on the pivotal numbers of Democratic- or Republican-nominated judges.

Lock-In

All of this is not to ignore attempts to devolve authority to the states on certain matters, often supported by presidents and certainly by congressional partisan coalitions (and sometimes bipartisan coalitions). Presidents Nixon and Reagan heralded different forms of so-called New Federalism that sought to allocate national money to the states but giving the states leeway in how to spend it. They both claimed philosophically to be decentralizers, but their presidencies played out quite differently than this philosophical position.[77] Reagan, for

---

[74] See Campbell (1997) and Carmines and Stimson (1989). See Coleman (1996) for an interesting perspective that presidential power largely destroyed party organization at the society level. See also Converse (1964), Scott (2000), Engstrom and Kernell (2000), Petrocik (1981), Cotter and Bibby (1980), and Cotter, Gibson, Bibby, and Huckshorn (1984).

[75] Claggett, Flanigan, and Zingale (1984).

[76] The evidence for this is well accepted and clear. See the work of Martin and Quinn (http://mqscores.wustl.edu/). Their evidence and overall conclusions are corroborated by many others.

[77] See Ferejohn and Weingast (1997), Donahue (1997), and Donahue and Pollack (2001).

instance, promoted policies that withheld transportation money from states that failed to comply with federal liquor standards. States have over time won authority to set their own speed limits within federal guidelines as opposed to one uniform speed limit. And most notably, the welfare reforms of the 1990s were substantively meaningful policy devolutions where states gained new-found authority to set their own standards for awarding means-tested welfare benefits.[78] Finally, George W. Bush, like his Republican predecessors, claimed to advocate for more states' rights, but in many of his promoted policies on medical care, internal security, and education, he ended up setting as many national standards as he devolved.[79]

The distinction between devolution and decentralization, however, is useful here. True decentralization involves giving back to the subunits authority that could only be given back to the central unit with the assent of the subunit. All of the changes in the previous paragraph entailed devolution where the Congress could unilaterally rescind the change and recentralize. Proposals for true decentralization since the New Deal have been meager or died after the state leaders realized their futility.[80] They either never reached a level of

---

[78] See Conlan (1998); Peterson (1995); Peterson, Rabe, and Wong (1986); and Goldwin and Schambra (1987). See Ottosen (1992) for a hopeful view.

[79] It is interesting, in light of federal education policy since 2002 (No Child Left Behind), to ponder this quote from William F. Russell, the dean of the Teachers College of Columbia University in 1934, in response to a proposal from congressional Democrats and from FDR to provide educational assistance to the states: "You can put authority over poor people at Washington; you can grant power to deal with the unemployed ... but if you put schools in this class, no matter how great their need for aid may be, discretionary authority and power will inevitably grow at Washington" (Teaford 2002, 130). The proposal by the Democrats in 1934 foundered on the controversial politics over potentially funding Catholic schools.

[80] Eskridge and Ferejohn (1994) offer a nuanced account about the current levels of state authority, and in particular, focus attention on how the Supreme Court has protected the states from national encroachment in many instances. In their words, the Court "has usually protected the integrity of state government and state police power ... from being displaced by national regulation as long as the exercise of these powers has not had substantial spillover effects" (1360). In making their arguments, they point to many examples, especially from cases involving the Commerce Clause, when the Court decided against nationalization. The Court, in their view, is a key player preserving state autonomy and thus U.S. federalism.The Eskridge and Ferejohn arguments, however, are mostly about how the Courts have constrained Congress at times, and the political conditions under which that will likely occur. They offer a "structural account," they say, which means that they connect the configuration of political preferences among the occupants of the major institutions (primarily the Supreme Court and Congress) to the outcomes of battles over federalism, as opposed to an account that would focus more on the development of legal theory among jurists. But the president is surprisingly absent from their account. They admit at the end of their article that if their theory is right, "national courts are unlikely to have either the desire ... or the opportunity ... to restrain *sustained* congressional assertions of authority over the states" [emphasis mine] (1398). But my account of U.S. federalism is that many of the key assertions of authority over the states, not only sustained but made permanent, have come from the executive, and even though they have typically had the blessing of Congress, the president should be the focus of an account of the lock-in of centralization.

legitimacy needed for parties or candidates to campaign on them, or Congress dissected or debated them without genuine motivation to take action.[81]

In the 1950s, the Republicans were serious about at least campaigning on decentralization. The end result, however, is telling. Dwight D. Eisenhower ran for reelection as president in 1956, promising to decentralize U.S. government on the idea that the New Deal-era centralizations had gone too far. The 1956 Republican Party Convention, which enthusiastically renominated him as their presidential candidate, approved a platform stating, "We hold that the strict division of powers and primary responsibility of State and local governments must be maintained, and that the centralization of powers in the national Government leads to expansion of the mastery of our lives … We are unalterably opposed to unwarranted growth of centralized Federal power."[82]

Soon after winning his reelection, Eisenhower formed the Joint Federal-State Action Committee, comprised mostly of governors, but also several members of the presidents' cabinet and staff who were generally sympathetic with the goal of decentralization. It made its recommendations in 1959. The committee's conclusions were rather meager given the scope of national government spending and activity since the New Deal in the 1930s. Two federal programs, it recommended, should be eliminated and turned back over to the states: federal grants for vocational training and for municipal wastewater treatment. When it came time to implement the recommendations, governors around the country complained of having to fashion new ways to raise money to pay for these programs. Critics complained that the loss of federal control over vocational training and municipal waste treatment would be a net loss for the country as a whole. Even governors who were initially supportive of the committee backed away from the recommendations. The committee's proposals ultimately died.

As for proposals that are not taken seriously but perhaps ought to be, the Tea Party in 2010 and 2011, an insurgent movement within the Republican Party, proposed repealing the Seventeenth Amendment, which would return the method of choosing senators to the state governments, if states chose, as opposed to the U.S. Constitutional mandate that they be directly elected.

Instead, in our modern system, the behavior of senators is telling. Many of the states are microcosms of the country itself, albeit tilting one way or another ideologically, and senators – being popularly elected – see themselves as bearers of ideological representation on issues of national scope. This is different than representing the state government and seeking to protect some measure of state autonomy from national encroachment. That task has been left to the governors, and they have little, if any, de facto voice in national policy making.

---

[81] For more on this point, see DiIulio and Kettl (1995). See also Williamson (1990).
[82] Republican Party (1956).

To summarize, executive centralization in the American context involved strengthening the presidency and executive branch bureaucracies with more capacity for extracting resources, more ability to make unilateral policy decisions, and more authority to influence the interpretation of the federal bargain. The trajectory of U.S. federalism was one of momentum toward executive centralization, with ratchets in a central direction at key moments. The glue holding the centralization in place was an evolving partisanship in the mid-twentieth century that linked people's political fates across vertical levels of authority within the U.S. federal system. Linking partisan goals at the state and congressional levels to presidential success, combined with the institutional change of directly elected senators, opened doors to assertions of presidential authority. These assertions, although displaying dubious political legitimacy at the outset, became more and more accepted over time. In the New Deal, both representative and executive centralization occurred, and in large doses. But it was the nature of that executive centralization in the 1930s and 1940s that fundamentally changed the character of the U.S. federation. It put into the hands of the executive two kinds of policy decisions: what policy areas were going to be centralized and what specific policies would fall under the umbrella of the centralized policy areas. Executive centralization also linked the state political party organizations to national policy programs led mostly by the president or presidential candidates.

Madison's vision – as described in one of his famous *Federalist Papers* (Number 39) – was of a national government that was a blend of representation by the people and by the states.[83] One possible interpretation of this paper, and the only way I see that it has a coherent logic, is that Madison desired to have state governments represented directly in the national government, through the Senate, and through the choosing of electors for the Electoral College in the presidential contest. Through the nineteenth century, Madison's vision was, by and large, intact. States were represented de jure and de facto in the national government, and centralization decisions were made by a process that included the states. The states were included in processes of assenting to the principle of centralization in a policy area, and then were included in the process of deciding policy. Of special importance was the degree to which, after the Jackson presidency and then after the Civil War, the states and their representatives in Congress pushed back hard against a permanent national presence in their states and a permanently large national bureaucracy.

Today the American Republic, after passing the crucial threshold leading to lock-in, is governed mostly by an executive-led partisan coalition that still has vestiges of input from the states, but not directly from the state governments, and only loosely from representatives in Congress who represent the states. The elements of lock-in discussed in Chapter 2 are securely present: the president leads a partisan group that reaches down to the subunit level,

---

[83] Madison, Hamilton, and Jay [1787–88] (2003).

has the resources of both bureaucracy and money to divide and conquer any potential coalition to decentralize, and can shape the interpretation of the federal bargain by having agenda control over who becomes federal judges.

While the framework offered in this chapter is distinctive, many of the facts may be well known for those familiar with U.S. political history. Within the context of the overall argument in this book, the chapter lays the groundwork for the other cases. It offers a list of elements to look for when we move to the other cases that for many readers will be less familiar.

4

Church

By some measures the largest and oldest organization in the world, the Roman Catholic Church (the Church hereafter), is a marvel of endurance, as well as a fascinating case of institutional evolution. This chapter summarizes key moments in Church history that demonstrate the ways in which its evolution is similar to the other cases highlighted in this book. Subunit leaders have repeatedly assented to representative centralization and, sometimes with great consequence, large enough groups of them have assented to executive centralization. The leaders across multiple levels of Church governance have formed partisan groups pursuing common policies, and most importantly, separated into groupings around the goals of the top leaders. The Church ratcheted toward executive centralization (especially since the mid-nineteenth century). As a result of the executive centralization and partisanship, the Church has locked into a period of centralization with predominant authority residing in the executive above the subunits and the central representative body.

According to Roman Catholic tradition, Jesus Christ founded the Church during his life and then when the Holy Spirit was sent to the Apostles after Christ's death, the Church began its public ministry. Bishops today are considered descendants of the Apostles. Governance in the Church has long resembled Western European monarchism from medieval and Renaissance times, including the corresponding hierarchical, vassal relationships. Bishops govern the various sees, which are local areas of responsibility (typically geographically defined), like dukes and princes, and altogether serve as the Church hierarchy. Peter the Apostle by tradition was the first pope. By the fact that he and Saint Paul were martyred and buried in Rome, the city and its Christian leaders were accorded special status. Today the Church uses the term pope to refer to the bishop of Rome who traces a direct line of succession back to Saint Peter.

Despite the many trials and challenges to papal authority since ancient times, the pope governs the Church as an absolute monarch. He is, in effect, a king over the princes and dukes (bishops) although without hereditary succession.[1] The core position of the Church – the one that has emerged over time and is codified in canon law – is that the pope is supreme in his realm, with final and absolute legislative, executive, and judicial authority. Similarly, bishops are supreme in their realms. Cardinals, an elite subset of bishops, elect the pope. Religious orders, meanwhile, serve as different kinds of subunits, although with ultimate subservience to the pope. Bishops' and other subunit leaders' legitimacy derives from their allegiance to the pope and to Church tradition. The hierarchy consisting of the pope and the bishops together hold the patrimony of the Church, which totals one billion members today.

The Church has for a long time been ambitious in seeking conformity by influencing the nature of belief and controlling the religious ritual practice of its members everywhere. Issues of governance, not surprisingly, have been recurring sources of conflict in the Church. Who among the hierarchy ought to have authority over whom? How much authority should central Church leaders have over subunit leaders? On what issues should local subunits have autonomy to make their own decisions? How much diversity of practice and belief should be tolerated?[2] The overall conclusion of this chapter is that the Church has locked into a system of considerable centralized authority for the reasons identified in earlier chapters. In broad strokes, the Church has increasingly centralized over time, both in terms of doctrinal and organizational authority emanating and being enforced from Rome, and in terms of executive centralization to the papacy itself.[3]

Centralization in the Church has two components: centralization to Rome that includes the hierarchy of bishops as a representative body, and the consolidation of executive (papal) power. A major element of the latter component has been the strong presence of the Curia, the most loyal bishops and people in the Vatican who surround the pope and are his most direct agents in the hierarchy. The lock-in toward Roman rule in recent centuries has occurred because of the increase in papal power, which has waxed and waned but mostly waxed, especially in the last 150 years. Although the broader group of bishops have

---

[1] This monarchical view was readily promulgated by the previous pope. As reported by the Associated Press (on the online version of the *New York Times*, June 6, 2012), "Pope Benedict XVI has praised Queen Elizabeth II's 'noble vision of the role of a Christian monarch' in a note congratulating her on her diamond jubilee." But note the irony in the next passage, with the pope heralding democracy: "In a message released Wednesday by the Vatican, Benedict said the British monarch has over the past 60 years been an 'inspiring example of dedication to duty and a commitment to maintaining the principles of freedom, justice and democracy.'"

[2] *Canon Law* (1995) describes in great detail the de jure hierarchical relationships in the Church. See also De Thomasis (1984).

[3] The idea that the Church has centralized over time is a consistent theme in Church history and contemporary commentary. See Bellitto (2002), Burke-Young (1999), Cheetham (1982), Greeley (2004), Kung (1981), McBrien (1997 and 2008), McClory (1997), O'Malley (2008 and 2010), Reese (1996), and Steinfels (2003).

sometimes pushed back collectively against papal power at key moments, enough of them approved of executive strengthening. Of importance for our story, executive centralization occurred when questions of representative versus executive centralization came to a head and resolutions tilted in favor of the pope's absolute authority. This occurred because enough bishops were convinced that they would also collectively benefit from moves toward more executive authority. The partisan forces benefiting from papal strength won out over those benefiting from more decentralized governance.

The time scale for the Church – literally thousands of years – marks it as a qualitatively different kind of case from the others in this book. Over the entire course of its history, the Church has gone through many periods of centralization and decentralization. We could choose any 200-year period and examine it in detail and compare it to our other cases. Although I will summarize certain moments occurring throughout the entire history, special emphasis will be on issues of Church governance between the bishops and the pope since the mid-nineteenth century. Much has changed between the 1850s and today, but there has existed commonality in the underlying issues and in the language and understanding of the controversies over governance that confront the Church. Throughout this span, the Church has experienced stress over how to coexist with modern, secular states. Moreover, fault lines have developed over the appropriate amount of central authority lodged in the pope in Rome relative to multiple levels of subunits (e.g., national churches, dioceses, parishes, religious orders). The language used today – such as "collegiality," "subsidiarity," and "infallibility" – emerged in regular Church discourse in the nineteenth century.

The time scale also affects our discursive endpoint. The present period is quite centralized, and to say that it is locked-in is not to say that in some future century or millennium the Church will not decentralize. Rather, the current resolution of the primary governance questions – that the pope is the final authority on all Church matters – will last for a very long time (for reasons discussed later). For the foreseeable future, executive centralization – both Roman and papal – is here to stay.

Federalism and Separation of Powers

Massive time scales present one challenge to our inferences about the Church and our comparison of it with other institutions. Another challenge for understanding the history of governance of the Church relative to our other cases is that Church historians intertwine theological arguments with evaluations and justifications of authority. Our focus is on the Church as an organization.[4] Assertions of authority in the Church by the pope and the bishops, and evaluations of these assertions by historians, who are also often theologians, are

---

[4] Wilde (2007) and DiMaggio (1997) strive to hold the same focus.

justified in theological terms. Theological principles regarding ecclesiastical authority can complicate matters related to operational authority. The terminology of the Church can be opaque, and the translation into more familiar language is imprecise. This is true when characterizing the principles of governance overall. Three theological and philosophical positions on Church governance are especially relevant to our story: conciliarism, subsidiarity, and collegiality. These philosophical concepts, each one controversial and also vague enough to gather adherents across various factions within the Church, animated the heated debates and fractious conflicts over governance in Church history.

Conciliarism was an idea that threaded through internal Church politics from the Middle Ages to the early modern period.[5] Conciliarists held the doctrine that an official Church council, which by the early Renaissance was called by popes and welcomed by most of the world's bishops, constitutes a governing body that has authority to determine Church policy. The notion faded away after aggressive efforts by popes to smother it. Subsidiarity arose in the mid-nineteenth century and was formally promulgated with a papal encyclical in 1931. It has become part of the official catechism, and generally means that higher order authorities should not take away the autonomy of lower order authorities or individuals to make decisions and to act unless there is an explicit justification rooted in the common good. Subsidiarity was intended to be the Church's philosophical strike against totalitarianism, on the idea that collectivism for its own sake was wrong.[6] However, it was later used to justify greater legitimacy and autonomy for bishops in their sees. (Subsidiarity is also a concept used in the documents of the European Union; see Chapter 6). Collegiality, like subsidiarity, remains a part of Church discourse and is related to conciliarism. Some would say it is the modern version of conciliarism. Collegiality refers to the idea that the collection of bishops either in council or in synod co-governs with the pope.[7] During the Second Vatican Council (1962–65) and immediately afterward, the practical meaning of collegiality was debated and it seemed as if the Church would end up with a genuine system of separation of powers with actual co-governance. During the council itself, the proceedings for a time resembled collegiality in this co-governance sense. Yet a more hierarchical version of collegiality became the official position of the Church following an interpretive document written by the pope that unambiguously claimed papal superiority (discussed later in this chapter).

All three concepts address questions about the degree to which the Church is or has been governed in a federated manner and under principles resembling separation of powers. We can think of a bishop's autonomy as a

[5] See Oakley (1969 and 2003) and Tierney (1955).
[6] See Nicodemus (1969), Burkhard (1998), Kaufman (1988), and Johnson (1990).
[7] See Burke-Young (1999), Cheetham (1982), Duffy (2002), McBrien (1997 and 2008), O'Malley (2008 and 2010), Reese (1996), Steinfels (2003) and Wilde (2007).

vertical relationship of subunit to central unit, thus raising issues common to federations.[8] We can think of the pope's authority relative to the bishops collectively as the horizontal relationship of representative body to the executive. This raises issues of the degree to which governing power is shared. Both vertical and horizontal relationships have reoccurred as contentious issues needing settlement, although in general, vertical authority has not been seriously threatened by the bishops as a whole, as they have assented to representative centralization (with exceptions noted in this chapter). In contrast, over the long history of the Church there were periods, some of them quite long, when the horizontal relationship was in flux and even reversed. At times long ago, papal authority was not absolute and was occasionally below that of the collective of bishops. Certainly, whichever direction it went – whether papal power temporarily superseded that of the whole of the bishops or vice versa – it was the result of struggle and controversy threatening the unity, if not the existence, of the Church.

The documents of the Church – its canon law and various encyclicals that rely on language from ancient, medieval, and Renaissance times – of course, do not describe Church governance using terminology of federalism and separation of powers. These terms gained traction in Europe during the Renaissance and the Enlightenment, although federalism certainly has roots from ancient times. In some cases, the Church implicitly avows the more contemporary concepts, and openly refers to a monarchical model. Federalism, for instance, is a concept fundamentally about coming to terms with diverse subunits with overlapping but separate interests who wish to pool their sovereignty. Canon law today, in contrast, states that each subunit (known as a particular church formally) is an embodiment of the one, universal church and is in essence the same. "The hierarchical order is conceived as a structural order of divine right which serves the people of God."[9] The universal Church is present in every location that has Church institutions. "Bishops should not be thought of as vicars of the Pope. His authority ... confirms and defends that of the bishops."[10] While this is the Church's formal perspective, I am frankly uncertain as to what this means in the practice of governance. It is a question of theological interpretation that I will leave to others.[11]

---

[8] In a similar way, we can substitute the leaders of religious orders and leaders of other particular churches for bishops in these arguments, although the bishops hold special place in the hierarchy.

[9] Kaufman (1988, 17).

[10] *Catechism,* passage 895.

[11] After discussions with Church officials and in reading articles and Church documents, my best guess is that the Church's stance means that within each subunit, the leader (bishop) is to rule supremely just like the pope rules supremely and that their joint authority is God-given. Particular churches are manifestations of the universal Church in a specific location. It raises the interesting question, nevertheless, of whether a federated institution can be one in which each subunit – in theory anyway – is not considered to be different and therefore deserving of autonomy, but is rather "the same" in some metaphysical sense, as the entire body of the Church and as

Subsidiarity, nevertheless, places the Church's philosophical position close to the ideas of federation. As a starting point for subsidiarity, the Church's twentieth-century position was that the lower-order units – individual human beings and particularly (local) churches – have God-given integrity deserving of protection and special, inviolate status. "It is a grave evil and a disturbance of right order to assign to a greater and higher association what lesser and subordinate organizations can do."[12] The default for the Church, in theory, is decentralized authority; authority at a higher order has to be justified on the basis that the lower level units are being helped "with a view to the common good."[13] Subsidiarity, some say, has become a code word for "shared authority" and other words, like *communion* are really code words for "centralization." Subsidiarity, in fact, says nothing about the locus of authority, but instead about "how power is used."[14]

Collegiality, meanwhile, also remains alive as a concept in Church governance. By one interpretation, it does have elements that appear consistent with separation of powers. The bishops collectively are the decision-making body of the Church. The pope leads the bishops, with his role more as an agenda setter and with a veto, rather than as a king over his vassals.[15] But the interpretation officially stated by the Church is more monarchical. In this sense, collegiality in no way implies that the bishops are a counterweight, or co-govern as equals, with the pope. There is no separation at all. The bishops only govern the Church when the pope sits at their head, and he has ultimate authority to veto or approve their actions.[16]

Abstract philosophical concepts aside, of more direct interest to us here are the interpretations of governance when applied to actual practice, and how the interpretation and practice have changed over time. Certainly the gap between what the Church communicates and what actually happens can widen. Conciliarism, as mentioned, no longer has a following and has been declared null within the Church. Some commentators on Vatican II (discussed later in this chapter) have suggested that the way events unfolded in the first half of the council in practice was consistent with the more "liberal" interpretation of collegiality, implying a practical version of separation of powers if not a parliamentary governance model.[17]

The Church has by varying degrees over the course of its history operated like a federation, and has generally had a potential separation of powers

the other subunits. How can their interests conflict, as they in practice do? Perhaps the Church's position is that interests of subunit and central unit do not really conflict, but that someone who concludes thus (e.g., a rogue bishop) has erred.

[12] Pius XI, *Quadrigesimo Anno*.
[13] *Catechism*, passage 1883.
[14] De La Bedoyere (2002, 120) makes this point, and the quotes are from his book.
[15] This very American point of view can be gleaned from Reese (1996) and O'Malley (2008), for example.
[16] *Lumen Gentium*, Chapter III, section 22.
[17] See Wilde (2007).

character in its governance structure. It has resembled a federation since its very beginnings, and true to any federation, the balance between central unit and subunits can become contested and evolves. The early form of the Church consisted of Christian communities spread around Eurasia and Northern Africa, headed by bishops who were chosen by local people. The Church has since been composed of geographic subunits that have degrees of autonomy that change over time. The subunits are considered to have special status and could govern their realm (diocese or religious orders) without centralized authority if necessary. There is a codified authority relationship between subunits and the central unit. Leaders of the subunits (bishops) together form a representative body at the central level that can make rules binding on subunits. Based on a broad definition from Chapter 2, the Church easily qualifies as "federated."

By the late second century, it seemed to be well understood that the Roman bishop was above the other bishops, and that he could settle their disputes.[18] (The term *pope*, however, was not used until the ninth century at the earliest.) He could rebuke other bishops, but not publicly. Thus, the form we know today was in place early on: the bishops, each representing a geographic subunit and led by the bishop of Rome, collectively constitute the representative body of the Church. An executive governs either alongside the bishops or lords over them, depending on the moment in history.

Assent to Representative Centralization

Representative centralization in Church history has been about vertical relationships primarily, with bishops and local or national Church communities having varying degrees of autonomy relative to the collective Church hierarchy centered in Rome (and nowadays, the Vatican). In general, the collection of bishops throughout Church history has supported the hierarchical authority of which they play a central part. The purpose of this section is to establish that bishops have demonstrated assent to orthodoxy, something that they themselves created collectively through their actions. They have historically granted the central unit in the Church substantial authority to stamp out heretics and establish uniform doctrine and liturgical practice.

To the extent that the bishop is a personification of Rome, Roman authority within the global church has been in the institutional interests of bishops in governing their own territories. To remain a bishop within the Church has in general meant assenting implicitly to the notion that Rome sets standards for liturgical behavior, theological belief, and – to a lesser extent – Church administration. Bishops in Church history have functioned as two things: (1) leaders of their sees and thus, representatives of Rome locally, and (2) representatives in synods or councils in Rome and thus, representatives of the local Church to the

---

[18] The Introduction and first chapter of Cheetham (1982) describe the development of Rome as the central locus of authority.

central unit. The dual nature of the bishops' role means that over the centuries, bishops have virtually by definition, assented to centralization toward Rome. Within their own sees, bishops are considered supreme and represent Church hierarchy to other clergy and laity who operate within their domains. Under canon law they are like mini-popes, holding all final executive, legislative, and judicial power within their realms.[19]

Although they represent their diocese in Rome, they also represent Rome to their diocese. For most bishops, the successful exercise of their authority within their sees is based on the recognition of Rome as the final administrative authority on all religious matters within the Church. Furthermore, the fact that they did not exercise their options to exit the Church indicated a form of consent to Roman authority. Most bishops have had opportunities to exit the Church entirely and join other denominations that are much less centralized. Bishops have left the Church; there have been numerous schisms, not to mention the Protestant Reformation, which opened up many opportunities to remain Christian but in a setting of a decentralized religious tradition.

In a council or synod, the bishops collectively become the hierarchy of the Church, and they take on a role of pursuing uniform doctrine for Catholics everywhere to adopt and follow. These councils have had numerous opportunities to keep Rome weak and to create a mostly decentralized Church,[20] but these were never the lasting results of such councils.

This is not to discount rogue bishops throughout history, or to downplay threats (both past and present) from groups of bishops to secede or defect, or to discount the many divisions among bishops. Bishops have in the past literally waged war against each other and against Rome. They occasionally bribed, murdered, and lied their way into consideration for being pope or to promote their favorite papal candidates. Young children have been named bishops as payment to a family for favors and some bishops have, by necessity at certain times, shown much more loyalty to their national, secular leaders than to Rome and the pope. National churches, in the form of the collection of bishops from a particular country with various ties to the national government, were substantial counterweights to Rome within the Church.[21] Where their loyalties lay depended very much on the specific political situations in their own areas, which determined who appointed the bishops and who controlled Church property upon the death of a bishop.

Thus, although most bishops have viewed their authority as coming from their commitment to Roman rule, note two other possibilities for bishops: their potential roguishness from centralized Church control or organizing against a particular pope or rival group of bishops. The former is objecting to or defecting from the idea of central authority within the Church, and throughout

[19] See Reese (1989).
[20] See Bellitto (2002), and Bulman and Parrella (2006).
[21] See Coppa (1998, chapters 2–5) and Pollard (2005).

recent Church history, this is more of an aberration than the norm. It virtually qualifies as leaving the Church entirely. The latter has more often been objecting to the particular application of central authority by specific people, and of that there has been plenty in the long history of the Church.

To summarize, the inescapable fact is that over the centuries, the bishops when they gather in Church councils have remained supportive of a centralized Church with uniform doctrine and ritual. In numerous Church councils, the bishops have collectively assented to doctrinal orthodoxy and rigorous enforcement of Church norms. The bishops have supported this simply as a defining feature of being Catholic. Roman Catholicism, what it means to be Catholic as opposed to another religious denomination, is loyalty to the core theology promulgated by Rome.

Bishops Challenging Popes

The definition of "Rome" as the central authority in the Church, however, has been contested and fluid. It has sometimes meant the collection of bishops, other times the pope, and occasionally the pope's vast bureaucracy (led by the Curia).[22] Often it has meant a combination of all three. The central political struggles within the Church since the nineteenth century have not been primarily about whether and to what degree Rome should be the central authority, but rather, whether bishops should approve representative centralization alone or move beyond that to executive centralization. The divisions were enhanced by the extreme forms of executive centralization proposed by popes and their supporters; the popes have historically wanted little to do with sharing powers on an equal footing with the representative body of bishops.

The earliest Church councils to settle questions of theology and of governance were not called by popes, and popes virtually never attended. Emperor Constantine, for instance, called the Great Nicene Council (325), which decided on measures to deal with the Arian heresy and established the core Church creed that is still invoked today. Councils often included large groups of bishops ambitious for more power within the Church collectively; bishops at numerous councils – such as at Constance (1414–18), Basel (1431–39), Lateran (1512–17), and Trent (1545–63) – pushed for reforms, often over the heads of popes.[23] By then it was the norm that popes called the councils together, and they were often surprised by proposals brought by reformers among the bishops. These reforms sought to establish stricter guidelines for the behavior of clergy and bishops, the status of religious orders, the education of seminarians, and to distinguish Church doctrine from heresies (and in later eras, Protestantism).

[22] See Henn (2000).
[23] Bellitto (2002) and Bulman and Parrella (2006).

Large groups of bishops have challenged papal authority on many occasions. At the Council of Constance, for example, the bishops passed a measure declaring the council itself as the final decider over Church governance and doctrine, and over individual popes (discussed again later in this chapter). Pope Martin V called a council soon thereafter in Pavia (1423) – it was quickly moved to Siena because of the plague – but it dissolved right away because of strong anti-papal sentiment among the bishops who pursued their own collective authority over the pope.[24]

Popes have had some of their economic powers curtailed by other groups within the Church, namely, elements of the Roman or Vatican bureaucracy headed by bishops. Restrictions on financial decisions were the natural consequence of abuses. Urban VIII (1623–44), who reigned during the Thirty Years War and led an army to gain more territory for papal lands, was embarrassed in front of the cardinals and his bureaucracy for plundering the Church's treasury. He agreed to guidelines on papal spending drawn up by the cardinals at the time.[25] These guidelines have largely stuck in place. Popes in modern times have tended to go along with fiscal procedures officially approved by others.[26] To do otherwise would be unseemly, and considered as undercutting their religious prestige.

The bishops have often divided into partisan groups around their support for papal power relative to the bishops. How much authority such a council should have relative to the pope is a question that reoccurred for centuries and for which there was deep disagreement leading to schism, bloodshed, and divisions among Catholics. Battles over conciliarism in the fifteenth century, for example, go to the very heart of the question of whether they were assenting to representative centralization or executive centralization. During the era of the Great Schism, there were as many as three rivals to the papacy in the late fourteenth and early fifteenth centuries. At the time, the Church was divided into factions loyal to the various claimants.[27] The Councils of Pisa (1409) and Constance (1414) were organized to settle the question of which, among the rivals, was to be the true pope. The Pisan Council, called when there were two claimants, chose a third person, Alexander V. This decision made matters worse, because there were now three claimants to the papacy instead of two. The schism persisted. At Constance a few years later, the council decided to appoint another new person altogether, the man who became Martin V. Choosing one of the existing claimants would not have settled the matter. Their decision stuck because King Sigismund of Germany – the most powerful ruler in Europe at the time – declared that the council's decision was binding on all, including those claiming to be pope and on Martin V.[28]

---

[24] Bellitto (2002) and Bulman and Parrella (2006).
[25] Cheetham (1982, 122).
[26] Pollard (2005).
[27] Today the Church recognizes only one person at any point in time in that era as the "true" pope, with the others being anti-popes.
[28] Cheetham (1982, 172–74).

The conciliarism promulgated by the Councils of Pisa and Constance raised intriguing and potentially explosive questions about Church governance. The strong form of conciliarism held that the council is above the pope in authority; a weaker version held that while the council is in session, the pope co-decides with the bishops, but outside of councils, the pope governs supremely. By that point in Church history, a conclave of cardinals decided on the next pope after a pope died or stepped down voluntarily (similar to today). The Constance Council, however, occurred at a moment when the pope, whoever it was among the three claimants, was very much alive and nominally holding the office. So if in principle there was a "true" pope (in a theological sense), that pope would need to step down in acquiescence to the council's choice. Indeed, the council explicitly declared that it could override the ordination of any of the popes or anti-popes, and that it had the authority to settle who was to lead the Church. The bishops at Constance, in not choosing from among the three claimants, but rather choosing a fourth (Martin V), implied that, even though one of the popes might have been the "true" pope – the heir of St. Peter – the council's decision was final. It did not rest with the pope.[29] It was the strong version of conciliarism and quite radical, although arguably one borne of necessity given the persistence of the schism.

After Constance, the question remained: how far to push the idea that the pope was not in fact supreme but needed to accept the decisions of the council of bishops? The bishops at the council of Constance were divided. They all agreed that in this instance, the council could act as supreme authority to choose a pope, just as conclaves could following the pope's death. Conciliarists felt this authority should be made permanent, whereas others, called papists, believed that authority should be temporary and apply only to the question of settling the schism. According to papists, once chosen, Martin V lorded supreme over the entire Church, including the collection of bishops and the cardinals who chose him. Naturally, Martin V agreed, and he became an ardent papist thereafter. It was said that the word "council" filled Martin with horror.[30] He vigorously took action against the hard-core conciliarists.

Amid this conflict, whether the council of bishops or the pope was to emerge supreme following the settlement of the schism was determined by the strength of outside powers aligned with the different sides. The pope after Martin V (Eugenius IV) largely rejected conciliarism, but agreed – under pressure from Sigismund – that the council of bishops could act independent of him on the suppression of heresy, unity with the East, and on reform of Church finances. By deciding which issues they had authority on, however, Eugenius was implicitly rejecting the idea that he was subordinate to the collection of bishops.

[29] Which one was the "true" pope was the subject of conflict at the time. Official Church historians later settled the question – none of them. According to official Vatican documents, there was an interregnum from 1415–17.

[30] Cheetham (1982, 173).

The council of bishops subsequently chose an alternative pope (which is officially an anti-pope in Church records) after being dissatisfied with Eugenius, but ultimately the secular rulers of Europe, along with Sigismund, sided with Eugenius. The anti-pope, Felix, and his supporters lost their claims to authority. The council of bishops, soon thereafter, became irrelevant for a time because the secular rulers of Europe sided with the pope against them.

Conciliarism shows up in various guises throughout the next few centuries, but supporters of the idea had formidable papal opponents. When Julius II (1503–13) led bloody wars on the Italian peninsula, a schismatic council formed in Pisa to depose him. He responded by calling his own council at Lateran, which undercut the schism and forced, sometimes by arms, dissident bishops and cardinals back into the fold. Popes for several hundred years, once chosen, repeatedly railed against the notion of conciliarism, even if they had been conciliarists in their previous roles. They published bulls (i.e., authoritative documents) and excommunicated those advocating the idea that the pope should be subordinate to or share power with any council. Yet later councils continued to try to assert their authority, including in Vatican II (discussed later).

The bishops tried to rein in popes in other ways as well, with limited success. During the Renaissance, which was a wretched time for the papacy owing to abominable behavior by holders of the office, it was common for the cardinals during a conclave to sign a "capitulation," an agreement that whoever was chosen as pope would agree to have his actions subject to control by a council of cardinals. Clement VI, for example, had a tumultuous reign. He earned his reputation for materialistic excess, aggressive assertions of papal power, and deep entanglements in politics among European monarchs. Soon after he died in December 1352, the cardinals met in conclave in Avignon to choose his successor. Partly in response to Clement's papacy, the cardinals vowed to restrict the power of the next pope by subjecting his decisions to a two-thirds majority vote of the College of Cardinals. They signed a capitulation swearing to uphold the agreement should he become pope. One of the cardinals, Etienne Aubert, was elected, and took the name Innocent VI. Among Innocent's first acts as pope was the repudiation of the capitulation agreement. He not only paid out 75,000 gold florins to the other cardinals, but he declared the capitulation nonbinding and illegal. By the standards of the time, Innocent VI used his powers as pope wisely and with mercy toward opponents. He nevertheless ruled in a manner that in no way resembled power sharing with the cardinals or any other group within the Church. His rule was supreme.

Later popes, many of whom also signed such agreements, also repudiated them afterward. Pius II (1458–64), an avowed conciliarist prior to his election, agreed in the conclave to have some control over him by the "Sacred College," but he then completely ignored the agreement and punished conciliarists during his reign. Various popes thereafter would ignore capitulation statements, having signed them to win the approval of their cardinal colleagues during the conclaves. Finally, Innocent XII issued a papal bull in 1695 condemning all pre-election pacts.[31]

In retrospect, it is difficult to understand how anyone ever thought capitulation agreements would work – assuming that a gentlemen's agreement rather than a method of enforcement would stick. However, the cardinals were essentially proposing a form of separation of powers: the executive (pope) and the representational body for the remainder of the Church at the time (College of Cardinals) would govern together, each needing to approve changes to policies and rules. These were in reality unenforceable contracts between the group of cardinals and the new pope. The contracts or agreements were made irrelevant after the election of popes who repudiated them. The pope clearly had the upper hand in enforcement or inducements after the fact. The reasons for papal dominance are varied, including the support of secular rulers, sheer resource levels at the pope's disposal, and skill at dividing the cardinals by buying some off and threatening others.

The basic divisions among bishops and Catholic rulers for many centuries in Europe were because of differences over where legitimate authority lay.[32] Conciliarists and papists were important examples of partisan groupings that came together to pursue common political goals within the Church. There were divisions across the centuries among bishops over the right of secular rulers to name bishops (called lay investiture), over whether the Eastern emperor deserved deference equal to the pope or at all, and over which claimant to the papacy among multiple claimants was the rightful holder of the seat. Bishops have also formed partisan groups over matters other than the authority relationships within the hierarchy or between Rome and other powers. They have divided over questions of religious dogma, over loyalties to specific secular rules and national governments, and even in our own time, over secular political questions.

We can roughly categorize the Church's history of federated governance since 1000 as follows. From the eleventh to sixteenth centuries, the Church was highly centralized, often representing the dominant governing authority in all of Europe, with the Roman pope supreme in both secular and religious realms. Its response to Protestantism was briefly to strengthen central control. The seventeenth and eighteenth centuries saw Rome's authority wane dramatically given the rising power of secular governments and the increased influence of Catholic monarchs over internal Church affairs. As the Church lost all secular authority by the nineteenth century, Rome regained internal (i.e., religious) centralized authority over its subunits. Over a 110-year process begun in the 1850s and ending in the 1960s, the Church codified that authority in canon law.

When they lived in periods of relative decentralization, such as the seventeenth and eighteenth centuries, many bishops could govern their sees in

---

[31] This account follows the description of Burke-Young (1999).
[32] Searle (1974) has an overview of the crucial era of the Counter–Reformation.

diverse manners with little control by Rome. Diversity across the subunits of the Church was not so much allowed or sanctioned by Rome, but was instead the reality that had to be tolerated lest the Church be destroyed by more powerful secular governments. In the seventeenth century, French kings declared that the pope had no jurisdiction over the French Church and installed independent assemblies of the French clergy to decide national Church matters. This Gallican position and political movement was declared invalid by popes like Innocent XI, but with French bishops largely siding with the king, there was little the pope could do.[33]

When they lived in periods of relative centralization, such as the eleventh through sixteenth centuries and in our present time, bishops often had to toe the line theologically, liturgically, and administratively. The questions settled at councils or by popes were over which line to toe. When the questions were settled by councils, the bishops acted as partisan groups within a semi-legislative setting seeking to turn the Church in one direction or the other. The Council at Trent, for example, held vigorous debates over whether to compromise on issues that might ease relationships with Protestants, such as the possibility of allowing clerical marriage and wine for the laity at mass. Bishops from Spain and Germany banded together to pursue such changes, but lost out to the more conservative bishops who supported Paul III's position refusing such reforms. Later, during the time periods of the Vatican Councils (I and II), the bishops were divided into partisan groups over the relationship of the Church to the modern world. By and large, the liberals pushing for more openness won the partisan battles when these issues made the agenda. The bishops were also divided over the appropriate authority of the pope relative to the bishops and national churches. As we will see, these issues of Church openness to the world and Church governance became linked.

Early Popes Asserting Authority

As previously discussed, the main representatives of the Church's geographic subunits – the bishops – have largely assented to representative centralization, although it is important to emphasize that this refers to the bishops who stayed within the Church's fold. It does not refer to all bishops, because some left the Church or dissented to such a degree that they were removed. But assenting to executive centralization was another matter, as we have seen. The bishops, either en masse or in large groupings, have at times asserted their authority relative to the pope. And the bishops have occasionally formed partisan groups around theological and organizational questions with the understanding that they needed to coordinate their actions if they wanted to achieve change within Church policy. Yet up to our own time, bishops who challenged papal authority ultimately lost.

[33] Cheetham (1982, 227–29).

The pope's role as the supreme ruler – the one bishop to rule over the others – has been hard won, and as we have seen, inconstant over time. Papal governance has been anything but serene. Devastating wars have been fought between Christian armies (some of them organized by popes) divided on the questions of whether the pope ruled absolutely or not, whether he was an Antichrist, or whether he was merely one Christian leader among many. Popes have been ignored and often ridiculed by bishops, clergy, and the laity throughout the centuries. They have been chased out of Rome by the Roman people and clergy, and by foreign armies (sometimes the armies of Catholic monarchs). They have been held under siege, arrested, kidnapped, and probably murdered. They have led armies, had harems, and even maneuvered to secure the papacy for a bastard son.[34] The history of the papacy is quite sordid, and even scatological in at least one instance. A conclave of cardinals in 1241 was pressured by the Senate of Rome to choose a pope quickly. Ten cardinals were put in a lowly room and deprived of quality food and medical care to hasten the decision. The story goes that the guards standing on the roof defecated through holes in the ceiling onto the cardinals. The cardinal chosen to be pope – Celestine IV – died sixteen days later of exhaustion from the episode, leading to a period without a pope for two years.[35]

The numerous ups and downs of authority of the pope relative to other leaders within the Church have several consistent patterns. Popes needed to assert their authority and build institutional structure around that authority to have it remain in place, and when authority ratcheted toward the pope, the bishops – or at least large groups of bishops – have assented. Thus, although some bishops have been the main challengers at times, at other times bishops – either by consensus or in large groupings – have approved of papal power.

Papal history – besides offering entertaining stories of intrigue, politics, violence, and bravery – also includes examples of specific popes known for having been centralizers.[36] Pope Danasus (366–84), for instance, held an early council that, as part of its work, ranked the sees in order of precedence. Rome was declared supreme over all the others. The next few popes, such as Innocent (402–17), made it clear that appeals regarding theological and spiritual matters, and matters of jurisdiction, were to come to Rome for settlement. And Leo the Great (440–61), a great centralizer, reminded bishops often of the supremacy of the Roman bishop over others. He relied on faked letters from the Apostle James, supposedly indicating that St. Peter passed on to Clement (officially the second pope according to the Church) the powers of supremacy over Christendom.[37]

---

[34] For generally critical histories of papal power, see Kung (1981) and McBrien (1997). See also Duffy (2002).

[35] Recounted in Cheetham (1982, 136).

[36] See O'Malley (2010) and McBrien (1997).

[37] There is no consensus among historians on whether Leo knew the letters were fake.

Much later, at a time when popes rivaled emperors and kings for rule over wide swaths of European territory, Nicholas II (1059–61) called the Lateran synod in 1059 to regularize the process of choosing the pope. According to the synod, cardinals – the select few among bishops who would form the pope's senate – would choose the next pope. Nicholas II's greatest mark on the papacy, however, was in establishing the Curia, the government of the Church. Led by the cardinals, the Curia was modeled after monarchical courts and attendants in use at the time in Europe, and what we would today call the bureaucracy that implements policy. The Curia grew in size and importance, and continues today as the key mechanism for maintaining papal authority within the Church.

Gregory VII (1073–85), who was pope shortly after Nicholas II (Alexander II was between) published *Dictatus Papae*, declaring that the pope is supreme over the Church and implied as well that he was supreme over the German, Frankish, and Byzantine monarchs. This was not received well by the monarchs. Later, when Gregory excommunicated German King Henry IV – not once but twice – Henry backed an anti-pope. A war ensued between supporters of each. The papal forces ultimately triumphed and the ensuing era marked the height of secular power for the papacy in Europe. The pope was for a time the most powerful ruler in Europe, both secular and religious.

Secular Challenges to Papal Authority

The secular aspects of papal power would slowly fade after the Middle Ages and then dramatically decrease by the sixteenth century, especially in two domains: 1) control of land and territory, and 2) influence on European politics. The trends in secular and ecclesiastical authority were anything but smooth and constant, but the beginning and ending are clear: the pope's relative authority without and within the Church ended in opposite places. Taking the long view, over hundreds of years, papal power in secular terms declined virtually to nothing, whereas ecclesiastical power became absolute.[38]

Popes, beginning in the early Renaissance, struggled for supremacy within European politics against monarchs and later, against republican governments; popes repeatedly lost the battle for secular control over land, resources, and Rome itself. After the Reformation, threats to papal authority from within the Church came not from conciliarism, but instead from Catholic secular rulers and bishops loyal to national governments. The more the popes tried to hold on to secular power, the more the monarchs of Europe (many of them Catholic, but others Protestant) humiliated them.[39]

For much of the time, the loss of secular power meant a loss of power over subunits within the Church, especially in parts of Europe. The French, Spanish,

[38] See Coppa (1998) and Pollard (2005).
[39] Evans and Thomas (1991).

and German leaders, for example – through various forms of government between the fourteenth and twentieth centuries – wished to reserve the right to run local sees and national churches. This included the authority to choose bishops, dispose of church land and assets as necessary, and ignore papal rulings and pronouncements. Some monarchs, especially in France (as discussed), declared that the pope had simply no jurisdiction over who would be bishops in their lands, nor could they control taxation schemes for funding local churches. Popes for centuries held territory, including the papal lands in what is now Italy, until 1870 and governed it like a secular ruler. These lands were stripped away, the last being in the aftermath of the creation of the Kingdom of Italy following revolution. Republican governments were no better for popes. For long periods of time after the French Revolution, there were two parallel churches in France, the official one sanctioned and controlled by the government, and the "true" church that followed Rome and listened to the pope.[40] The latter, as its only means of survival, operated mostly underground.

Popes, by the end of the seventeenth century, were largely irrelevant to the many conflicts among European nations and were therefore repeatedly pushed around. Secular encroachment extended to the selection of the pope. Gregory XV (1621–23) started a trend of permitting increased involvement by secular rulers in influencing the cardinals' choice upon the death of the pope. He was forced to reform procedures in the conclaves, granting each monarch of France, Spain, and the Holy Roman Emperor, a right of veto. This veto, either explicit or implicit, lasted until the early twentieth century. In the last known instance, Emperor Joseph of Austria vetoed Cardinal Rampolla's candidacy to become pope in 1903.[41]

Changes in papal power in these contradictory directions were linked. Popes were coerced – often by force of arms – to lose secular power, but in the bargain with national governments in Europe and in moments of institutional crisis among the bishops, they gained ecclesiastical power. Such bargains included concordats (similar to treaties) with secular rulers. These concordats described divisions of authority between Rome and the national government over appointments, land, and wealth. Depending on the country and the ruler, they could give the pope more or less authority over national churches. Later concordats mostly gave popes increasing latitude in managing Church affairs within the country in exchange for acknowledging secular sovereignty and confessional diversity (i.e., Protestantism was tolerated). Piece by piece, concordats gave Rome increasing authority to appoint bishops. One of the linchpins of modern papal power today – the authority to appoint bishops – resides almost entirely with Rome, although this was won at the expense of losing Church influence in the affairs of secular governments. (The appointment of bishops remains a delicate issue today in a few countries, such as China and Vietnam.)

[40] Cheetham (1982, 242–45).
[41] Cheetham (1982, 221). See Burke-Young (1999, 66) for a discussion of these vetoes.

Vatican I

From the French Revolution in the late eighteenth century to the late nineteenth century, the Church underwent the wrenching transition just summarized. It was once an institution holding substantial secular power throughout Europe, with control over large areas of territory in what is now central Italy (the papal states), possessing deep connections to monarchies in several of the most powerful states and empires of Europe, and freely operating as quasi-governments in theocratic local territories in many countries. It evolved into an institution without formal secular power, devoted almost solely to religious matters and facing hostility on all sides – from liberalized governments and Protestants to secular monarchs antithetical to the Church's mission. Especially relevant for Church governance was the rising tide of liberalism and republicanism in parts of Europe, and specifically the political changes occurring in France and Italy.[42]

In France during the nineteenth century, the government swung back and forth between republican government and monarchy, but in either case, relations with Rome were poor. The monarchs bullied the popes. Republican governments were deeply hostile to the clergy, and saw papal defenders, such as the French Jesuits and Vatican-appointed bishops, as opponents of revolutionary French values and institutions. Dissident French priests promoted rationalism and liberalism that were anathema to the Church hierarchy. Meanwhile, in Italy, the revolution that began in 1848 to expel Austria from Italian lands and make Italy a republic pitted the pope against nationalist forces that eventually invaded Rome and forced the pope, Pius IX, to flee south of the city to Gaeta.

Pius IX has a revealing history. He began his term in 1846 as a liberalizer, a promoter within Italy of a constitutional monarchy, and a leader open to secular government in Rome and within the papal territories. But after he was chased out of Rome in 1848, he turned adamantly against any form of republicanism and appealed to the Catholic powers of Europe, especially France, for assistance. When French troops helped to chase republicans out of Rome in 1850, Pius IX was briefly restored as Roman ruler under French protection, and was determined to stamp out republican and nationalist ideas from what territories remained as part of papal lands and in Rome itself. His harsh, oppressive tactics turned much of the population within his own territories against him.[43]

Pius's reaction was part of an overall Church effort to oppose the political transformations in Europe. The transformations by this time were the capstones of the long process of denuding the Church of secular authority and limiting its moral standing worldwide. Most of the hierarchy, including the popes, remained deeply opposed to freedom of religious conscience, democracy,

---

[42] See Costigan (2005) for a full account of the approach of Vatican I.
[43] See McBrien (1997), Coppa (1998), and Cheetham (1982) for full accounts.

rationalism, and separation of Church and state – all of which increasingly comprised the central planks of government in Europe, especially in France and Italy. This opposition marginalized the Church among intellectuals and many ordinary citizens, not to mention splitting the bishops and clergy into different partisan groupings. The term "liberal" referred to a host of trends permeating Europe – the notions of equality and republican government coming out of the American and French Revolutions, freedom of thought and expression, religious tolerance, and more generally, a loosening of old hierarchies and established modes of personal conduct. All of these, it was thought by the Church hierarchy, led to less morality among populations and should be fought tooth and nail. Pope Gregory XVI (1831–46), for instance, published a bull in 1832 prohibiting Catholics from voting, running for office, or cooperating in any way with new, liberal governments.

In reaction to these political events and to the overall loss of secular power by the papacy, the ultramontanism movement gained ground among bishops, clergy, and certain elements of the monarchy in Europe. First advocated by Jesuits in the sixteenth century, it was especially grounded among religious clergy in France throughout the nineteenth century. Ultramontanism had two related aspects. First, advocates asserted theologically that the pope should be the supreme, unquestioned authority within the Church. Second, by the nineteenth century, it applied to those who believed that a strong papacy was practically the best bulwark against the excesses of liberalism and republicanism. The ultramontanists collectively, although not necessarily in an organized manner, pursued policy changes within the Church. Papal infallibility became an idea the ultramontanists latched onto.[44]

Pius IX called for Vatican I to bring the bishops together in the midst of this tremendous upheaval in Europe including the reaction by ultramontanists. With the concept of monarchy under assault in Europe generally, Pius IX felt threatened not only by secular powers, but also from within the Church. Besides a desire to make an official, bishop-supported statement opposing the "errors" in contemporary European political and culture, including especially rationalism and liberalism, he wanted the council to approve the idea that the pope was supreme and did not need council assent to papal statements.[45] Aligning himself implicitly with the ultramontanists, he wanted to assert Roman – and particularly papal – control over the Church, but he wanted the assent of the bishops.

Note the paradox of asking the council to approve its own limited authority and making the pope the ultimate decision maker. He was asking for assent to extreme executive centralization by the representative body, and he eventually got it, although in limited and contested form. Pius IX recognized the paradox

---

[44] See Costigan (2005), McBrien (2008), and Cheetham (1982).

[45] See Bellitto (2002, 122) and the extended discussion in his book for a full account. Also, see O'Malley (2008), Kung (1981), Bulman and Parrella (2006), and McBrien (1997 and 2008).

and thus worded his pronouncements carefully in a way that would end up influencing the later Vatican II Council nearly 100 years in the future. The council and the pope were "collegial," but the council met under the pope's authority.[46]

There were various groups at odds during the First Vatican Council. The two with clear agendas were the ultramontanists, who wanted fealty to a supreme pope who ruled completely, and the so-called liberals, who wanted the Church to come to terms with modernity, liberalism, science, and separation of Church and state. A third group, called "inopportunists," were comfortable with weaker forms of papal infallibility, but thought the timing was bad to assert it given the situation in Italy and the need for comfortable relations with Protestant governments.[47]

Debates over papal infallibility during the council were heated. Liberals worried about papal dominance shutting off relations with Protestant rulers and countries with strict separation of church and state. One Dominican theologian and cardinal who was wary of too much papal autonomy but sought a compromise said that he thought the model should be, "What the pope taught was infallible, but the pope himself was not infallible." Furthermore, the pope was well understood to be the most important among the bishops, but he should not act separately from the bishops. Pius IX opposed this view and signaled his affinity with the ultramontanists. He met with this Dominican cardinal and indicating displeasure said, "I am tradition. I am the Church."[48]

After three weeks of debate, a compromise was approved overwhelmingly (533 to 2) after a large portion of dissenters (60 bishops) bolted the council. To a degree, the Dominican cardinal's view – not the extreme version favored by the ultramontanists – prevailed. Infallibility was said to apply not to the pope himself, but to his teaching authority. Furthermore, infallibility was only relevant on matters of faith and morals, not church governance. Infallible proclamations could only come when he spoke ex cathedra, but the pope did not need to be with the bishops to do so. Another category was set – irreformable statements – that included papal decrees. These were not infallible, in the sense of being utterly free from error. Soon after the final vote on infallibility – during recess – the council disbanded because of the start of the Franco-Prussian war. When the French troops protecting the pope left to fight against Prussia, the pope was defenseless against republican forces in Italy. The hierarchy fled Rome, and papal lands were seized by the Italians. Rome was occupied by Italian forces when Italy was finally united, north and south. The pope was forced into prisoner status within Vatican walls, his secular power completely destroyed. Brief by historical standards, the council lasted only nine months, cut short by the approach of Italian troops.[49]

---

[46] O'Malley (2008).
[47] McBrien (2008).
[48] Bellitto (2002, 122).
[49] This account follows that of Bellitto (2002).

Besides their place in the roiling European politics at the time, Vatican I and the infallibility doctrine have complicated legacies.[50] Infallibility has been formally invoked only once since Vatican I (in 1954 by Pius XII), so some argue it has had limited effect theologically. Arguably, it has also been of little tangible importance to governance in the Church, including in the overall centralization toward papal power. Consistent with this view, historians state that evidence suggests if the council had been allowed to continue, it would have declared that the college of bishops, when presided over by the pope, is also infallible.[51] Such a move would have opened Church governance to a degree of collective decision-making authority over theological matters and set the Church on a potentially different path. It implies that the favored position of the ultramontanists did not hold sway among a majority and that the preponderance of bishops were in a frame of mind to limit papal authority. If this is true regarding the prevailing sentiment among bishops, it explains why Vatican I did not really settle questions of papal power relative to the bishops, but merely pushed the questions off to a future time. The uncertainty over the meaning of infallibility for governance in the Church lingered.

In evaluating the history of the Church in the wake of Vatican I, we cannot ignore what happened afterward, especially at Vatican II. The statement about infallibility evolved out of broader political movements within the Church and in Europe. The doctrine that emerged from the council was more limited than its popular reputation implies; nevertheless, on several dimensions the council did have the effect of continuing religious centralization throughout the nineteenth century. The invocation of infallibility had lasting implications.

A large consequence of the transformation of the Church from secular to spiritual power had to do with changes over what could be offered to leaders of subunits, and what those leaders could offer to members of the Church within their domains. The Church previously had been a governing unit dispensing material favors and the usual things secular monarchs offer to vassals. Then it was a Church left only with the primary purpose of setting uniform standards of religious and moral conduct. The Church no longer had demonstrable material benefits to give, other than to appoint bishops where it could. The sources of large material benefits to any societal group were now secular governments, and the Church was left only with religious authority.[52]

In reaction to this loss of material beneficence, the Roman hierarchy, led by the pope, has pushed for more intellectual influence. Rome thus used increasing numbers of papal encyclicals to announce the official position of the Church on controversial issues confronting all people. Moreover, those encyclicals were grander in scope, pronouncing on theological matters and behavioral

[50] See McClory (1997) for a full treatment. See also P. Collins (1997).
[51] Wilde (2007, 60).
[52] Many others have made this point. See Kung (1981) for a particularly critical view. See also R. Collins (2009).

matters of interest to Catholics everywhere. Throughout the nineteenth century, "Catholics increasingly looked to 'Rome' not only as a court of final appeal but for answers to all questions."[53]

The push-back by liberals within the Church to this assumption of authority was partly in support of modern ideas of deliberative and representative government, and thus was a reaction to the idea that like a monarch, the pope was the final decider. At issue at the time of Vatican I were profound discourses within the Church over whether it would govern itself as an absolute monarchy or as something else resembling the trend in secular governments: decision making that directly included a strong representative body (the bishops collectively). Concepts of modern governance, including separation of powers, were in the air, and the council was the Church's counterresponse and it led to continued centralization. While ostensibly papal infallibility applied to theological matters only, the council's decision emphatically signaled the importance of maintaining the monarchical model of governance.[54] The call by Pius IX for infallibility was only part of his overall message. He regularly called for complete obedience by the bishops, and deplored diversity of Catholic thought and liturgy.

A large proportion of bishops, especially those aligned with the Curia, played an assenting role. Vatican I presents somewhat of a puzzle regarding the incentives of the bishops to go along with papal infallibility – why approve the diminution of their collective authority? It is important to realize, however, that infallibility of the central authority served as a unifying principle and helped many bishops achieve legitimacy relative to their secular governments. The answer to the puzzle, therefore, has to do with the nature of partisanship among the bishops, especially those with sympathies toward ultramontanism.

The bishops present at the council, nearly all of whom assented to papal infallibility, likely did so for reasons having to do with their own status within their realms. The partisan orientations of the bishops within the Church and within their national context became linked to the status, not only of Rome as the center of the Church, but of the papacy specifically. It was a partisan position of the ultramontanists that complete papal authority over the bishops was the necessary bulwark against liberalism and modernism, two concepts alive in Europe that threatened the positions of many bishops in their territories. But it was also a reaction against complete replacement of the Church as a secular governing unit. Thus, the bishops present at the council who assented to an extreme form of executive centralization did so because their partisan interests aligned with the specific theological, political, and cultural positions of the pope at the time (and in their expectation for the foreseeable future). Enough bishops reasoned that the fraying of papal power could lead to the fraying of Roman authority, which could mean a fraying of the authority of the bishop

[53] O'Malley (2008, 56).
[54] Kung (1981).

within his realm. Like the office of the papacy itself, the office of the local bishop had lost its secular role and its ability to dispense material benefits to Catholics. The only role left was spiritual, and so papal infallibility strengthened the spiritual authority of the one who represented the pope at the local level. To lose the spiritual authority of Rome was to lose the spiritual authority of the local bishop.

Vatican II

Popes in the decades after Vatican I were generally stern and remained defiant against the prevailing trends in secular government, science, and culture. They faced continued threats from secular leaders, and had complicated and controversial relationships with fascist leaders in Spain, Italy, and Germany. The hierarchy of the Church by the 1930s considered communism to be its greatest global enemy, a stance that distorted its priorities in dealing with fascism and Nazism. After an unfortunate delay, Pius XI eventually showed bravery during World War II in speaking out against the Axis, and although perhaps not enough in retrospect, he took a critical stance against Hitler. Following the war and the Holocaust, the Church led in contradictory directions. It softened its opposition to secular democracy and even encouraged Catholics to participate and vote for Christian Democratic parties. Pius XII opened the Church to dialogues over science and loosened up some elements of the liturgy. The Church became a proponent of an international human rights legal regime with powers to hold governments accountable for atrocities, and moved toward better relationships with Jews and other Christian faiths.

None of these changes, however, heralded any concrete movement away from complete papal power. Pius XII railed against dissident theologians, and never once consulted with the group of cardinals, even when he unilaterally defined the assumption of Mary ex cathedra (thus infallibly).[55] Even though the Church was opening slightly but unmistakably to the modern world, it still was a surprise when a new pope named in 1958 found reasons to reopen formally some of the earlier debates from Vatican I. When John XXIII called the Second Vatican Council in 1962, the Roman Curia was dominated by Italian conservative bishops who saw little reason for changes that might come from a council. Many were caught off guard by the pope's call.

A portion within the Curia eventually warmed up to the idea of a council in order to encourage the bishops as a whole to settle what was unsettled after Vatican I. They wanted the new council to ratify in definitive terms the authoritative teachings of the Church headed by the pope. Some of these conservative bishops wanted what Pius IX earlier sought and mostly won at Vatican I: assent once again by the bishops to executive centralization. Alternately, many theologians and liberal Church intellectuals – based on the notion of collegiality that

55 Coppa (1998, 210).

arose during Vatican I – held out hope that the Church might move away from complete centralized control. At least philosophically and in canon law, the governing relationship between the bishops and the pope appeared to remain unsettled, so both sides saw opportunities.

Vatican II occurred in four sessions for more than four years. The council dealt with a host of matters relevant to the Church and society, issuing sixteen documents expounding on a vast spectrum of issues, including ecumenism, the liturgy, the life of clergy, and Christian education. It was widely seen as a liberalizing council, one that brought the Church into the modern world and to a better relationship with the modern world. The council oriented the Church favorably toward science and toward modern concepts in politics, law, and culture, including religious freedom, feminism, democracy, human rights, and the legitimacy of secular rule. Some have argued that the council was more pastoral than legislative and judicial.[56] Yet the council did wrestle with questions of governance, twisting and turning over the fundamental question of papal authority.

The council opened in a manner that revealed deep disagreements between two sides that came to be known as the majority liberals and the minority conservatives (hereafter, liberals and conservatives). The conservatives began the council predominating on the body controlling the agenda, and promulgated a set of deliberative and voting rules designed to affirm documents preserving the status quo in the Church and offered few changes. But in the first session, several surprising events reshaped the agenda and disrupted the expected flow of the council. The liberals succeeded, aided somewhat by John XXIII and by sheer organizational will, in upending the hold the conservatives had on the agenda, and introduced bold proposals for change. Most of their proposals passed by an overwhelming majority vote, including documents establishing the vernacular mass instead of the universal Latin, statements on the importance of ecumenism, the value of the laity in the Church, improving relationships with Jews and Protestants, and establishing that the Church was newly supportive of religious freedom (as opposed to holding to the position that religious freedom merely allowed people to be condemned because they were not Catholic). On numerous measures, the liberals triumphed over their conservative opponents.

The geographic groupings of bishops correlated with ideological groupings. In general, conservatives were from Italy and Spain, with strong voices among those in the Curia or in dioceses in or near Rome. They not only wanted to preserve papal and Roman authority, but also saw the trends occurring among bishops in other parts of the world as deeply troubling; their openness to religious liberty, ecumenism, feminism, and forms of socialism to be in various ways against orthodoxy. They wanted the council to reaffirm the Roman line and push back. The liberals were generally bishops from North America, Latin

---

[56] This is the main argument of O'Malley (2008).

America, Africa, Asia, and the countries in Europe with Protestant-majority populations. They had tremendous stakes in having the Church open up to alternative cultural and political forms. Although they differed somewhat over details, they agreed on the need for reforms, and on a large number of issues they won by virtue of their numbers and their political savvy.

The process by which the liberals triumphed was as important as the final decisions. John XXIII tolerated and even encouraged a separation of powers character to the proceedings. With the support of John XXIII, decision making involved proposals being drafted and debated first by groups of bishops organized sometimes by ideology, but more often by geography. These were then brought to the entire group of bishops for debate and vote. Episcopal conferences among bishops from a given country were organized and met regularly. In many cases, these Episcopal conferences across multiple countries formed coalitions of the ideologically like-minded, and worked on drafts for sections of the documents. They were much better organized than their conservative counterparts.[57] There was a palpable sense of representational deliberation in the first session of the council. Groups of bishops representing regions or countries with overlapping ideological interests brought to the discussion subunit voices. These interests were being represented within a body that had decision-making authority over Church doctrine and dogma. The vote of the bishops in plenary were final acts of decision making, at least while John XXIII held the papacy. In fact, although the decision-making rules generally required a two-third support by all the bishops to approve a document, John XXIII stepped in to permit documents receiving a majority but not quite the requisite two-thirds support.

It is not entirely clear what John XXIII thought about the specific liberalizing documents being passed, and whether he was allowing documents to be passed even when he disagreed with them. What is clear is that John XXIII was committed to the process of the council permitting the college of bishops to decide, a process in which in his view (and the view of the victorious liberals) the Holy Spirit was working through the participants. His stance on process infuriated conservatives, especially those within the Curia. He valued deliberation, advice, and new information, as when he established the Papal Commission on Birth Control in March 1963.

John XXIII died before the start of the second session. One of his closest advisors, who took the name Paul VI, was chosen quickly in conclave. Paul VI made his mark right away when just prior to the opening of the second session, he announced reforms of the Curia. He signaled a willingness to continue permitting the bishops as a group to vote on Church documents. The council after Paul VI's assumption to the papacy continued to pass liberalizing documents that had been in formation. Paul VI encouraged the participation of women, the laity, and non-Christian observers at the council, and in a crucial move toward

---

[57] Wilde (2007, chapter 2).

the end of the council, pressed for the establishment of a continuing synod of bishops that would last after the council was over. He traveled abroad to the Holy Land and India, signaling that the pope was no longer a prisoner of the Vatican.[58] When he permitted a more varied liturgy enabling local churches to alter worship styles toward local culture, the decision rankled conservatives.

Paul VI, however, differed from John XXIII in style and also substance. He became more actively involved than John XXIII by remaining informed and offering his views occasionally. Although his reforms of the Curia occurred against the wishes of many conservatives, he was also more receptive to their entreaties than was John XXIII. He ended up drawing lines not to be crossed in ways that John XXIII did not, exercising both agenda control and a veto that ultimately undermined a view of collegiality, suggesting separation of powers or shared powers. After being warned in secret by groups of conservatives, he explicitly removed key items off the council's agenda – on birth control, priestly celibacy, additional reforms of the Curia, and collegiality – when it appeared that matters might go in directions he did not like for the Church.

The final turn of events caps off Vatican II as a signature moment in our story. As different as the Vatican II Council was from Vatican I, in the end, it landed in a place that largely confirmed the more conservative position of Vatican I on papal authority, and even clarified and codified that position. The actions of popes following the council confirmed the lock-in to executive centralization. The majority of bishops did not necessarily assent to this move as much as they were outflanked by the pope.

In the third session, after a draft was submitted on a crucial document – what would become *Lumen Gentium*, which outlined the governing model of the Church – Paul VI offered his suggested revisions, not all of which were approved by the drafting group of bishops. The fact that the pope's suggestions were not followed entirely was itself an affront to the conservatives and alarmed the Curia. They were aghast by the process and by what was in the document. The monarchical model of the Church was at risk by having the council suggest a model of co-governance, including elements not entirely approved by the pope. Paul VI was eventually contacted formally in a letter by a group of conservatives warning him against the consequences of collegiality. They predicted in the letter that if the document were accepted as is, the very governing foundation of the papacy would collapse. Their reference to the style of governance they wanted to maintain says it all: if the document as written passed, "The church would be changed from monarchical to 'episcopalian' and collegial, and would do so, supposedly, by reason of divine ordinance."[59] They encouraged the pope to take the parts of the document on collegiality off the agenda.

[58] O'Malley (2008, 198).
[59] Quoted in O'Malley (2008, 202).

Lumen Gentium was nevertheless on the verge of passing with language about collegiality that continued to trouble conservatives. Ostensibly, it appeared as if the conservatives won:

[T]he college or body of bishops has no authority unless it is understood together with the Roman Pontiff ... The pope's power of primary over all, both pastors and faithful, remains whole and intact ... The Roman Pontiff has full, supreme, and universal power over the Church ... The order of bishops ... is also the subject of supreme and full power over the universal Church, provided we understand this body together with its head the Roman Pontiff and never with this head. This power can be exercised only with the consent of the Roman Pontiff.[60]

Conservatives were concerned, however, that this language implied that the bishops were in fact also supreme powers over the Church along with the pope, although only when the pope was acting as head of the bishops. If not clarified, the conservatives argued, this could be taken to mean that the pope has supreme authority only if he resides as head of all the bishops. They believed *Lumen Gentium* implied that the pope needed to act in concert with the bishops to be supreme.[61]

It has been said that Paul VI wept when informed of the potential interpretation of the document to limit his authority. As part of a set of recommendations to the council in its final session, Paul VI sent a supposed clarification on the language about collegiality contained in *Lumen Gentium*, a document termed "Nota Praevia." Paul VI wanted the note to be in the introduction to *Lumen Gentium* but it ended up as an appendix. It stated that, "The College [of bishops] is not always 'fully active'; rather it acts as a college in the strict sense only from time to time and only with the consent of its head."[62] It is never to act independently of its head. Then in his Apostolic letter, *Motu Proprio, Apostolica Sollicitudo*, Paul VI formally established the Synod of bishops, stating that it has "the function of providing information and offering advice. It can also enjoy the power of making decisions when such power is conferred upon it by the Roman Pontiff; in this case, it belongs to him to ratify the decisions of the Synod."[63] The bishops had no authority independent of the pope and their decisions would need to be ratified by the pope.

This formulation by the pope did not seem to contradict the earlier language and still was vague. But for some reason, it mollified the conservatives and they overwhelmingly approved it and *Lumen Gentium*, as did the liberals. But seen in retrospect, especially in light of subsequent actions by Paul VI on birth control and actions by later popes, it is clear that what had happened within the council in terms of decision-making process had briefly opened the door

---

[60] *Lumen Gentium*, section 22.
[61] Ferrara and Woods (2002, 88).
[62] *Lumen Gentium*, section 4.
[63] Paul IV (1965).

to something that supporters of papal primacy wanted closed. The possibility of making the Church a system that included co-governance with a representative body emerged during the council largely through its practice. The bishops were seriously flirting with formalizing such a system of co-governance between the council of bishops and the pope, but the language attempting to codify it was not enough. The impetus for a liberal version of collegiality came largely because of the new influence of bishops from outside of Europe. It also came about because of the experience of many bishops within Europe living under democratic governments with thriving Church institutions in their realms. Democracy could work not only as a principle in operating nation-states, but also as a principle for governing the Church, they argued. Unlike during the period of Vatican I, papal dominance within the Church was not seen as a necessary hedge against encroaching, dangerous ideas from the secular world. Instead, the liberals saw an absolutist papacy as antiquated and out of tune with the times and the new scholarship on the workings of the early Church. It also seemed destined to lead to a loss of prestige by bishops outside of Europe in their own realms.

Paul VI decided otherwise, and made sure that the vague language was applied in a manner indicating that he was firmly above the council of bishops in Church hierarchy. The council was ending and Paul VI's timing was opportune for him: he would be the one to call the council to close and to call a synod thereafter. It was a successful move to thwart efforts to spread authority across units within the Church, making sure that absolute monarchy remained the model of governance.[64] Paul VI's actions were manifest in his subsequent decisions over birth control. He continued to allow the committee on birth control to work throughout the years of the council and then after their work was done, he considered their final recommendations as providing "evidence as would enable [the teaching authority of the Church] to give an apt reply on this matter."[65] The commission, although divided, opened the door to the Church approving artificial birth control for married couples.[66]

The pope's authoritative document, *Humanae Vitae*, goes on: "However, the conclusions arrived at by the Commission could not be considered by Us as definitive and absolutely certain, dispensing Us from the duty of examining

[64] Henn's (2000, 151–52) reflections on this are interesting:

[*Lumen Gentium*] brings into sharp focus once again the question of how many subjects of such authority there are in the church. There seem to be only three possible responses to this question: (1) there is one subject of supreme authority, the pope, from whom all other authority flows; (2) there are two subjects, inadequately distinct – the pope alone and the pope together with the college of bishops; and (3) there is one subject, the college of bishops, but the pope may exercise the supreme authority of the college freely, as he deems appropriate, in virtue of his role as its head ... Wide-ranging agreement by theologians about how the subjects or subjects of full and supreme authority are to be understood and related obviously has not yet been achieved." See also Oakley (1969).

[65] *Humanae Vitae*, section 5.
[66] McClory (1995) has a full account.

personally this serious question ... We, by virtue of the Mandate entrusted to Us by Christ, intend to give Our reply to this series of grave questions."[67]

Paul VI then pens the following words regarding a prohibition that hundreds of millions of Catholics have flouted in practice:

"[E]xcluded is any action which either before, at the moment of, or after sexual intercourse, is specifically intended to prevent procreation – whether as an end or as a means ... The laws that the Most High God has engraved in [man's] very nature ... [T]hese laws must be wisely and lovingly observed."[68]

Beyond the prohibition on artificial birth control, the key move for *Humanae Vitae* was procedural, removing the issue of birth control from the College of Bishops or from a future synod to be voted on.[69] The bishops collectively would almost surely have supported the majority position of the commission, but the pope's supreme interpretive authority won out over the collective interpretive skills of the world's bishops.

Lock-In

The two Vatican councils of 1870 and the 1960s stand out as the crucial moments shaping modern Church governance. Vatican II saw the resurgence of the idea of collegiality, and an ardent push by a majority of bishops to create a separation of powers system within the Church. Paul VI and his successors, however, effectively killed real collegiality for the foreseeable future. Thereafter, the executive centralization wrought by both Vatican I and II remained in place because of the actions of later popes, especially John Paul II. This important pope took actions to lock-in Paul's interpretation and ensure a long legacy. His actions were intended to bury the idea of separation of powers within the Church for the long term. He purged the bishops of liberals, appointed bishops with ideas clearly in line with his own thinking on theological matters, administrative matters, and especially on the role of the papacy relative to the bishops. Benedict XVI and Francis continued along the same path. Through their absolute appointment powers, and their absolute powers to interpret canon law, including the role of the papacy in governance, and through their abilities to use Vatican resources to punish, reward, and divide potential coalitions agitating for change, these modern popes have locked-in papal dominance of the Church, or in our terms, extreme executive centralization.

An argument could be made that the Church is, in fact, devolved in authority, which is its source of strength. As previously mentioned, the subunits of the Church are known in canon law as particular churches, and although there are a variety of types, the most common form is a diocese or archdiocese.

---

[67] *Humanae Vitae*, section 6.
[68] *Humanae Vitae*, sections 14 and 31.
[69] See Drane (1969) for a critical view.

All particular churches are headed by bishops or their equivalents. A few particular churches, such as the Coptic and Armenian Catholic Churches, have their own rites and their leaders, known as patriarchs, are chosen by local custom (although formally approved by the pope). The leaders of these particular churches have virtually complete control over the administration of Church practice within their domains. According to canon law, the bishops have final lawmaking and judicial authority in their particular churches. With the exception of matters explicitly described in canon law as the prerogative of the pope, there is no vehicle for overriding the bishop or appealing his decisions on matters within his jurisdiction. Within dioceses, pastors and priests are given wide latitude to govern their parishes and religious orders provided they conform to Church doctrine. Oversight comes mostly on the basis of responding to complaints rather than active monitoring of day-to-day operations. The Church is a remarkable federated system held together by a set of institutions that combine clear lines of authority, devolution, and flexibility.

The Church is remarkable not only because of the longevity and durability of its basic structure, but because it can combine flexibility and uniformity across a global scale. Despite the recent history of executive centralization, the Church (contrary to popular image) does change over time in substantial ways. It has reformed itself numerous times, both organizationally and doctrinally. In recent centuries, it changed doctrine in response to humanism, the rise of democracy and human rights, and changes in international finance. At one time the Church sanctioned slavery and the execution of heretics; today it steadfastly pronounces against unwarranted violence and coercion, using a standard of what is "unwarranted" from international human rights documents.

Its liturgy, moreover, has changed dramatically over decades and centuries, and continues to evolve. The U.S. branch of the Church, for example, recently tinkered with the English language version of the mass to make it conform more to original Latin versions. Yet today you will hear the same liturgy (albeit in the local language) in Vietnam, Brazil, Canada, and Angola. That is, even though some music will be different and local customs will shape the experience, you will hear the same words spoken in the prayers, the prayers conducted in the same order, and the same understanding of what is going on at the liturgy. Its federated character allows for this local flavor and consistency together.

Nevertheless, the Church remains a deeply centralized institution toward executive authority. Centralization starts with the pope but runs throughout the Church. The authority of Rome is unquestioned and ultimately supreme, and within dioceses, the same can be said for the bishop's authority. The central authority wielded by the pope is manifest through a vast bureaucracy, the Curia. The Vatican oversees the global church by choosing bishops; collecting and allocating resources; setting up new dioceses; deciding on doctrine; disciplining theologians; settling conflicts and controversies that arise across and within religious orders, dioceses, and national churches; and managing the pope's schedule. Within dioceses, bureaucracies operate seminaries and school systems, run social service agencies, communicate and coordinate across parishes, place personnel (including clergy) within Church units, and manage the bishop's schedule. Hierarchy manifest through bureaucracy pervades multiple levels of the Church.

At least in theory today, the bishops are not supposed to be mere stewards of Rome, even though it ends up being that way in practice. The modern understanding in theological terms is that, once chosen, a bishop's authority to govern comes directly from God and not through Rome. Bishops are, in Church terminology, ordained to their positions, which means that they are not agents of Rome but govern their realms fully and completely. This is more a theological matter than a practical one, and was firmly established in canon law only within the last century. Although bishops have the freedom to make a huge number of decisions on their own, on quite weighty matters in everyday governance without consulting Rome, this does not mean they have full autonomy. Bishops today are appointed by Rome; therefore, bishops can be (and have been) removed by Rome if they depart substantially from Church teaching or behave contrary to Church law.

Rome permits devolution to the diocese, but there is little true decentralization. On day-to-day governance, there are constant questions over which level – the diocese or Rome – has the legitimate authority on specific policy issues. Rome, for instance, has the final authority over all theological matters of doctrine and translations of liturgical texts to be used in religious ceremonies. Bishops have, according to canon law, full authority to set up or close down seminaries within their dioceses, and to grant dispensations to the faithful. The mix of central or subunit authority across various policy issues is complicated by the fact that at any moment, Rome can revoke any autonomy the bishops have.

In an interesting twist, the Vatican – in response to the ongoing child sexual abuse scandals – has adopted legal strategies that reveal a deep contradiction. It has repeatedly held the position that any liability for negligence by the Church for clerical sexual abuse resides at lower levels – with dioceses, particular churches, parishes, schools, or religious orders. In other words, the Vatican should not be held liable in U.S. or European courts because the subunits are autonomous.[70] Meanwhile, the Vatican has also recalled bishops who acted inappropriately and has promulgated new rules for clerical training and for the training of lay ministers, and has mandated new procedures that all subunits must follow, all in response to the abuse scandals. To avoid legal liability,

---

[70] U.S. federal courts have consented to this interpretation, repeatedly siding with the view that individuals in the United States working for the Church – clergy or lay – are employees of dioceses and not of the Vatican. Thus, in August 2012, a federal district court in Oregon held that the Vatican was not liable for sexual abuse by priests because it was not the employer of the priests. See Associated Press (August 20, 2012).

the Church presents itself as highly decentralized, but as an organization, it reveals its underlying centralized model of control in trying to minimize future problems.[71]

Papal dominance appears to be locked-in. The pope not only controls a massive bureaucracy that can collect and dispense resources among all formal subunits of the Church, he also controls the appointment of bishops and cardinals, sets the agenda for the Church (including any Church councils), and has final authority to interpret canon law, including the powers of the papacy itself. The people in those roles have not been afraid to use that authority and to remind others repeatedly of that authority.[72]

John Paul II even changed the voting rules for the conclave before he died, and by one interpretation, did so to ensure that conservative bishops collectively would have enough weight to choose a conservative pope.[73] The standard rule for choosing a pope in conclave was that a two-thirds super majority was required to approve a man for the papacy. In 1996, John Paul II declared that if a decision had not been made after thirty rounds of voting, the rule would change to simple majority – any proportion more than 50 percent. The argument goes that he believed there were enough votes among the cardinals to support his style of pope, but not enough to pass the two-third threshold. This is a time-honored way to ensure one's legacy: change the rules in favor of one's own faction to capture the successor position.[74]

It is common to hear people refer to the Church as one in a current "crisis." Whether someone considers the Church in crisis, and if so, which crisis the person identifies or how he or she states it, say as much about the person's attitude toward the Church and to organized Christian religious institutions as it does about the Church itself. Regardless of whether the present time qualifies as a crisis, the Church does face dilemmas borne of deep divisions among its members, among its leaders, and among its external critics. Some consider it not orthodox enough, whereas others consider it too orthodox. It is either too hierarchical, or its hierarchy only weakly influences its subunits and members. It is either inflexible to its detriment, or has been too flexible to its detriment.

If we focus solely on the several present crises without an historical perspective, however, we miss a key point about the Church: it has often been in crisis throughout its long history, and it has often changed and reformed.

---

[71] See Fogarty (2004), Wilbourn (1996), and Chopko (2003).

[72] There is a saying in the Church: *Roma locuta, causa finata* – "Rome has spoken, the matter is settled."

[73] See Baumgartner (2003) and Tobin (2003).

[74] Another interpretation challenges this view. John Paul II was exposed to theoretical results from social-choice theory, and knew the importance of institutional design. He also knew of the possibility of voting cycles and wanted to avoid a locked or prolonged conclave – the theme of Maltzman, Schwartzberg, and Sigelman (2006). They argue that John Paul II had appointed 80 percent of the cardinals by 1995 and thus had plenty for a two-thirds voting threshold.

Popes at times took advantage of external threats to consolidate power away from councils of bishops or cardinals. Like the U.S. government cases and GM (Chapter 5), it has ratcheted toward historically unprecedented executive authority. If the Church were ever to decentralize, it may take a crisis that implicates the papacy to such a degree that no large group of subunit representatives see it in their partisan interests to maintain papal dominance.[75] It has happened before, although in schismatic, unhappy times for the Church.

[75] See Fogarty (2004).

5

Corporation

For many years during the twentieth century, General Motors (GM) was the world's largest industrial corporation by various measures, including number of employees and sales. Each year between 1933–2007, it sold more vehicles than any other manufacturer in the world. Despite its near collapse a few years ago, GM still lives on and maintains a substantial presence in the global automotive industry.[1] In fact, by 2011, it had regained its place as the number one seller of vehicles.[2]

The mighty GM of decades past left a distinctive imprint on the modern corporation. It offered a model of organizational structure that many other corporations followed in the middle part of the twentieth century. Organizational theorists have assiduously studied GM and its corporate leaders, and generations of business school students have analyzed GM's early corporate structure.[3] Like any huge organization, GM has constantly worked to balance decentralization and centralization, to craft the right model of federated governance. During its formative decades, it was led by innovators who devised and carried out reorganizations while maintaining a highly productive balance between

---

[1] The GM of today is not legally the same one that sprang up in the early twentieth century to become the largest corporation in the world. That corporation was broken apart with the U.S. portion declaring bankruptcy in 2009. It was reformed and listed on the New York Stock Exchange in 2010 with the U.S. Government as the majority stockholder, and with substantial holdings by the government of Canada and the autoworkers' unions of the two countries. The legal difference between the old and new GM follows from a technicality and we can treat them as the same throughout this chapter and book.

[2] From self-reports by the companies themselves, GM sold about 9 million vehicles worldwide in 2011, and the next largest, the Volkswagen Group, sold around 8.2 million vehicles. By 2013, however, Toyota had regained the top spot as selling the most vehicles.

[3] Chandler's earliest works on organizations referred directly to GM as the centerpiece. See Chandler (1977) for a summary of his research. Peter Drucker based his major book (1946) on the GM model of organization. See also Drucker (1972).

decentralized autonomy and centralized control of strategy. As with our other cases, the balance at GM between subunit autonomy and central authority was never static, and it was not the result of broad consensus among leaders. Rather, GM's institutional structure and the resulting settlements on authority were contested and repeatedly forged through political conflict within the leadership.

Like the other cases in this book, there was an overall direction to the changes in authority that occurred at GM. Its history, especially its first four decades, aptly illustrates our themes: the striking of a federal bargain, how representative and executive centralization can occur, and how executive centralization builds on itself and becomes difficult to reverse. GM began as a holding corporation for car companies in 1908. The leaders of the individual companies that were part of GM assented to initial centralization on the understanding that they would maintain autonomy and be represented in the central, corporate bodies that make important decisions. They assented to as much representative centralization as could be expected in a business corporation. Over time, executives in the central unit at GM asserted authority while struggling to maintain the support of subunit leaders and investors who saw their fates linked to the success of corporate leaders' specific ideas. The trajectory was toward corporate authority over subunits (vertical authority) and executive authority over representative bodies (horizontal). And like our other cases, these were related. Crucially, it was the contest for authority within the central unit (horizontal) that ultimately shaped the degree of centralization (vertical). Finally, by the late 1950s, executive centralization had locked-in.

Federated Beginnings

GM's path from a highly decentralized holding company to locked-in executive centralization started with the initial vision and actions of its founder, Billy Durant.[4] Different than other early auto executives in the United States because he was not an engineer or inventor, Durant was mostly a salesman and a purveyor of financial schemes to raise capital for the creation of new companies. Henry Ford, Ransom Olds, Benjamin Briscoe, David Dunbar Buick, and Henry Leland – the men who with Durant shaped the early American automotive industry – were all tinkering with the design of automobiles and engines in pursuit of a reliable, saleable vehicle. Like many of them, Durant worked first in the business of manufacturing and marketing horse-drawn vehicles. By 1900, he had recognized the huge potential for the automobile as a consumer product. Along with Ford, Durant paid close attention to the means of production and profit margins. He envisioned before anyone else the full-service automobile company, starting from raw materials and ending with the sale of a car to a consumer. To get to that, however, he needed to knit existing companies together.

---

[4] For an admiring account, see Gustin (1973).

Durant believed that larger was better when it came to companies. Deeply concerned about how many different automakers were in the market, Durant in 1908 invited four of the leading manufacturers in the country to lunch in Detroit to discuss the possibility of a merger. He proposed forming a holding company to avoid murderous competition and to push smaller companies out of business. Ford, Buick, Reo, and Maxwell-Briscoe were represented at the meeting. Henry Ford reportedly said nothing, and let it be known later that he was skeptical throughout. He subsequently made it clear that he would go it alone, telling others that the key was having cars be as inexpensive as possible for consumers. Durant, in contrast, told the others that constant innovation and dividing up the market share among the leading manufacturers were the keys to success.[5] As it would turn out, these differences in philosophy largely capture the basic approaches of the Ford Motor Company and General Motors for several decades thereafter.

The result of the initial meeting and other meetings that followed was a merger between Oldsmobile and Buick; Durant incorporated the holding company in September 1908. Durant's vision was to create the largest automobile company, but one decentralized enough to turn the talent loose to make innovations and, ultimately, profits. The looseness of reins planned for the component auto companies unnerved others, who assented to even more centralized control than Durant wanted. According to Durant, when Briscoe heard of Durant's plans for the holding company, Briscoe joked, "Ho! Ho! Durant is for states' rights; I am for union."[6]

As head of GM, Durant devoted his attention to stock schemes, buying companies, and hiring talented auto men. His tenure was dynamic but turbulent. Already by 1909, Durant had purchased eleven companies, and later, in 1917, he brought the heavyweight Chevrolet into GM. In 1919, there were seventeen auto or parts divisions under Durant at GM. He used creative financing to buy these competitors, and more than once got into serious problems with bankers and debtors. He lost control of the company to financiers in 1910, but regained it in 1916, then lost it for good in 1920. He was forced out that year by GM's major investors, which included J. P. Morgan and the du Pont family.[7]

From the beginning, largely owing to Durant's philosophy and his way of doing business, GM had the markings of a federated organization with subunit input into decision making in the corporate central unit. The companies Durant bought were generally left alone to make and market their cars. Each car

---

[5] This meeting is recounted in various books and articles. See Cray (1980) for a lively account.

[6] Quoted in Yanik (2009, 49).

[7] Durant never again worked for GM, and never even returned to GM's offices. For the rest of his life, Durant watched from the outside as the company he started blossomed into the largest industrial corporation in the world. In his last years, he managed a bowling alley in Flint, Michigan. To honor his status as its founder, GM secretly paid him a pension until he died in 1947. See Gustin (1973), Cray (1980), and Pelfrey (2006). For the data on numbers of companies and chronology, Cray (1980) summarizes these in a useful manner.

company that joined starting in 1909 and continuing until 1920 was promised autonomy to develop and market its vehicles. They would effectively collude to take advantage of the rapidly growing automobile market, to compete altogether against Ford and others, and to share the benefits of unified sources for financing. Wilfred Leland's agreement in 1909 with Durant was typical. Son of Henry Leland, founder of Cadillac and Lincoln, Wilfred was owner of Cadillac and agreed to sell his company to GM. Wilfred wanted assurances that he would be left alone to do what he wanted, with no interference. Durant for the most part complied.[8] While the auto companies had informal input, there was not much the central unit did other than serve as a forum for collusion.

Decentralized Governance

By the end of 1920, with Durant gone, the du Pont family in Delaware had controlling interest in GM. Pierre du Pont was president and together with Alfred Sloan as vice president, they began operating the company. Sloan had joined GM a few years earlier as part a group of business leaders folding their own United Motors Company into GM. Sloan and du Pont agreed that Durant permitted too much decentralization in the corporation, and they felt that greater central control would increase profits. Later, when Sloan was president of GM, he referred to the era of Durant disparagingly as "decentralization with a vengeance."[9] Although du Pont and Sloan wanted to preserve the benefits of decentralization in driving innovation, they also saw the downside of the lack of coordination and runaway speculation by the division leaders regarding new markets.

Although du Pont and Sloan agreed on the need for more centralization, they differed over how much to push in that direction and what centralization meant. Seen from the outside, and given GM's huge profitability and increasing size over time, these two were a dream pairing for the prosperity of GM through the Depression, the Second World War and into the 1950s.[10] But Sloan had fundamental differences of opinion with du Pont and the company's major owners – and with other executives – over the appropriate degree of autonomy for the auto divisions and their voice in running the corporation. Sloan and the investors especially disagreed over the subunit representation in central decision making.

Sloan had for several years proposed a form of corporate governance that was innovative, but seemed risky to investors. It continued portions of Durant's federated model and added formalized representation by the subunits at the central level in a committee with real decision-making authority. Sloan's

---

[8] Cray (1980, 81).

[9] Sloan (1964, 30).

[10] Sloan ran the company from various positions, as president and CEO from 1923–37, then as CEO and chairman of the board from 1937–46, and then as chairman of the board from 1946–56.

original plan as described to du Pont was a corporate form of separation of powers with subunit representation. A finance committee, dominated by investors and especially by du Pont, would approve finances and new investments, while an executive committee, comprised of managers and the heads of the auto divisions (chaired by Sloan himself) would make strategic decisions for the corporation. Sloan's idea was that matters would reach the executive committee only if they affected more than one division. Otherwise, the individual divisions' managers would have autonomy to make tactical and some strategic decisions. There were even distinct accounting standards within the different auto divisions under Sloan's plan.[11] This was the instantiation of GM's version of the M-Form of corporate organization that gained much attention.[12]

The M-Form would become famous in corporate governance circles as a model that blended centralized strategic control with decentralized tactical control. The basic idea was to enable those with the most knowledge of specific product markets – the ones actually designing, making, and selling the products from local divisions – to have discretion in how to increase their market share and maximize profits. The corporate central units would coordinate the activities of the local divisions to avoid competition with each other, and would also give incentives for the local divisions to add to the corporation's overall profits and make decisions on overall corporate strategy. In the simplest and purest of terms, the M-Form located strategic decisions at the central level and tactical decisions specific to product markets at the local level.

Within the M-Form, however, there is tremendous room for variation.[13] Du Pont and his fellow investors in these initial years balked at aspects of Sloan's model, especially the representational parts. They envisioned a different version of the M-Form, and instituted a qualitatively different kind of centralization. Three-quarters of the executive committee would be seated with investors, and there would be no divisional representation. A third central committee, operations, would represent the auto division managers, but would have little power. Du Pont also fired the Durant-era divisional managers, forced the auto divisions to hand over profits to the corporation and to have a common accounting system, and gave the finance committee veto power over large expenditures by the divisions. Du Pont believed, not unreasonably, that the auto divisions, if they were represented in central committees, would advocate for their own individual interests and not collectively for the interests of investors. He wanted to avoid partisanship within the central committees based on those advocating for particular auto divisions.[14]

---

[11] Freeland (2001, chapter 2).
[12] Mott (1924), Pound (1934), Freeland (2001), Drucker (1946), Chandler (1977), Cooley (2005), and Brown (1927).
[13] This is one of Freeland's (2001) main points, that the M-Form was a vague blueprint and GM's executives fought over the devilish details.
[14] Freeland (2001, 52–58).

When du Pont's plan was implemented in 1921, it did not go well. In fairness, Sloan had a hand in making it unsuccessful, but so did the legacy of Durant's decentralization. The leaders of the auto divisions, even those appointed by du Pont, felt betrayed in that they believed the whole point of the corporation, via Durant's vision, was to grow through innovation by the separate, and mostly autonomous, divisions. They resented du Pont's plans right off, and were suspicious not only of motivations by the central unit, but also of any engineering or marketing suggestions that came from the central unit. The resentment boiled to the surface when du Pont in 1921 tried to force all the divisions to adopt a new technology for all vehicles, an air-cooled engine. Du Pont faced immediate resistance from the divisions over this central mandate. They delayed implementation and found excuses that infuriated du Pont. Sloan, unconvinced by the need for the air-cooled engine, made promises to du Pont but in the end dragged his feet and failed to enforce du Pont's directives. The air-cooled engine proposal died in a slow, and to du Pont, frustrating process.[15]

Given how decentralized GM was under Durant, and how much it was in reality a collection of auto companies held together loosely through a set of papers filed in Michigan and New Jersey by Durant, it is no surprise that the first attempts to impose anything on the subunits failed. Certainly the subunits had enough control over resources that by their lack of assent to du Pont's proposed increased centralization, the air-cooled engine initiative failed. But more than this, centralization also failed because of vigorous disagreements within the central unit over the role of subunit representation. Sloan at this time generally preferred to grant the divisions considerable representation on powerful committees and also grant them autonomy in their own affairs because he acknowledged their diverse expertise. Du Pont wished for a stronger hand by investors and by the central management of GM because he wanted to avoid partisan infighting. Du Pont's frustration with the divisions led to his voluntary resignation as president in 1923. He turned the reins over to Sloan, but stayed on as chairman of the board. These initial differences over governing philosophy between du Pont and Sloan persisted for the next several decades.

The corporation was in these early years teetering between being truly decentralized and merely devolved, even with Sloan's vision looking to the latter. Under Durant – and for a few years after – it was surely decentralized, with de facto subunit assent necessary for central policies that affected them. The air-cooled engine fiasco demonstrated that. The evolution under Sloan was a gradual move toward a more centralized system, albeit one of palpable devolution. Not long after Sloan took over, the central unit was in a stronger position but the divisions still retained tremendous autonomy. The central unit gradually gained the authority to reverse the autonomy given to the divisions at any time.

---

[15] There are numerous accounts of the air-cooled engine controversy. See Freeland (2001, 58–64). See also accounts in Cray (1980), Keller (1989), Sloan (1964), and Pound (1934).

The example of the air-cooled engine, when the divisions maintained the collective strength to thwart centralized schemes, bothered Sloan even though he was not upset by that specific outcome. Sloan knew that their collective capacity could haunt him next time around. He set about to change the structure so that he could gain subunit assent for centralized policies and his central authority over any of them individually. Sloan, by "trading sovereignty for support [of subunits] ... [he] actually enhanced [his] own power."[16] Sloan's corporate model at the time reflected this recognition that central policies enjoying little support from the divisions would not fly. His motivation, as stated in memoirs and in internal memos, was to emphasize within GM corporate decisions that are made consensually. By this he meant that the divisions were, on the whole, on board with the direction of the corporation and were rarely going to be imposed upon by the central management without their consent.

Whereas the ideal of divisional representation appealed to Sloan, one hitch to his plans was the power of the investors, who naturally believed that they were the constituency needing predominant representation in corporate decision making, not the divisions. There were essentially three groups with overlapping but often competing institutional interests in GM: owners, the leaders of the divisions, and the corporate managers. The owners focused on profitability above all. The leaders of such divisions as Buick, Cadillac, Chevrolet, and Oldsmobile competed among themselves for resources, but they had a shared interest in governance structures that gave the divisions representational weight on key corporate committees. And finally, corporate managers with Sloan as the leader believed they had the expertise to run the corporation and sought autonomy from the owners, but also their ready approval for financing proposed new investments. In these formative years, Sloan clearly needed access to investors' resources, but he also needed divisions' consent. One of Sloan's early legacies as a corporate leader was his ability to thread this needle, keeping investors at bay while permitting subunit autonomy and often earning the assent of both groups.[17]

He pushed forth the defining elements of his version of the M-Form. Operating subunits were to have substantial autonomy to design and make specific products, whereas central corporate management would assist the subunits in such a way that would avoid favoritism yet maintain central strategic control over the corporation. The auto divisions would make their own tactical decisions whereas the central corporation would make broad strategic decisions. As it played out in GM, and consistent with GM's origins, the coordination was a form of industrial collusion. For many decades, each division produced a line of products that did not compete with any other product produced by the corporation. The mission was to segment the market; Chevrolet would produce

---

[16] Freeland (2001, 269).
[17] Not only does Sloan (1964) himself admit as much, but many others agree with him. See Sheehan (1958), Pound (1934), Pelfrey (2006), *Newsweek* (1963), and Drucker (1946).

stylish cars priced to be slightly above Ford's lowest-priced cars, on the idea that consumers would be willing to pay a bit more for styling. Buick would produce car a notch above Chevrolet in price and then Oldsmobile one notch above Buick. Finally, Cadillac would target the top of the market. There were other subunits devoted to trucks and busses. Subunit production and marketing (and labor negotiation in later decades) would be coordinated so that the corporation could take advantage of economies of scale, but the subunits would also be empowered to make tactical decisions to take advantage of their expertise within their segments of the market.[18]

As we have already seen in the differences between du Pont and Sloan, there is much room for variations in terms of who has authority to make decisions within this kind of model. Sloan fought for his version, what has been called a "corrupted" M-Form, where central managers (especially himself) could run the company largely free of meddling investors' dictates.[19] But as long as the investors could speak through a strong voice of a single person like du Pont, corporate management – not to mention the separate divisional managers – would not have the kind of autonomy Sloan believed necessary to continue innovation that leads to growth.

Sloan did what he could for devolution and especially for subunit representation. As expected, he sought to put more divisional managers on the executive committee in 1923, but the investors forbade it. Sloan then, in a crucial move, sought go around the investors and demonstrate to them that he deserved their trust when he grew the company despite not adhering exactly to their wishes. Starting in 1923, he took steps to strengthen the power of the operations committee, which represented the divisions. He redefined the kinds of questions that it would deal with to include broader strategic matters. As in any collective decision-making setting, controlling the agenda and defining terms mattered a great deal. When crucial moments arose, for the purposes of determining what under the M-Form would be decided by central corporate management (strategic) and by the auto divisions (tactical), Sloan tended to side with a broad definition of what was tactical to expand the authority of the divisions to manage their own affairs.[20] He would do this often throughout this long tenure, although less consistently as time went on.

Divisional autonomy, reasoned Sloan, was related to his own authority, but he sometimes had to sacrifice the former to obtain more of the latter. Not surprisingly, Sloan wanted more autonomy from the board of directors to run the corporation, and he largely succeeded in earning this central managerial autonomy. Although he sought considerable discretion for divisional managers to run their auto divisions, Sloan prioritized his own autonomy from investors above all. He felt forced to make the trade-off repeatedly after the mid-1920s.

---

[18] Mott (1924), Pound (1934), Freeland (2001), Drucker (1946), Chandler (1977), Cooley (2005), and Brown (1927).

[19] As mentioned previously in a footnote, this is one of the central themes of Freeland (2001).

[20] Freeland (2001, 80).

Executive Centralization

The ideas on governance that Sloan pursued within GM were not fixed but instead evolved, especially in response to such outside events as the Depression and World War II. Periods of centralization and decentralization that occurred over the next few decades were both responses to external forces and also Sloan's seizing opportunities to gain more managerial autonomy from the owners, even if the divisions lost out in the process at times.

By way of summary, between 1933 and the 1950s, the corporation vacillated between strong central control and substantial divisional autonomy. We can consider several key executive-centralization thresholds. Certainly the prior move from Durant to du Pont in 1920 was a moment of executive centralization, but it was ineffective and brief, and was reversed when Sloan's ascent to the presidency in 1923 marked a move toward a more representative centralization. Sloan was always a strong executive, but he would, as much as possible in a corporate context, permit the subunits to share in governance. He was not advocating democracy; rather, that the subunits be a part of the governing structure of the corporation. During and just after Sloan's term, GM experienced two bouts of executive centralization: in 1933 (a second threshold), and then in the mid-1950s, with the latter bout surviving and sticking in place (a third threshold).[21] In between, in the 1940s, GM permitted a remarkable degree of devolution within both representative and executive centralization. Two things were changing at GM during this period: the degree of subunit autonomy, which went back and forth; and the degree to which it was merely a corporation led by central managers and owners or whether its governance model was to include subunit representation. Subunit representation also went back and forth. The two things were correlated in that subunit autonomy came at times when the subunits were part of central committees making important decisions.

Note the use of the word "devolution", instead of decentralization, when referring to the 1940s. This implies that GM had by that time already locked-in to a degree of centralization; true decentralization either did not or could not take place. I address toward the end of this chapter which GM threshold fundamentally changed the corporation to locked-in centralization.

The lack of spending money by Americans during the Depression caused many corporations to focus less on innovation and more on lower-cost, high-volume sales. GM, in response to the economic downturn, simplified production toward less-expensive cars in all divisions. Central management reined in expenditures in all divisions during the time of economic contraction. To cut costs, operations were consolidated; divisions shared facilities and had

---

[21] For observing the trajectories and the various reorganizations, most helpful are the General Motors annual reports, which nearly always include organizational charts plus the names of the executives on the boards. From those names, one can then find biographies of the men, including which units within GM they may have headed.

common parts and processes. Thus, operating decisions affected more than one division. This necessitated decision making at the central level.

Corporate leaders correspondingly centralized authority away from the divisions. Beginning especially in 1933, with Sloan's initiative, GM reduced the role of division managers on the corporate committees and centralized aspects of operations that were formerly the province of the divisions. Given what he considered to be increasing partisan fighting across divisions on the operations committee, Sloan got fed up and eliminated the committee in 1933, retaining an executive committee and a finance committee. He took the division leaders off of the executive committee and by this time, he had put men at the head of divisions who broadly supported his vision for the corporation. The division leaders nevertheless complained about the changes, but to no avail. This was quite a change from the previous decade when the division leaders had flexed their collective muscle over the air-cooled engine.

Sloan, concerned that investors would force cost-cutting to a degree that damaged the overall survivability of the corporation, used centralization away from the divisions as a means to make owners more comfortable with increasing managerial autonomy from the investors themselves. A major reorganization in 1937 centralized even further, and eliminated division representation in committees charged with making any strategic decisions. The executive and finance committees were scrapped, replaced by an overall policy committee that delegated operational decisions to an administrative committee. The divisions had marginal input into the administrative committee when consulted. More importantly, the policy committee – by Sloan's design – was dominated by central executives and not investors. Sloan further sought to wall off the investors from decision making by blurring the responsibilities of the policy and administrative committees, with both being dominated by central managers.

The changing environment within labor relations also justified this centralization, in the view of Sloan and other central executives. The Wagner Act of 1935 permitted corporate-wide labor negotiations as opposed to specific labor agreements for each division. Likewise, new government regulations coming out of the New Deal required corporate-level compliance, and it made sense to establish policies applying to every division from centralized committees.

By the time war came, GM was quite centralized with little governing input at the central level by the divisions. Yet surprisingly, the corporation was profitable despite depression, and the financial results for investors seemed to vindicate the centralization and also undercut complaints of division leaders. The 1930s centralization was soon to be reversed, but it had a lasting legacy.

At first, when military contracts became the obvious direction for GM during the war, the policy committee's reaction was to continue and even enhance centralization. This soon became unworkable given the many specialized products, and Sloan argued for more divisional representation and autonomy. Another attempt was then made to establish a new War Administrative Committee (WAC), which was the previous administrative committee, formally separated from the policy committee, to make military contract decisions. This time, division leaders were represented. Leaders of the three largest divisions had a formal vote on the WAC, although they only had authority to react and approve proposals made by small policy groups comprised entirely of central managers. The WAC, however, in spite of limited divisional input, gave substantial autonomy to divisions to pursue military contracts on their own. The structure of representation – the limit of three division leaders plus their role only as approvers – led to divisional autonomy, but stunted the role of the WAC as a representative body. Division leaders "had real input" but were limited in "the extent to which they could engage in partisan politics" on this committee.[22]

The devolution to the divisions made sense at the time. From 1942–45, GM virtually ceased making autos for private citizens and was oriented toward defense production. With Sloan's approval, divisions were free by 1942 to bid on and accept government defense contracts on their own. Again, his thinking was to take advantage of the expertise within divisions to exploit the opportunities brought about by copious defense spending, and he sought to avoid investor disapproval by including only a moderate amount of division representation in the central unit.

Yet this representation was still too much for the investors. In 1944, the investors weighed in and complained about the WAC being once again too much a forum for partisan infighting, and forced Sloan to return to the previous model of an administrative committee alongside the policy committee. Sloan complied formally, but got his way by adding in 1945 even more division leaders to the administrative committee. An investor charged that the administrative committee now "was beset by partisan bargaining that stemmed from the presence of division managers and group executives."[23] Sloan replied as follows: "I accept the fact that there are on the Administrative Committee executives who [have conflicting interests] … However … it is far better to have differences … identified, laid on the table face up and discussed … If we set up an organization of supermen, [it] will become more and more separated from what is going on in the business … We [would have] not only legislation without representation, but legislation without knowledge."[24] Lammot du Pont then wrote to Sloan that "the governing committee of a corporation is not … set up to secure cooperation, but is … set up to *rule* the business of the corporation."[25] The differences of opinion between the men from the 1920s had continued into the 1940s. Note also the language they used: legislation, representation, conflicting interests, partisanship. Sloan and the investors acknowledged partisanship among the division leaders, but differed on the desirability of hashing out partisanship brought into the central committees.

[22] Freeland (2001, 156).
[23] Quoted in Freeland (2001, 169).
[24] Quoted in Freeland (2001, 172 – edits both Freeland's and my own).
[25] Quoted in Freeland (2001, 173 – emphasis original in du Pont's letter).

Management instigated another major reorganization after the war in 1946, and its design reflected a compromise between Sloan and the investors suspicious of divisional input at the central unit, although it did little to reduce the tensions. Under the reorganization, three committees would make corporate decisions: a financial policy committee, which could veto anything and would be dominated by investors and central managers; an operations policy committee with mostly central managers and some divisional leaders; and an administrative committee that was heavy on divisional leaders. The last was advisory to the operations policy committee. The divisional leaders felt left out, but they could take some comfort in the new chief executive officer (CEO), Charles Wilson, who took over after Sloan stepped down in 1946.[26]

Wilson was renowned in industrial circles for his skillful management of war-time production by the corporation. GM had supplied a huge proportion of vehicles, tanks, airplanes, and engine products to the U.S. war effort. Given his success in that role, Wilson was later asked by President Eisenhower to be Secretary of Defense in 1953. It was Wilson's famous remark during his confirmation hearings for that post that "what was good for General Motors was good for the country and vice versa."[27] Wilson considered himself an operations person and typically sided with divisional leaders against the so-called financial side on the financial policy committee. So indirectly for a time, the divisional leaders were helped by the executive leadership siding with them systematically over corporate decisions.

Post-war economic growth led to huge expansion and profitability for GM. One important evolutionary change in the late 1940s was not seen as a form of centralization but rather, as a logical step toward more efficiency. In retrospect, it was another turning point for GM's internal governance, especially in a reshaping of the partisan landscape among subunit leaders. Corporate management created a new set of units in charge of the corporate divisions that performed functions that cut across all the auto divisions. The Fischer Body division had been around for a long time, but new units were added, such as the engine and assembly divisions. GM's creation of more of these new units added new institutional interests in the mix – the general operations people sided more often than not with central management on questions of governance against the investors and the auto divisions. Wilson added more of the leaders of the operational subunits to the operations policy committee as a way to strengthen his hand against the financial executives. The balance of decision-making authority had turned in a somewhat different direction, but still away from the divisional leaders and toward a more diverse set of central executives. Representation of managers increased on the central committees. Their interests cut across all the auto divisions. They could recognize (or saw

---

[26] Sloan remained chairman of the board until 1956, leaving Wilson to run the corporation.
[27] That remark and other confrontations soured enthusiasm among several senators for him, but he was approved nevertheless.

from their perspective) the harm done through a lack of coordination and competition across subunits.

Harlow Curtice took over as president and CEO in 1953 after Wilson left to join the government. Like his predecessor, Curtice was considered an operations person, which meant he greatly valued the particular technical expertise that divisional managers had to offer. He resented and resisted the interference of the "finance" people within the corporate leadership. At first, Curtice approved of divisional representation in central committees. Largely as a way to shift power at the central level away from the financial types – the owners and finance managers – Curtice added representatives from the divisions to the major boards and committees of GM. He began his tenure and governed the corporation for several years with robust input from division managers, and felt that as long as operations people like him ran GM, everything would be fine. In his initial governing philosophy, he seemed much like Sloan.

Then several years into Curtice's tenure, the corporation began to slide toward a different kind of centralization, neither the kind favored by the investors nor the kind Sloan promoted. Curtice pulled back on earlier commitments to Sloan's vision, and not only removed division managers from corporate governance, but also began to meddle in divisional affairs to the consternation of managers of the various divisions. As an operations person, Curtice also felt he could interfere in the internal business within the divisions. Unfortunately for divisional autonomy, Curtice became more autocratic as his time in leadership went on. Curtice began to bully the divisional managers, meddle in their affairs, and reduce their role in the central committees to mere listeners to his harangues rather than as representatives with voice. He said during this time, "the best committee is the committee of one." Curtice offended both owners and divisional managers in his autocratic style. To his credit, or despite his managerial style, GM in the mid- to late 1950s experienced record profits and market share.

In response to the general frustration among owners and corporate managers resulting from Curtice's methods, GM reorganized yet again in 1958 after Curtice left the company. The reorganization in one sense returned to an older model, with a finance committee dominated by investors and an executive committee dominated by central managers and some subunit leaders. But of key importance is that the representation of subunits on the executive committee in this new model was not the auto divisions, but the operations units like engine, assembly, and body. The automotive division leaders were relegated to a very weak administrative committee with virtually no voice in corporate strategy. The new top leaders, Frederic Donner as chairman of the board and John Gordon as president, sought part of what Sloan always wanted in terms of gaining for corporate management more autonomy from owners. The du Pont family, because of government anti-trust suits, had lost their controlling interest in GM, and the investors were laying low to avoid more government suits. But Donner and Gordon did not pursue the representative side of

Sloan's vision. They eliminated divisional managers from corporate committees making strategic decisions.

The 1958 reorganization has been regarded by scholars as a key turning point for GM. Henceforth, divisional managers would have virtually no input over corporate strategy, and would have little resources or autonomy to innovate on their own without corporate approval. The corporation would be governed mostly by central managers, overseen on financial matters by an owner-dominated board. Furthermore, GM itself would create its own internal engineering units to develop new technologies and ideas for cars, and then pass along directives to the divisions to incorporate the innovations into their vehicles. Major engineering advances and new prototypes for cars would be directed and decided on mostly by central management. By the 1960s, GM was recognized formally and in reality as an executive centralized corporation with a strict separation between strategy (handled by corporate management) and tactics (handled by divisions but with routine interference by central management). The days of what has been called "participatory decentralization" at GM were over and according to the terms used in this book, the weakness of divisional subunits relative to executive authority became locked-in. Pierre du Pont, who died in 1954, would have been pleased.[28]

The changes in the late 1950s can be seen partially as a result of the decline of Sloan's vision for the company. Conflicts within the corporate central unit between management and owners for a long time shaped the nature of centralization and decentralization in GM in fundamental ways. Sloan protected the divisions and promoted their cases within the corporation more than any GM leader since his tenure. On the whole, throughout his three decades at the helm, Sloan sought a more decentralized version of the M-Form than the owners and other managers wanted. He applied the brake on centralization within GM, in the sense that he favored more divisional autonomy and more divisional voice in central management decisions than the owners. He cleverly fended off owners when they tried to disrupt his plans for a relatively decentralized corporation. But he also had a hand in centralization. Sloan was at the central helm, not only of running the company, but also of building coalitions in favor of governance schemes that determined how the company would be run in the future. Above all, he wanted managerial autonomy from owners and in fighting for that he had to sacrifice much autonomy and representation of divisional subunits. Once again, we see the consequences for vertical authority (between central and subunit) of the conflicts over horizontal authority (in this case between investors and central management).[29]

---

[28] This ending of participatory decentralization by 1958 is a major theme of Freeland (2001).

[29] There was an interesting and revealing conflict between Drucker and Sloan over GM's model of governance. When Drucker's 1946 book came out extolling GM's model of decentralized governance, Sloan was unimpressed, and in his own memoirs disparages Drucker's account (Sloan, 1964), claiming that Drucker's proscriptions for large corporations were disastrous.

Partisanship

The overall changes at GM were the result of much more than merely passing the baton from Sloan to other leaders. What solidified the changes wrought by the top leadership was the evolving partisanship within the corporation among managers at various levels in the subunit and the central unit. As summarized previously, GM passed several thresholds in its early history. For most of the time before the final threshold was passed in the late 1950s, the auto divisions formed the core components of the corporation with gravitas and representation in central decision making. Subunits were at one time auto divisions (with the exception of Fischer Body) that could in principle stand alone as companies, but had banded together to achieve some efficiencies and market advantages from cooperation.

Between 1920–58, GM's governing philosophy oscillated between emphasizing the benefits of having auto divisions with autonomy and a voice inside the corporation and emphasizing the benefits of centralized control. The overall story, however, is one of gradual weakening of the auto divisions as autonomous entities. It was not a monotonic move toward centralization; there were moments when the auto divisions emerged strengthened from reorganizations. Divisional managers with loyalties to their auto divisions were not so passive in the beginning, and they dragged their feet with du Pont in the early 1920s and made their voices heard through the early 1930s. However, as the leaders of the divisions were replaced gradually by those with more loyalties to the central corporation, and as the divisions lost representation in meaningful central corporate bodies, the formerly stand-alone auto companies became not only less influential in how the corporation was run, but also less stand-alone. With the addition of corporate subunits that produced industrialized parts used by all the auto divisions – body, assembly, engine – and their increasing voice within the corporation, partisanship among the overall group of subunits changed. Now substantial portions of the subunit leadership saw their interests as aligned with central corporate management against both the major investors and the other subunit leaders of the auto divisions. The moves toward executive centralization occurred in stages, but it was a ratcheting toward centralized control that occasionally fell backward until the 1950s when it no longer included meaningful subunit input.

After each threshold was passed, the auto divisions became increasingly agents of central management with little voice in central corporate decisions. But the final threshold in the 1950s has not been reversed. The story is not so much one of legal or financial control wielded by the corporate center – in principle, it always had that even from the earliest days of the corporation – as it is an internal political story of how different interests coalesced or divided in pursuit of more autonomy, voice, and resources. The ratchets in GM's executive centralization occurred when Sloan, Wilson, and Curtice – seeking to increase their own executive autonomy and authority – found allies at various points among different groups – operational unit leaders, fellow central managers, and a few investors – for institutional changes with lasting legacies.

Lock-in

In becoming a much more centralized corporation, GM – as it passed three thresholds – lost its character as a federated institution with a corporate version of separation of power.

Threshold One – early 1920s (reversed somewhat later)
Threshold Two – early 1930s (led to lock-in, but permitted substantial devolution)
Threshold Three – late 1950s (even deeper lock-in)

The first threshold came in the 1920s when the purest vision of Durant – give the auto divisions great autonomy – was dropped in favor of the more moderate M-Form. The second (lock-in) threshold occurred during the Depression, and what happened afterward was telling. The post-Depression devolution set a precedent that any decentralizing or centralizing moves would be done, not because the subunits pressed for it, but because central management decided it was the wise thing to do. The 1940s devolution was not a return to the Durant days of true decentralization. The subunit autonomy was granted by the central unit, which could just as easily take that authority back. Besides becoming staffed with Sloan loyalists, the subunits were now merely permitted to make decisions, rather than actually asserting their autonomy and being part of the deliberations over how much autonomy they should have. The situation after the 1930s threshold was reaffirmed in the late 1950s with a third threshold. Further depth to the lock-in came when divisional representation in corporate decision making largely ceased to exist after the 1958 reorganization.

Solidified in the 1950s, GM's executive centralization has been identified as a major cause of the corporation's overall decline.[30] The argument often made is that it had become too large to be nimble enough to respond to changing global forces. It could not respond effectively to competition from foreign automakers, rising gasoline prices, and aggressive new federal regulators. When critics charge that a given corporation has become so large that it cannot nimbly react to new market conditions, they often point to literature from the 1970s and 1980s on GM.

In the case of GM, its inability to act nimbly may not have been because of its size, but because it lacked subunit autonomy. Looking back on it, and informed by other similar cases, it is hardly surprising that eventually GM ceased being a relatively decentralized, federated institution and became an institution organized with a set of agents (divisions) serving the needs of a dominant principal (the corporation). There were after centralization few checks on central corporate authority to determine the representational scheme, to interpret which

---

[30] See Abernathy (1978), Cray (1980), Drucker (1972), and Whitman (1999).

issues were for the corporation to make and which issues were for the auto divisions to make, and to extract resources from the subunits without some form of consent by the subunits. True decentralization is almost impossible to imagine now for GM or for other industrial corporations, as GM and others long ago passed the relevant thresholds in centralization. Today at GM, the auto divisions are marketing units and bear little resemblance to the autonomous companies that formed the basis of GM.[31]

Is it sustainable to have a large corporation governed by a system where subunits have the kind of autonomy reserved for the American states in the U.S. political system (whereby the central unit cannot legally encroach on certain spheres of action in the subunit), and where there exists constitutional decentralization, with real subunit representation on the bodies that make decisions over centralization and decentralization? It may be that the kind of governance of business corporations that admits a certain degree of true decentralization, with subunits represented in central decision making, is not realistic for the modern corporation, or maybe for corporations as large as GM. Perhaps if GM had not moved first beyond Durant-style, extreme decentralization, then second beyond the earliest Sloan plans for subunit representation and moderate decentralization, and finally third to an organization where the subunits are basically marketing vehicles for centrally planned products, then it would not have survived. It could be that the centralization that took place, which I am deeming irreversible and implying has harmed GM, is not realistic. Perhaps the GM story tells us it is not sustainable. In that case, those who advocate for true decentralization within corporations (or those who run units bought up by larger corporations and who hope for real autonomy and voice in their internal affairs) should either get such autonomy and voice codified airtight in contracts or recognize the futility of the decentralization cause.

In evaluating Sloan's vision of strategic centralization and operational devolution, the details matter over how the executive body in the central unit gradually insulated itself from investors, and more importantly for our purposes, the representational voice of the subunits. In similar fashion to political federations and other types of federated institutions, specific crises gave the executive side leeway to strengthen its powers and solidified more autonomy within the central unit for the bodies that worked more for the executive than for the representational body. The executive could essentially do away with subunit representation, and the corporation would move beyond a separation of powers system to a system with executive control (at least vis-à-vis the subunits).

For example, in the GM case regarding the M-Form, who decides what decisions were categorized as "strategic" and what decisions were categorized as "operational"? Apparently, Sloan himself made many of these decisions, so he acted as a supreme judge part of the time. But he was also acting as executive (company president), so this put him in the position of being the one to benefit

---

[31] Davis, Diekmann, and Tinsley (1994).

from decisions that tended to lump things in the "strategic" category if it were clear that the auto divisions were opposed to his views on a given matter.[32]

Against the notion that GM has locked-in to centralization, it could be claimed that the company in fact did devolve on occasion after the 1950s. Consider the reorganization plan adopted and implemented by CEO Roger Smith in 1984, the so-called GM10. The GM10 plan under Smith was audacious and ambitious, costing the corporation $18 million. It was framed as an effort to remake GM into a post-Sloan corporation. Smith's goals were to eliminate redundancy and inefficiencies. He formed two groups of divisions – the CPC (Chevrolet-Pontiac-Canada) and BOC (Buick-Oldsmobile-Cadillac) – and made each of them consolidate their design and assembly across their component divisions. He eliminated Fischer Body and several other corporate divisions and folded them into the new groups. The CPC group would supposedly make smaller cars whereas the BOC group would supposedly make larger cars.

By any reckoning, Smith's GM10 reorganization was a disaster.[33] When the details were worked out, it was discovered that it was not really possible to divide the tasks of the company into small car jobs and large car jobs. For example, the CPC ended up making Cadillacs because that turned out to be more efficient. The two groups could not "stand-alone" as was planned because they needed each other. Moreover, the reorganization added an entire layer of new bureaucracy to the corporation – the group managers – with interests apart from the auto divisions and the central management. This new bureaucracy added additional politics and additional costs to the corporation. Finally, many employees within the company, especially those working for former units like Fischer Body, became unhappy and resentful of central management. They did not have any loyalty to the new groups, either. Resentment toward the central unit might be fine if loyalty to auto divisions keeps employees working hard. If employees have no loyalty to the units, however, this can spell trouble. It did for GM.

Smith also created the Saturn Corporation in the 1980s, a remarkable experiment in creating a relatively autonomous automobile company within what was by then no longer a federated corporate organization.[34] Saturn, it is important to note here, was a creation by the central management of the corporation, not an idea that bubbled up from lower levels of GM. Smith wanted to build a small car with lower labor costs so that it had a chance of being profitable. Previous attempts to build a fuel-efficient, small car at GM failed even before

---

[32] Freeland (2001, 109–10).

[33] See Monks and Minow (2007) for an account of the GM10. The negative, postmortem judgments are prominent in news coverage in *Fortune* and general-interest magazines like *Time* in 1992 (see Taylor [1992], for example). I also learned much in conversation with Marina Whitman, who was an executive at GM at the time.

[34] Detailed information about the Saturn experiment can be found in Rubinstein and Kochan (2001).

production because, it has been argued, of the high labor and production costs in the upper Midwest.

By having various states compete to host Saturn (Tennessee ultimately won) and bid by using tax deferments or easements and upfront government-built infrastructure, the initial costs of setting up the company were low. The company would not be bound by the interconnecting financial and manufacturing relationships that had been built up across the other GM auto divisions. Saturn's employees originally were outside of the United Auto Workers (UAW) negotiating framework that bound the entire corporation, and employees were given a stake in Saturn in return for lower wages. And most important for our purposes, Saturn managers were given autonomy over many matters. Saturn was, as the advertising stated, a "different kind of company." It would essentially stand or fall on its own, at least in theory.

Unfortunately for GM, the Saturn experiment in devolution did not last long. It began well, but then about a decade after its creation, the company stopped succeeding economically. The central managers at GM on several occasions ended up forcing Saturn to make decisions that flouted the original design principles of autonomy. For example, the central corporation refused to allow Saturn to expand its production because the central unit determined that Saturn had excess capacity. In the end, Saturn became just another division of GM. It ultimately folded in 2009 after GM could not find a buyer for it.

Long before the 1980s, GM had ceased to be a federated corporate organization that could move authority vertically and enable subunits to be innovative on their own. Thus, attempts to reform, to be flexible, to devolve, were all clunky and hard to sustain by the 1980s. Smith's GM10 reorganization was a strange mixture of centralization and decentralization. He wanted the groups to be autonomous, but took authority away from or eliminated certain subunits. The Saturn attempt was a one-shot experiment at devolution that worked for a time but did not survive. The failure was not necessarily owing to design flaws in how Saturn was organized or governed, but had deeper roots in GM's business model in the automobile industry. Nevertheless, the position Saturn settled into confirms the main historical argument being made here, that subunits since the late 1950s (and maybe earlier in the 1930s) have not been the core constituent units in the corporation with representation in central decision making.

GM represents a cautionary tale. Three overlapping audiences – those studying corporate governance, those studying federated organizations in general, and those studying federated institutions of either organizations or governments – can consider GM a prime example of the tendency of central units to kill the wealth-producing goose. GM offers an example of how efforts to improve efficiency with centralized schemes created interests at the central level that were either jealous or distrustful of autonomous auto divisions. GM, like most other large corporations with subunits, has operated on the idea that there is ideal balance between central control and subunit control. The balancing point shifted over time so that the executive central unit ultimately won out, with essentially no checks on its authority by the subunits. Although it could pretend it was a relatively decentralized corporation, and both inside and outside the company it could peddle the idea that divisional autonomy was what made GM tick (or Sloan's notion of decision making by consensus), in truth its degree of centralization and decentralization was moving all the time, mostly and finally by the 1950s in the direction of the central executives.

True to form as a corporate leader by example, the standard for large corporations in the United States followed GM. The basic, largely experimental idea from the origins of GM was used less and less (for exceptions, see Chapter 7). Rarely would large corporations be run like federations with the possibility of reasonably autonomous subunits and decision-making authority given to a representative body made up of those subunits' representatives.[35] Executive centralized control won out, and in this instance, eliminating representational committees on which subunits were seated.

[35] See Davis, Diekmann, and Tinsley (1994).

6

International Political Union

Among our four main cases, the European Union (EU) has the least complete history in the sense that it has not ratcheted toward intensive executive centralization. The EU has not locked-in in the same way as the other cases. The citizens of the EU member countries coexist in a complex, sprawling international union that has unmistakably trended toward representative centralization. They live in a system where uneven but enormously consequential authority is wielded by a government in Brussels that has final authority above nation-state governments on a host of important policy issues.

It is tempting for two reasons to put the focus on the inevitable, and say that the EU has "not yet ratcheted" toward executive centralization and is "not yet locked-in." First, there were moments in the recent past when the member states in the EU appeared to be on the verge of approving changes that would lead toward substantial executive centralization, but they stepped back. Second, and related, recent circumstances will possibly lead them to take that leap. There are, as of this writing, loud calls for more centralization within the EU in response to economic crises and even stalwart opponents of a stronger EU executive among the member states – the governments of Germany and France, for instance – have shown more openness toward common economic policies decided on by an executive and backed up by rigorous enforcement. In 2013, the EU set the stage for a dramatic strengthening over the next few years of banking regulation by central administrators.

The key institutional question confronting the EU, however, makes it only a temptation to add the word "yet." Locked-in executive centralization is not inevitable. The leaders of the member states face difficult choices ahead, choices that directly correlate with the main ideas in this book. To deal with crises like those of 2011 and 2012, which involved a spiraling downward into unsustainable debt by certain economies within the Eurozone, the member states may need to assent to a stronger, more singular EU executive authority. To do so may require establishment of institutions in the central executive unit that will lead to a lock-in of centralization, and a loss of flexibility in the future. From a political scientist's perspective (and apropos of our ideas here), a fundamental question facing the EU is which governing direction it will take. Will it strengthen the EU executive in a manner reflecting the virtues of a parliamentary system where the executive is routinely and constantly responsible to representative units within the central unit? Or will it strengthen the EU executive in a manner reflecting the kind of authority common in a presidential system with day-to-day independence from the representative bodies and with responsibility toward elsewhere (perhaps voters directly)?

In sum, the question for the EU is whether it will continue to rely mostly on decision-making procedures in Brussels based on a model of representative centralization as opposed to a model of executive centralization. The arguments in this book based on our other cases suggest that the latter choice, which will be tempting to make under duress, invites lock-in.

EU Form of Government

Among the most important developments on the world stage since the 1950s, European political and economic integration has brought about a set of institutions of governance that are hard to categorize. The EU is notoriously difficult to describe in precise and recognizable terms because it is a novelty.[1] What is not in doubt is that the EU is a trading bloc, a currency union, and most of all, a single market. These elements have made the EU one of the main examples of political institutions epitomizing, and some would say accelerating, the pace of globalization. Through the pooling of sovereignty, the member states of the EU have reduced barriers of trade and immigration and created the conditions for continual exchanges of cultural, financial, and personal factors across national borders. The single market brought about by EU institutions is truly a marvel of social engineering, changing the lives of Europeans and affecting the world economy in fundamental ways.[2] It was brought about through the political will of member-state leaders who have often faced popular hostility when making decisions that in retrospect were economically of huge benefit to most Europeans.

The EU functions as a political system designed more or less following principles of federalism, and to some degree, separation of powers. It is not a nation-state; the central powers and the legal bases do not suggest a full-fledged federal republic in the way of the United States, Canada, Brazil, Australia, or Germany. Rather, it is an international political union, knit together not as tightly as these

---

[1] Many writers wrestle with categorization. See Hitchcock (2002), Hix (2005), Hooghe and Marks (2001), Keohane and Hoffman (1991), Mattli (1999), McKay (2001), Scharpf (1999), Siedentopp (2001), Bartolini (2005), Elazar (2001), and Goldstein (2001).
[2] See, for instance, Franzese and Hays (2006). Verdun (2000) has an engaging account.

federations, but it is also stronger than what would be called a confederation. There are real teeth to the enforcement of EU law by the central unit.

The EU is certainly federated in the sense described in Chapter 2. The member states act as subunits that can be granted authority or can have authority taken away by the central unit, and they can individually govern themselves if necessary. The EU binds together its member states more closely than do other international unions or association such as the OAS, NAFTA, ASEAN, or the UN.[3] Especially after a set of reforms initiated in the 1980s, the member states have pooled (some would say lost) a good deal of sovereignty in the process of forming or joining the EU. The central EU government can pass laws enforceable on the member states and on the citizens of those member states. Unanimity of the member-state governments is not necessary to pass most kinds of laws. Thus, member states can have laws imposed on them that they did not formally approve in a collective vote. Furthermore, the EU functions as a legal system with a community of legal professionals and a set of concepts and precedents studied in law school curricula around the continent.[4] The treaties ratified over the decades together act like a federal constitution forming the underlying legal basis for the union itself. European law is now quite broadly applied to many areas of life in the member states, and the Court of Justice (ECJ) can override lower courts, including the supreme courts of the member states.

As for separation of powers, some of the pieces are there, albeit in complicated form. The EU's governing structure bears resemblance to the U.S. system in several of its component parts. The Council is like the original U.S. Senate, representing the member-state governments. By Council, the reference is actually to two related bodies: the European Council, which consists of the heads of state, and the Council of Ministers, which – through a series of layered councils – consists of government ministers from the member states. It is common to refer to the European Council and the Council of Ministers altogether as "the Council." The EU Parliament acts like the U.S. House of Representatives. It is directly elected by EU citizens in contests operated by the member states, but under EU regulations. The Council of Ministers and the Parliament must both approve laws and regulations of the EU, and in this regard also jointly resemble the U.S. bicameral legislative system. On judicial matters having to do with European law, the ECJ is the final word on the interpretation of laws and of the treaties, thus mirroring the U.S. Supreme Court.

The main difference is the executive, which is not a single person. The Commission, a body currently consisting of one member from each state, was for a long time considered the primary executive unit. Commissioners are

---

[3] These acronyms stand for, respectively, Organization of American States, North American Free-Trade Agreement, Association of South East Asian Nations, and United Nations.

[4] See Stone-Sweet and Sandholz (1997) and Alter (2001) for a discussion of the implications of the creation of a legal community of lawyers and judges steeped in European law.

appointed by the European Council and approved by the Parliament. Yet in a process that gained momentum in the 2000s and culminated in the Lisbon treaty reforms (taking force in 2009), the EU executive authority became fragmented across multiple units, effectively diluting the Commission's power. The Commission still has executive powers and is represented by the Commission president who is elected by the Council. Since the Lisbon Treaty, the European Council also elects its own president, a formal title currently occupied by Herman Van Rompuy from Belgium, who has thus far made few waves within the EU. The Council and Commission jointly appoint a high representative who shares executive authority on matters of foreign policy and trade, and who formally sits on both bodies. The European Council of Ministers, meanwhile, is chaired by a president, a position occupied in rotating fashion among the heads of state of the twenty-seven member countries. There is also the key role played by the president of the European Central Bank, who has in recent years gained considerable policy-making autonomy relative to his putative bosses on the European Council.[5]

The existence of the multiple executive units is widely considered a weakness, inviting derision in international circles. It is both instructive and amusing to see the EU making policy pronouncements today with three and sometimes four people standing at microphones – the Commission president, the president of the European Council, the president of the Council of Ministers, and the high representative. The official stance is that the multiplicity reflects the sense that the EU is a collective of sovereign countries and not a single political unit. In reality, this multiplicity is because there is no settled understanding of what office has primacy under which circumstances, and more importantly, how much authority an EU executive ought to have. This is why several leaders show up to speak to the press when the EU makes pronouncements or attends international meetings.

In assessing whether the EU's overall governing structure resembles separation of powers, we could argue about the finer points, such as if, for example, the main executive body (Commission) is really separate and not directly responsible to the two representative assemblies (Council and Parliament). In an interesting institutional twist that makes the EU seem like a parliamentary system, the preponderance of agenda powers for legislation rest at the Commission and the Commissioners can be removed by the Parliament. This would be as if in the United States the power to propose legislation to Congress rested solely with a unit within the executive branch whose leaders could be removed by Congress. At the same time, the fragmentation of the executive

---

[5] Although expressing an exaggeration, the following quote accurately captures the sense of increasing authority during times of crisis: "In terms of unelected people, [Draghi, the ECB President] is by far the most powerful in the democratic world" (quote from Franklin Allen, a professor of finance and economics at the University of Pennsylvania's Wharton School, as recounted in Kulish and Ewing 2012).

into multiple positions with various reporting lines and responsibilities to and from the Parliament and Council makes the EU lack the clarity and tidiness of a parliamentary system and gives it a strong resemblance to separation of powers. It would be more accurate to say that there is separation of executive authority along with some separation of powers. In practice, authority is highly fragmented horizontally across the governing units in the EU, but without the clean boundaries between legislative and executive levels that we find in the United States.

Other aspects of the EU are also consistent with its status as a functioning political system, and it even has state-like qualities.[6] The EU bureaucracy is relatively large, with codified rules for hiring, promotion, and compensation. EU bureaucrats are paid well and have an ethos of being protectors of the goals of the union and not advancing the interests of the member states.[7] There are party groups that operate within the parliament, acting within the chamber similar to the parties in national parliaments (more later on this).[8] These party groups are at times European-focused, and not merely collections of member-state parties. Like Washington, D.C., there are vibrant lobbying scenes in Brussels and Strasbourg, with thousands of interest groups and paid lobbyists pressing their case on the EU government. This is testament to the weight placed on EU law in determining the economic health of particular industries and social groups.

Assent to Representative Centralization

All of this describes the EU in its current form. The EU, however, began in a simpler form and was highly decentralized, evolving to the present state over decades. Most of the important moves toward centralization in the EU happened with the overt consent of its member-state subunits. After all, any new treaty or treaty change requires unanimous approval of the member states. The founding was a voluntary joining together of six countries into a customs union. Member states, of course, apply to join and thus are not forced to become part of the EU, and when they do apply, it requires unanimous approval of the existing member states to be admitted.

The founding occurred over a series of years, confirmed by the Treaty of Rome in 1957 when France, Germany, Italy, the Netherlands, Belgium, and Luxembourg agreed to form the European Community.[9] Previously in 1954, they had formed the European Coal and Steel Community, thereby creating a common market for those industrial products most needed for war production.

---

[6] This is the central theme of Hix (2005).

[7] For a sophisticated treatment of EU bureaucracy, see Franchino (2007).

[8] See Kreppel (2002), Hug (2002), and Hix, Noury, and Roland (2007).

[9] For readable accounts of the Founding and development of the EU, see Dinan (2010), Gabel (1998), Wallace and Wallace (2000), and Nugent (2004).

The original impetus was to bind together the German and French economies in such a manner that they could no longer fight each other with modern weapons because each could halt the supply of key raw materials. The governments of the other four countries involved saw their economies as so intertwined with those of France and Germany that it made obvious sense to reap common gains by reducing trade barriers among them all and erecting common barriers to outside countries. What began as an integrating customs union – intended to keep the peace between two long-time combatants – quickly became an organized force for economic growth among all its members.

The Treaty of Rome in 1957 created a limited customs union for the six countries, with procedures for adjudicating disputes among the member states. The executive arm of the new European Community would be the Commission. Often at odds with the Commission were ministers and bureaucrats who staffed the Council of Ministers, which represented the member states. The Council of Ministers made the major policy decisions for the EU, business in the Council was conducted according to unanimous rules, and all member states had to agree to any policy changes made at the European level. The treaty also established the ECJ.

The Commission after 1957 quickly grew in size and was seen right away as suspicious by member-state governments because it seemed a consistent force for aggrandizing the authority of Brussels when regulating transnational economic interactions. There was a certain momentum toward what critics perceived as executive centralization mostly in the form of new bureaus within the Commission and Council with limited but substantive powers to regulate.[10] In reality, however, any such powers were very limited and the changes strictly adhered to an extremely weak version of representative centralization because of unanimous voting rules in place on the Council. The requirement of unanimity for any policy changes meant that the Community was actually a highly decentralized international forum. The member states held onto their authority. Whatever authority the Commission wielded was grudgingly agreed to by the member states on the understanding that if a decision by the Commission offended a country enough, the Commission would back off.[11]

This power of veto and the decentralization it caused became an even stronger norm with the adoption of a named principle (The Luxembourg Compromise) that could be invoked when necessary. An important, although vague, concept keeping the Community together in the face of staunch defenders of national sovereignty for the late 1960s and 1970s, the Luxembourg Compromise emerged following what has been called "the empty chair crisis." The French, under President Charles De Gaulle, were chairing the Council meetings in 1965 when discussions began on a series of proposals made by

---

[10] See Hooghe (2001) and Majone (2002).

[11] There are differences of opinion on this point, but I am compelled most by the view that unanimous decision-rules were a huge constraint on the Commission. See Moravcsik (1998).

then-Commission president Walter Hallstein. In response to the proposals, the French, who could have merely voted the proposals down, did not want them even discussed. They left the Council meetings and refused to participate, leaving the chair's position empty. De Gaulle and his government were adamantly opposed to further reducing the authority of the member states relative to Brussels. It was enough that they were bound to abide by decisions of the ECJ on matters of interpretation of the Council's regulations.[12]

Only after the proposals by Hallstein were tabled months later did the French return to the Council. The episode not only maintained the unanimous decision-rules at the central level in the Community, but also reversed the momentum the Commission had in centralizing regulatory authority to Brussels. For another fourteen years, the Community remained limited in scope and with new members added, especially Britain in 1973, the Council held onto its status as the ultimate authority in the Community.

Two changes in the 1960s and 1970s represented a small break in member-state authority relative to Brussels. In retrospect, they were the beginning of a process of centralization – of a representative, but also legal nature – that peaked and finally ebbed in the 2000s. First, the European Parliament, which was until 1979 an assembly of people appointed by the parliaments of the members states, was now to be directly elected by voters in the members states. This divorced the formal link between the Parliament and the Council – because the parliaments of the member states elected representatives to both chambers – and set the stage for later changes that both strengthened the hand of the Parliament in legislative procedures and made the Parliament an independent, popularly elected, political force within the Community.

Second, the ECJ made a series of decisions culminating in the landmark Cassis de Dijon case (1979) that signaled a European legal order that was not simply international, but also supreme over member-state legal systems. Beginning with a decision in 1963, the Court asserted that European law had direct effect on individuals, meaning that it was akin to domestic law in how individuals could sue or be sued relying on EU-level statutes. It then asserted supremacy over national law in 1964 arguing that because the member states had entered into treaties creating a "Community of unlimited duration, having its own institutions, its own personality … its own legal capacity … the member states have limited their sovereign rights."[13] If there were a conflict between European laws and the laws of the member states, the Court decided, the laws created at the European level in Brussels were overriding. Together, these changes established the European legal system as qualitatively different from international law in terms of how it integrated the political systems. By common interpretation, the treaties formed the basis of a direct, governing structure for people living in the EU – not just through their member states.

---

[12] Dinan (2010, 36–38) gives a summary account of the crisis. See also, Monnet (1978).
[13] This quote is from European Court of Justice (1964). Also excerpted from Hix (2005, 122).

The practical meaning of this became clearer in 1974 when the Court ruled that national laws could not hinder the workings of the Community in any way. This was reinforced again in 1979 with the Cassis de Dijon decision. The Court decided in that 1979 case that countries could not limit the sale of a product within their territory if it could be sold in another member state, thus establishing the principle of mutual recognition. The consequences of the decision turned out to be profound, with similarities to the U.S. Supreme Court's interpretation of the Commerce Clause, as Cassis de Dijon was used to strike down national laws controlling commerce in almost any area. It meant that the logical conclusion was uniformity in regulation of commerce, thus the creation of a single market. Huge swaths of the member countries' economies were no longer subject to the regulatory authority of national governments. Depending on the products, regulatory authority would either be pooled at the European level, or governments would have to accept the regulatory standards of their fellow Community members.

The move to parliamentary elections seemed like a natural change to win more legitimacy among citizens and was not intended to centralize authority, although later it contributed to such an effect when combined with reforms of voting rules on the Council. In contrast, the court cases surprised some of the member-state governments and they were not happy, although there was little they could do short of dismantling the Court. One is hard pressed to argue that the member states openly assented to the Court's understanding; more accurately, they tolerated it for practical reasons. The German Constitutional Court's official position set out a workable, if not entirely logical, solution to the problem of handing sovereign authority to an international union that was not a nation state. The German court eventually ruled in 1993 on whether the pooled sovereignty represented by the ECJ decisions in the 1960s and 1970s and then in later treaties (Maastricht, discussed shortly) represented a violation of the sovereign rights of the German people. The German court decided that the legal assertions of the ECJ and the pretentions to sovereignty by the EU were not in accord with the German constitution, and that the German court could decide that EU actions were illegal under German Basic Law. However, the German government had voluntarily entered into the treaties creating the Community and (later) the Union and thus had agreed to, in the language of the EU, "transfer competencies" upward to a higher level. And as long as those treaties were in effect, EU law could in practical terms be supreme.[14]

The first major ratchet after the Treaty of Rome that was altogether assented to by the member states came in the mid-1980s, with the negotiations and final approval of the Single European Act (SEA). This treaty strengthened the

---

[14] See Hix (2005, 131–32). It is interesting that in 2012, the German government of Angela Merkel was considering a referendum to establish a law overturning the German court's interpretation, thus directly linking EU law to German law and not by virtue of the treaties. It is not clear the implications of such a move.

role of the Parliament in lawmaking, and most critically, allowed for super majority, as opposed to unanimous, voting in the Council to pass laws in many areas. It is hard to overstate the importance of the changes in the SEA for EU governance. These institutional changes opened the gates to a major centralization of authority toward Brussels. Although the result of the new rules under the SEA was billed as a pooling of sovereignty, it was, in fact, a tremendous loss of sovereignty for member states. The norm embodied in the Luxembourg Compromise was emasculated. No one could escape recognition of the fact that, together with the legal standard of mutual recognition from the Cassis de Dijon case, the citizens of the member states would be subject to laws that their sovereign governments had not approved.

It is worth asking: why would the member-state governments unanimously agree to give up their veto? This question and others like it lingered over the period of the 1980s and 1990s. From memoirs we get insights from leaders, and we can follow debates occurring within member-state parliaments.[15] A similar question (addressed shortly) asks why the government of Germany, in particular, agreed to pool decision-making authority in the creation of the Eurozone in the 1990s even though it already held primacy of influence over European economic – and specifically, monetary – affairs.

The answer to the questions raised by SEA and why nations gave up the veto mostly has to do with logic and the attendant political economy of economic liberalization of the single market, which in the 1980s was formalized as the overriding principle of economic governance in the Community. The EU had expanded by the time of the SEA to twelve member states and unanimity had become difficult to achieve. Even skeptics of Brussels, but promoters of the single market (like the U.K.'s prime minister, Margaret Thatcher), understood that the only way to enforce the principles of the single market was to allow for less-than-unanimous voting, because the single market involved opening up industries to free and fair competition.[16] If any member state could veto enforcement of the single market in a given industry, then the member state with the firms having the most advantageous market positions that would benefit the most from anti-competitive policies would certainly either veto enforcement policies or reign in the Commission, the implementer of the enforcement policies. In the language of social science, moving the single-market legislation along was an ongoing collective-action problem requiring the overcoming of individual temptation to free ride through cooperation enforced by a central authority. Put another way, it was like agreeing to a system of traffic laws and a traffic cop, even though you occasionally like to speed and do driving stunts in parking lots. The changes brought about by the SEA were promulgated by proponents of the single market and of a centralized monetary policy in the Commission, but also within the members countries, which ended up convincing all member

---

[15] See, for example, Thatcher (1993).
[16] This is clear in her memoirs; see Thatcher (1993).

governments of the desirability of limiting the veto only to extremely pertinent matters.[17]

Even though they recognized the seriousness of the changes, there was a silver lining for member governments. The changes allowed them to have their political cake and eat it too when they could vote against a single-market piece of legislation at the EU level, thus signaling to their home country industries that they cared for them and wished to protect their market position, while allowing the legislation to still pass for the good of the entire European economy and their own home country consumers. This process of agreement among member countries to liberalize industries, not always unanimously, was done industry by industry.[18] The Commission had earlier proposed in an important White Paper in 1985 a plan to establish the single market. For the most part, the Council and Parliament followed the plan. That it was all put together in a single document with a coherent logic reinforced the idea that to succeed, the single market needed all the pieces (i.e., industries) liberalized in place with few if any free riders among the interested economic actors within the member states. The member states behaved as if their leaders understood that all were making sacrifices in subjecting their industries to competition.

The next pair of treaty negotiations continued the momentum toward more representative centralization. The Maastricht Treaty (1992) created what would henceforth be called the European Union, and together with the Amsterdam Treaty (1997) further strengthened the Parliament, opened up new areas for super-majority voting in the Council, and created entirely new bureaucracies devoted to macroeconomic policies and foreign policy. The Amsterdam Treaty improved on the institutional features Maastricht had put in place.[19] Together they established a somewhat complicated legislative process that formalized bicameralism; for most policy issues, the Council and the Parliament had to approve laws and regulations.[20]

---

[17] A good example is recounted in Schmidt (2000). The Commission gave notice in 1992 of "possible" decisions – sanctions and fines – against member states if state monopolies persisted. It linked approval of state aid to a Greek national airline carrier to liberalization of Greek airports, insisting on the latter in return for looking the other way on the former. Soon, Ireland, Greece, Spain, and Italy complied with anti-monopoly regulations. When, in 1995, a new directive was passed on airport liberalization, only Germany and Austria opposed it. Commissioners credited the earlier enforcement of existing regulations for breaking of the anti-competition bloc against new regulations and exposing the two recalcitrant states. As Schmidt summarizes, "the Commission not only breaks the resistance of some member states but wins simultaneously strong supporters for a directive. It effectively *changes the member states' preferences* in its favor" (47).

[18] See Kollman (2003) for a formalized model based on this idea of industry-by-industry liberalization.

[19] See Tsebelis and Garrett (2001) for a critique of the Maastricht institutions.

[20] Hix (2005, chapter 3) has a detailed account of the legislative process as it evolved. Dinan (2010, chapter 11) has an updated description. Also, see Bueno de Mesquita and Stokman (1994), and Crombez (2001). For research on recent parliaments, see Jensen and Winzen (2012) and McElroy and Benoit (2012).

The major controversies in these negotiations were over institutional design, particularly over issues of federalism. The term federalism itself, in fact, bedeviled the negotiation for both the Maastricht and Amsterdam treaties. It meant different things in the different domestic political debates of countries. For the British and Danish, federalism meant centralizing authority to the European level and away from the member states, whereas in Germany it meant preserving member-state autonomy relative to the central unit in Brussels. As will be discussed, the U.K. government later expressed strong opposition to the use of the term regarding the EU because it implied nation-state qualities.[21]

As with our other cases, a vague concept enabled the participants in these crucial negotiations to avoid commitments over which level of government has authority over which policies. Borrowing from the Church, the member states invoked the idea of subsidiarity, and it is actually mentioned in the Maastricht Treaty. Subsidiarity shares the meaning in both Church and European political contexts: lower-level units should have the autonomy to make decisions unless it becomes necessary, or makes sense, for more highly aggregated units to set policies binding on the lower-level units. In a formal report issued by the heads of state jointly, they "stressed the need for [subsidiarity] to be strictly applied."[22] This essentially empty statement appeased some who were nervous about others' definitions of federalism. The troublesome and ongoing concern is determining when it is necessary, or when it makes sense (for reasons of efficiency or expediency), for more highly aggregated units to set policies. Put differently and more pointedly, who decides where decisions should be made? The Commission ironically made a report that the burden of proof for centralizing policies lay with the EU institutions, although it also warned against subsidiarity becoming a basis for complaints about unpopular EU actions.

These abstract questions over federalism and subsidiarity became practical when the countries addressed how common monetary and common currency policies were to be made and enforced. Disagreements over the degree of autonomy granted to central bankers relative to committees comprised of member-state government leaders dogged the negotiations. These controversies of federal governance and of representation at the central level have animated EU history since the early 1990s, and have two aspects related to questions of who has authority: the authority of Brussels relative to the member states, and the influence of the more powerful member states within the EU government in Brussels.

The Maastricht and Amsterdam treaties define three chronological stages to the creation of the single market, or what was by then known as the European Monetary Union (EMU). In stage one, which had already occurred, the SEA and the members of the European Union had agreed to create a single market so that goods, people, and money could flow freely across national borders.

[21] Dinan (2010, 92–93).
[22] Dinan (2010, 98). See Van Kersberen and Verbeek (2004).

Maastricht further formalized the idea that single-market, competitive-market principles would guide regulatory decisions at the European level. Negotiations at Maastricht and Amsterdam hammered out details on market liberalization. There were also decisions made over the impending unification of East and West Germany, and the potential for enlargement eastward to incorporate parts of the former Soviet Union. Stages two and three, as agreed to in the Maastricht Treaty, were, respectively, full coordination of monetary policy through a European Central Bank and European-level financial committees (accomplished in 1996), and establishment of a common currency, the Euro (fully accomplished in 2002).

By any reasonable standard, all three stages of EMU, but especially European monetary cohesiveness and the resulting Eurozone, were remarkable political achievements. Among the most striking aspects of these achievements is that the EU managed to smooth over or avoid differences among the major European countries to set the second and third stages of EMU in motion. The avoidance occurred when the U.K. and a few smaller countries were permitted to opt out of most of stages two and three. The smoothing over came when France and Germany bargained and won agreement. France gained some measure of political control over monetary policy through the financial committees on the European Council. Germany won a big victory in having the explicit policy goal of the European Central Bank (ECB) be the same as its own Bundesbank; that is, inflation control would be the primary goal set by the ECB.

Germany's role in EMU was an ongoing sticking point. Given the position of the two main protagonists in the negotiations over the institutions governing stages two and three of EMU – France and Germany – it is not clear exactly what Germany gained from the outcome of the Maastricht negotiations. As the largest economy in Europe, and as the country with the most stable and respectable currency in Continental Europe, by reputation the most independent central bank, and a track record spanning many decades of solid economic growth and low inflation, Germany was already dominant. Policies by the Bundesbank rippled through the other financial capitals of Europe with regularity. It would seem to have had much to lose and little to gain from full monetary coordination and common currency union within Western Europe.

Helmut Kohl's government in the early 1990s should have been expected to greet proposals to create the full EMU with skepticism. What did it have to gain from pooling sovereignty on monetary policy? Why the German government went along remains somewhat of a mystery to this day, although several answers can be proposed. One is primarily economic. Germany agreed to go along with stages two and three because the government became convinced by economic arguments that having a unified policy and currency would bring large efficiency gains. It would substantially reduce costs of trade among the member countries of the EU and this would benefit Germany as much as any other country, if not more.

A second answer focuses on political bargaining, and is commonly told in histories of the time period.[23] Germany badly wanted the other countries of Europe, especially France, to approve of German reunification and to put no roadblocks in front of having a united Germany being a full member of the EU, with a large number of seats in the European Parliament.[24] Germany was willing to trade off some independence and sovereignty on monetary affairs against earning that approval and that political influence within the other EU institutions. In fact, the story has a personal edge; Francois Mitterand and Helmut Kohl, according to observers, agreed over a series of personal meetings at summits to support each on a package deal: German support for all three stages of EMU, and French support for a unified Germany.[25]

The most compelling answer has to do with a trade-off for Germany but not a trade-off of one policy against another. Germany agreed to go along with the second and third stages of EMU when its leaders became convinced that, in our terms, European economic policy would be made by a centralized governing structure organized along representative lines and not executive lines. Moreover, the institutional design of representation had to be "fair" (i.e., favorable to large countries) for Germany. This runs against the common interpretation that Germany wanted more central bank independence and thus more executive autonomy. It was executive autonomy with the twist that the executive would be directly accountable to the member states in proportion to their economic and population size. In fact, Germany wanted assurance that it would play the leading role, dominating policymaking over monetary affairs at the European level regardless of how it would be decided. If governance would be taken over by executive bodies, those bodies would have to be immediately responsible to the European Council and in strengthening the Parliament, with seats apportioned by population and Germany having roughly one-quarter of the seats at the time, this gave Germany additional assurances of having its interests represented.[26]

This is not an answer about economic efficiency, or about bargaining across countries. Rather, it is a story of ambition for representation, and in the best-case scenario for Germany, predominant influence over policy. Germany decided to go along with the second and third stages of EMU because it valued becoming

---

[23] See Dinan (2010, chapters 4–5).
[24] See Dinan (2004, chapters 6–7).
[25] Dinan (2004, 236–37, 239–40, 244).
[26] It is difficult to summarize the relationship between this interpretation of the intention of the German government with what others write because others couch descriptions of German intentions differently. It is often stated, for instance, that Germans were – since the end of War World II – willing to sacrifice much to gain acceptance among other European countries, and that EMU was a sacrifice for them in order to assuage the fears of other countries of an enlarged Germany. This paragraph in the text about German ambitions for representation, however, gives my interpretation of their intentions given my knowledge of the subsequent behavior of the German government. I first wrote this interpretation in a working paper (Kollman 2006).

leader of a new European-level macroeconomic regime, and this could only take place if the centralized authority remained representational.

Given this predictable reasoning by Germany, why would the other governments go along? France in particular had reasons to be wary of German influence because both rightist and leftist political parties in France have historically been less focused on inflation in monetary policy than the German government. In other words, it was reasonable to believe that no matter who was in government in France, they were going to find themselves at odds with Germany over European economic policy. Yet France had much to gain by EMU even if Germany was going to throw its weight around. Without a centralized European monetary and economic policy, Germany would likely throw its weight around anyway. The strong German mark influenced all the other currencies and Germany's economic dominance, especially as the EU was poised to expand eastward, would only grow. For France, under a more centralized governance of the European economy, at least their government would have *some* say in the direction of policy as opposed to it being left to watch on the sidelines. If representation was going to be by size and economic strength, France would gain as well.

Thus, France and Germany agreed to link together EU economies and centralize authority in the 1990s on the condition that they remain represented in decision making on an ongoing basis. They may have looked into the future and may have seen different scenarios, but zero-sum outcomes were not realized between them. Future scenarios under representative centralization were better for both than the status quo. Germany agreed to a system where it would not be driving the bus alone; everyone else would be on the bus with them. It made sense for Germany as long as it was typically the main influence determining where the bus was going. For France, and for the other countries as well (minus the U.K. and several others that opted out), it was better to be on the bus influencing the driver than having Germany drive the bus alone.

Germany's sanguine predictions and its worries about the future of its representation under EMU have both borne out. Even though Germany is formally just one among equals in the governance of EMU, in reality it has more than the upper hand. It benefited in setting the goals for the Euro in laying the monetary basis for robust economic growth in the mid-2000s. Moreover, its policy goals dominate the ECB, it has the largest influence on who will become ECB governor, and it is not afraid to throw its weight around on fundamental decisions about economic policy more generally within the European Council. However, the linking together of economic fates has brought with it responsibilities for Germany to bail out other economies, something discussed later in this chapter.

Following these two monumental treaties – Maastricht and Amsterdam – the EU launched the Euro and expanded eastward and eventually incorporated twelve new countries. The expansion was seen as a boon economically overall for the existing member states, and had important geopolitical implications.

But it also, in some eyes, had the effect of weakening the momentum toward more centralization. A view often propounded in the U.K. (the most skeptical government, typically, toward Brussels' authority) was that with so many member states (twenty-seven as of this writing), and the increasing diversity of voices within EU representative institutions, it would be difficult to find enough consensus to pass meaningful policies strengthening the central EU government.[27]

The view that the growth of the EU to incorporate the new members and largely cover the continent would weaken Brussels may be correct in the short and medium term. But depending on the direction taken by the EU in institutional reform in response to crises over the next few years, the long run could mean a strengthening of the EU. Instead of keeping the EU weak, the twenty-seven member states might see the futility of their respective representative institutions taking decisive action, instead opting for a more executive model of centralized governance. Before discussing the debates that occurred in the 2000s and will continue to occur over this, let us first examine the changing partisanship within Europe in response to the representative centralization that took place in the 1980s and 1990s.

Partisan Changes

As with all of our cases, the most relevant change that occurred in partisanship in the EU has been the political shift, albeit gradual, from a system where the actors focused on geographically local concerns to a system with actors increasingly oriented toward influencing policy making at the central level.[28] Because the centralization agreed to by the member states was primarily representative as opposed to executive, the partisanship of most relevance was influencing collective decision making in forums such as the Parliament and the Council, and especially in summit meetings among heads of state, rather than in choosing the executive. The exception to this was the process of choosing Commissioners and influencing who would be Commission president and later on, president of the EU. Yet the process of choosing the Commission is revealing: partisan groups made sure that certain national interests were represented in the Commission rather than giving voice to who would be the executive, and more importantly, the member states changed EU institutions so that Parliament could fire commissioners if necessary.[29] The evolution of the design of the Commission revealed the representative character of EU institutions because the member states insisted on maintaining an ongoing check on Commission authority.

---

[27] See Nugent (2004) for various commentaries on this point about the United Kingdom.
[28] For an overview of EU history with a valuable perspective on partisanship, see Bartolini (2005). See also Benoit and Laver (2006).
[29] See Hooghe (2001) and Dinan (2010, chapter 7).

It bears repeating at this point an earlier caveat from Chapter 2. By partisanship, we can mean party labels as used to win elections, but we are not restricted by this definition. It can also mean political groupings that coordinate action in a conscious way to bring about policy changes at whatever governmental level is relevant. In Chapters 4 and 5 on the Church and GM, we referred to partisan groups of bishops or auto executives who together saw their fates as linked to the success or failure of specific proposals or policies.

In the history of the EU, however, actual party labels do matter and are relevant for evaluating the changes that cause centralization as well as changes that occur in response to centralization. In fact, entirely new partisan labels and organizations were created at the EU level to organize the politics of the Parliament. A somewhat more expansive view of partisanship matters as well: the groupings of member-state governments into coalitions to organize the business of the Council and to try and shape the direction of institutional change during treaty negotiations.

The evolution of partisanship toward a more European version occurred at various levels among national parties, voters, and European parliamentarians. At the nation-state level, domestic political parties in Europe competing for national elections took positions for and against European integration. By and large, center-left and center-right parties were for a long time generally pro-EU, whereas parties at the extreme left and right opposed European integration. Not surprisingly within the European Parliament, center-left and center-right members dominate and often collude together to vote for policies of integration against the other parties.[30] Of crucial importance is that the positions of the domestic political parties on European matters have become more nuanced. Thus, when they compete in national elections in the member states, the parties increasingly take positions on European-level policies that move beyond merely pro- or anti-EU integration. They actually espouse positions on how they will interact at the European level and provide details about what policies they will pursue.[31]

The move toward more European content in national-level elections has begun to trickle down to voters, although it has been a slow process. A common refrain in the scholarly literature on European elections for the Parliament is that these elections are second order, meaning that they are like referendums on national politicians and have little European content. Voters in Europe have never seemed to care much about what happens at the EU level, and choose among parties even in European elections for domestic reasons, either punishing the national incumbent parties or supporting minor parties to signal distinct policy preferences, or both. Although the evidence continues to support the conclusion that national politics significantly affect which parties win elections to the European Parliament, there is also considerable evidence in the

---

[30] Hix (2005, chapter 6), Kreppel (2001). See Caramani (2004) for an important account of how European party politics has changed over time. See also Coman (2009).
[31] Hix, Noury, and Roland (2007).

other direction. Scholars are detecting increasing evaluation of European-level politics in voters' choices at various levels of elections. This means that increasingly opinions about EU-level policies influence which party is supported in both national and European elections.[32]

As for what has occurred in the European Parliament, the evolution is heading in the same direction. In the early development of the Parliament following the 1979 decision to allow for direct elections, a process of formalizing party groups was established. Indeed, the set of rules required that any formalized group be comprised of representatives from more than two member states.[33] The two main party groups in the EU Parliament sprang up immediately: one representing parliamentarians elected from center-right parties within the member states (the two main ones were called the Christian Democratic Group and the European Conservative Group and now are called the European People's Party and the European Conservatives and Reformists) and another representing those elected from center-left parties (the main one now called the Progressive Alliance of Socialists and Democrats). There are also the Confederal Group of the European United Left-Nordic Green Left and the Group of Greens-European Free Alliance, and even the Europe of Freedom and Democracy Group representing anti-EU parliamentarians – those who, of all things, abhor the EU even though their jobs reside within an EU institution.

The party groups and parties within the European Parliament have become increasingly important and not only signal a change in response to centralization, but also have become influential in creating an ethos of joint interest across countries in ideologically coherent policy changes occurring at the EU level. Scholars have begun to detect an unmistakable trend toward voting decisions within the Parliament being made at least as much based on European party group as national interest. When members of the parliament face a conflict over supporting their national group or their party group, data show that they more and more choose their party group.[34]

---

[32] See Spillman (2012). Note also the increasingly important activity of trans-national party confederations. See Hix (2005, 186).

[33] Hix (2005, chapter 6), Kreppel (2001), and Coman (2009). The language here can be confusing. Officially, Europarties are specific parties within the European Parliament, such as the Party of European Socialists (PES). These can act like ordinary political parties in the legislative and electoral setting, although they often do not act like ordinary parties. For example, they rely heavily on national-level parties to conduct election campaigning. Then party groups officially are coalitions of Europarties, and these are loose coalitions that are heavily restricted in what they can do. The reasons are complicated, but mostly having to do with maintaining the value of Europarties and not diluting their purpose.

[34] This remains a controversial assertion and there are various interpretations of the data. I am most persuaded by the conclusion that over time, the party groups are increasingly trumping national interests in explaining voting behavior by members of parliament. Hix, Noury, and Roland (2007, chapter 7); Carubba, Gabel, Murrah, Clough, Montgomery, and Schambach (2006); Votewatch.eu (2012); Coman (2009); Hix and Noury (2009); Jensen and Winzen (2012); and McElroy and Benoit (2012).

Finally, among the heads of state comprising the European Council, they often formed coalitions to propose or oppose specific institutional proposals. These coalitions were sometimes based on size, echoing the conflicts surrounding the founding era in the United States. The largest countries would band together to support a particular institutional change favoring representation by population, for example, while the smallest countries would argue for more equality in representation. More recently, coalitions have formed around broad directions of economic policy; for instance, whether the EU should allow for government-led industry promotion or leave company fortunes to market forces alone.[35] Public divisions have arisen over the wisdom of the EU requiring labor-market reforms to engender more standardized labor laws across countries, and if such laws would be more uniform, what would be the centralized standards. As with any federated system with meaningful central authority, the conflicts occurring within the European Council blend together questions of authority – should the EU make decisions or the member states – with questions of policy – if the EU makes decisions, then which policies should be chosen? The increasing relevance of the latter brought about partisan coalitions across member-state governments, and not partisanship in the traditional sense of all Christian Democrats or all Socialists. Rather, it created coalitions relevant to the policy making at the EU level, with a center-rightist like former French president Nicholas Sarkozy cooperating with leftist leaders of smaller countries to counteract the push by rightist leaders of the U.K. and Germany (David Cameron and Angela Merkel, respectively).

In sum, the changes toward more centralization has meant that different sets of people voting for policies over, say, environmental regulations at the national level and at the EU level see their interests as linked across geographic space over continent-wide policy questions. This slow accretion toward politics (in the sense of contestation for power) being organized at the continental level has been somewhat a cause of EU centralization but mostly a consequence. The conclusion to draw from this summary of partisan changes in Europe coincident with representative centralization is that with these developments over recent decades, some of the pieces are there for the EU to increase executive centralization and keep it in place should it occur. Like our other cases, changing partisanship borne of representative centralization becomes the raw ingredient that can enable and then cement executive centralization.[36] That executive centralization has yet to occur, but there have been close calls since 2000.

Limiting Executive Centralization

Leaders of the member states in the EU wrestled continuously with difficult decisions over federalism and separation of powers in the early 2000s as the

---

[35] See Dinan (2010, chapter 8).
[36] For a view to how different factors reinforce each other in EU integration, see Pierson (1996).

union expanded to include twelve new members and the Eurozone became established with the common currency. The treaties of Nice (2001) and Lisbon (2007) mark important milestones for the EU both for reasons commonly given and for reasons not always recognized.

Negotiations among member states that began in 2000 were intended to deal with knotty institutional issues anticipating the incorporation of the new eastern members. The end result in the Nice Treaty was seen as a disappointment because the negotiations themselves were acrimonious and seemed to reveal pettiness over representational and financial issues. The French government in the process of negotiation suggested moves strengthening the EU executive. France alarmed the smaller countries by proposing a reduction in the number of Commissioners. The proposal, although leaving certain countries off the Commission, was motivated by a desire for a more nimble, autonomous executive. France also opposed changes in other aspects of representation, insisting on maintaining the same number of Council votes as Germany, to the consternation of the other member-state governments. Belgium and the Netherlands also quarreled over the number of votes on the Council. All the larger countries expressed strong interest in having a more rational allocation of Council votes based on population, while the smaller countries banded together to resist any such changes. They insisted that, for instance, Malta and Cyprus get three and four votes respectively whereas France and Germany each get twenty-nine, an allocation grossly in the smaller countries' favor if using population representation as the basis. Meanwhile, Germany sent strong signals that it would not bankroll the enlargement as much as others expected. This position by Germany would pay off later in the decade for many of the existing member countries (among the original fifteen prior to eastern enlargement) when resources were needed, not for the enlargement countries, but to bolster the economies of the existing members within the Eurozone.[37]

The Nice Treaty was eventually approved and interpreted as inducing minor changes that ended up being temporary.[38] It survived one failed referendum in Ireland; it was approved by a later one when more Irish turned out to vote. Even though they seemed petty at the time and soured the European public on the EU somewhat, the Nice negotiations continued a process of collective decision making of substantial importance related to the nature and appropriate degree of centralization. Take, for instance, part of the treaty that dealt with what was called "flexibility;" this has to do with the degree to which subsets of countries could integrate independently in certain policy areas. With the Nice Treaty, they all agreed that these subsets of countries could make such sub-agreements even without the approval of all the other countries. In other

---

[37] Dinan (2010, chapter 6) offers a helpful summary of these demands and the ultimate negotiated outcomes.

[38] See Dinan (2010, 144–45) for a typical interpretation.

words, unanimous approval was no longer required for these flexible agreements among subsets of countries.[39]

Nice was the first of three instances in the 2000s where the EU had opportunities to undertake substantial executive centralization. Instead, the member states tweaked and substantiated a representative version of centralized governance. When the governments of the member countries met again in 2004 to deal with institutional issues, this time chaired by former French president Valery Giscard d'Estaing, they actually set out to write a European Constitution. Billed as a constitutional convention of sorts and not an ordinary intergovernmental conference, it included academics, international nongovernmental organizations (NGOs), and interest group representatives to address the officials as they hammered out a document that was supposed to encompass all the previous treaties and solve recurring institutional design issues. Several of the proposed changes were in truth dramatic, and consequently controversial. The member-state governments agreed in the Constitutional Treaty to reduce the size of the Commission by the year 2014 (this was later rescinded by the Lisbon Treaty) and to elect a president of the Council as opposed to rotating the position among the members' heads of state. They also revised the voting rules for the Council and the Parliament so that laws could not be vetoed by a united coalition of the smallest member states. This came as an attempt to correct what was seen as a problem with the Nice voting formula.

Other proposals and counterproposals were revealing, if merely symbolic. At the insistence of the Blair government in the U.K., for example, the words "federal" and "federalism" were scrapped from the treaty. Also the high representative could not be renamed the "foreign minister." There was no need for a Charter on Fundamental Rights because the member states already protected such rights, according to the official positions of the British and Irish governments. "In general Britain wanted the revised treaties to give the EU as unconstitutional and unstatelike [sic] an appearance as possible." This position drew allies among other member countries as well.[40]

Like Nice, the Constitutional Treaty was seen by the public in negative terms given the reporting on the negotiations. But this time, the negotiated treaty never went into force because even though the member governments approved, the populations of France and the Netherlands rejected it in referenda.[41] Other countries planning to have referenda did not even bother. Some of the postmortems on the referendum outcomes referred to a nervousness about the symbolism of a European constitution, and all that it implied about the institutional and political supremacy asserted by Brussels. The new enlargement was viewed negatively among the public in Western Europe. These attitudes

---

[39] Dinan (2010, 123–24, 145).

[40] Quote from Dinan (2010, 151).

[41] Technically, the French referendum outcome was nonbinding, but combined with the Dutch referendum result, it basically killed the treaty.

only hardened with the proposed invitation to Turkey to join the Union. Polls showed declining public approval for the EU in almost every country, including those newly admitted from the east where public opinion had formerly been enthusiastic.[42]

Negotiations resumed again in 2006 and the countries formally met in 2007 to pick up the pieces from the failed constitutional treaty. What ended up passing – the Lisbon Treaty – altered some of the key formulas from before and signaled strong, reaffirming support for the defining features of the current EU, including fragmented executive authority and moderately strong representational centralization. The treaty went back to the model of a twenty-seven person Commission, one per member state, and went along with the notion of an elected president of the Council, although in the treaty the member states maintained the rotating presidency for the Council of Ministers below the foreign ministers. The High Representative would chair the Council of Foreign Ministers and also sit on the Commission, providing an explicit institutional bridge between the most powerful legislative unit in the EU and traditionally the key executive unit. This time around, complaints about representation came from the newest members, primarily Poland, but the older members closed ranks and the representational formulas mostly held firm. The treaty finalized a variant of the complicated voting system for legislation proposed in the previous constitutional treaty. To pass legislation, 55 percent of the member states had to approve, representing at least 65 percent of the population. The winning voting bloc must include at least fifteen member states (necessary in case there are many abstentions). It was also stipulated that it would take more than three member states to block legislation, thus ensuring that three large countries could not prevent action without the support of at least one other member state.[43]

The devil in these negotiations was indeed in the details for the member countries, and as the European public observed reports of those details being hammered out, they expressed less approval of the EU institutions and of their own countries' participation in the EU. That is unfortunate for those who see value in European integration. But in stepping back and evaluating their effect in total, the two treaties, Nice and Lisbon, successfully tracked and embodied the suspicions by many of the member states of a stronger, more singular EU executive. As the example of Germany in the Maastricht negotiations revealed, the worry for any given member-state government was over strengthening the executive and giving it autonomy, only to see that executive become captured by other member states to encroach on one's national sovereignty. The payoff of a strong executive who would solve collective problems and crises more

---

[42] There is a large literature on reactions to enlargement. See Hix and Noury (2009) for a summary. See also Europa.eu (2012a), and subsequent, updated versions, for the latest data. See Tillman (2012).

[43] For a good summary of the Lisbon Treaty reforms, see Europa.eu (2012b).

decisively has not been enough for the member states to give up their desire for representation in a centralized body with predominant authority. These treaty negotiations and outcomes are notable at least as much for what they did not do as for what they did accomplish.

Evidence of the fears of a rising European executive can be seen in whom they chose for positions following the treaty agreement. When the first election of the new European Council president took place in 2009, for instance, member-state governments – especially France and Germany – balked at electing Tony Blair. Aware of the history of the U.S. presidency and those of such other countries as Russia, the member-state leaders reasoned that someone of Blair's stature and drive might, with popular approval to resolve a given a crisis, build legitimacy and eventually bureaucracy to a degree that would outstrip the agreed-upon mandate from Lisbon. Thus, they elected Von Rompuy, a dutiful, low-profile leader who as of this writing has avoided trumpeting his own authority relative to the others in the executive unit – the Commission president and the president of the Council of Ministers. He was reelected to a second term in the post in 2012.

Another example is trade negotiation with countries outside the EU. After Maastricht specified common negotiations by the EU, there were two different interpretations of the language in the treaty: one by the Commission, which gave it sole competence to negotiate on trade, and one by the Council, which assumed the treaty meant a shared competence between the two bodies. The Commission requested a ruling by the ECJ in the early 1990s, and to its surprise, the ECJ ruled in favor of the Council. The ECJ ruled against the idea that the Commission alone could conclude trade agreements on services and intellectual property rights. Instead, the Commission and the Council would now both negotiate jointly with third countries on these matters. Other countries outside the EU might have initially found this situation strange, but they have become used to it and it enjoys the support of the member-state governments.[44]

This attitude and ability to stave off executive centralization among member-state governments may not survive many more crises. The financial crisis beginning in 2008 has continued to alarm people all over the world as it drags on, and, of course, it alarms the Europeans themselves. Threats of financial default by Greece, Ireland, Portugal, Spain, Slovenia, and Italy brought strong action by the wealthiest countries. Germany has felt the burden the most, and its government has struggled with deciding on the best policies to save the European economy in order to save the Germany economy. Popular calls from various quarters for a strengthened EU to govern the economy of the continent are rarely specific about the nature of the institutions required. Some explicitly ask for more executive autonomy and rigorous enforcement of agreed-upon fiscal and monetary rules. Leading scholars of EU governance repeatedly call for a

---

[44] Dinan (2010, 505).

continent-wide election of the Commission president.[45] In general, Germany as the most important player has balked at institutional designs creating a relatively autonomous, popularly supported executive that can make decisions without the formal input from the member states.

The history of institutional change in the EU is instructive when compared to the histories of our other cases. Like the United States, there was a founding, a growth in number of members, and a working out over time of which level of government ought to have or actually has authority over certain policy issues. Differently than the United States, however, and more like the Church and GM, have been the moments when the EU changed toward more centralization, which occurred during negotiations explicitly designed to address institutional questions. With the United States, centralization of all kinds occurred during crises, often in the buildup of legislative statutes and bureaucratic capacity over a relatively short period of time. Additionally, centralization occurred in the United States through accretion as much as through deliberate decision making. The EU's changes typically occurred during intergovernmental negotiations over new treaties specifying the details of decision-making institutions. Thus, like those present at Church councils or designing GM's reorganization plans, the heads of state at EU-level meetings were well aware that they were collectively deciding matters with long-term institutional implications for where authority would rest. However, those moments were also occurring in the context of immediate political controversies that shaped the decisions. Roughly every decade in the EU, the heads of state faced a new kind of constitutional convention, but they sometimes made weighty constitutional decisions based on short-term calculations about their own political survival given current events.

Much of the history of the EU can be characterized as a ratcheting of authority away from the member states of the EU toward the central government in Brussels through a series of treaty negotiations and several Court of Justice decisions. The story summarized in this chapter has familiar elements for those aware of EU history. My interpretation of these events centers on the constant tension among the member states and within the EU policy-making community over whether centralization, which had a certain momentum making it seem inevitable, would be of the representative kind or the executive kind. Of direct relevance to the arguments in this book, the partisanship among leaders in the member states and in Brussels evolved to break them into groupings based on linked interests in specific EU-level policy outcomes. Evolving in parallel with institutional changes at the EU level, partisanship changed from being geographically defined to being based on divisions over European-wide policies. Partisan cleavages increasingly split groups within countries and united groups across countries.

---

[45] See, for instance, Hix (2008).

Within the EU, the momentum toward centralization has slowed over fundamental questions. Take the concept of subsidiarity, which was in vogue as a concept in the 1990s, and occasionally arises again in EU jargon. But like the M-Form at GM or the "Necessary and Proper" clause in the United States, the term subsidiarity serves more as an agreement principle to enable people with fundamental conflicts over federated governance to move forward without establishing precise boundaries. Such flexible concepts allow for the creation of institutions that can make decisions on a case-by-case basis. As always, those agreeing typically look ahead expecting some kind of representation in those decisions on the cases. If they delegate to an executive body that is not directly answerable to them, they can lose the reins forever.

Events since 2000 have been a revelation about the limits of Brussels' authority. Although Brussels has tremendous authority to affect the conduct of business on the European continent, the EU still cannot tax citizens directly and it cannot compel member states to participate in foreign policy or military actions. The fact that these limitations ultimately restricted the degree of further centralization toward Brussels became clear when the member states split over the Iraq War in 2003 and 2004 (and thus could not craft a coherent European foreign policy for the Middle East and Gulf Region), and when the members states regularly flouted the previously agreed-upon economic policy targets as part of the Eurozone. Germany and France did not keep their promises about their own government budgets in mid-decade, promises made to cement unity around the Euro and the authority of the European Central Bank. Without stronger executive authority, the largest countries can treat the EU as more of a voluntary confederation as opposed to a federation.

Centralization in the EU does continue slowly, largely by the logic of the single market. Recent ECJ decisions (e.g., the Kohl and Decker cases) show how the Commission can make health care policies in the member states appear like single market and competition policies, with enormous consequences reducing the autonomy of states to determine their own spending priorities on health care.[46] Also using single-market legislation, the Commission can sometimes bully specific states into complying with the single-market provisions in a given industrial area. Then once those states have been forced to comply, they join the side of the collection of member states and the EU central unit that *wants* to enforce it on the states that have not yet complied. The Commission has the power, through selective enforcement, to turn opponents of a given interpretation of the single-market legislation into proponents, and builds super majorities this way. Member states do not like this and recognize that centralized, executive enforcement begets more favorable politics toward more

---

[46] See ECJ 28 April 1998, Decker-case C-120/95, ECJ 28 April 1998, Kohl-case C-158/96. See also Greer and Rauscher (2011) and Greer (2009).

centralization because of the nature of the issue and the enforcement discretion of the executive.[47]

A leading scholar makes the summary point well:

The formal and informal rules of the EU game have not developed randomly. Institutional choices are policy choices by other means. In the recurring institutional reform game that is EU politics, the actors have developed highly sophisticated institutional preferences, such as which policies should be tackled at the EU level ... However ... actors can never be certain of the long-term policy impact of institutional choices. But as they start to learn that the long-term consequences of institutional changes are uncertain, they become more conservative when designing rules, preferring to stick with the institutional status-quo than risk an undesirable policy outcome. As a result the EU has become harder to reform.[48]

If the main reason for the slowed momentum is the lack of assent by the member states to executive centralization, perhaps their government leaders are aware intuitively of lock-in – the conclusions of this book. Related and more likely, however, they each reason that vesting authority in an executive will likely speed up centralization again in the EU with two negative consequences for the member states: less autonomy and less representation in central decision making.

The EU has not yet locked into executive centralization, but it was close in the late 1990s, and has flirted on some policy dimensions. It stepped back when it enlarged to incorporate the Eastern and Southeastern European countries, and the nation-states, through the workings of the Council and through the assertions of the largest members, reasserted themselves within the EU. Nevertheless, the calls of late – with the Lisbon treaty and the creation of a single, elected president having a longer term – could mean that the EU will face the prospects of increasing executive centralization. If it happens in a way that creates truly European-level political parties that operate within the nation-states in their national elections, then there is a real chance of irreversibility. At stake is whether the EU will in the future tilt more toward a separation of powers system or in the other direction, and this above all will determine whether an EU executive will gain relative authority leading to lock-in.

---

[47] See Schmidt (2000).
[48] Hix (2005, 413).

7

The Elusive Balance

The previous four chapters recounted historical episodes from some of the world's most important federated institutions. The U.S. case is Exhibit A, a familiar example based on the overall design of its governing institutions. The well-known design features spring from the tenets of federation and separation of powers. Along with these design features is the well-established historical pattern of a strengthened presidency over time with increasing authority lodged in the executive branch. That increasing authority to the executive, combined with partisanship linked to capturing the presidency, are key to understanding how centralization to the national level and away from the subunits becomes locked-in. The subunit governments and representatives over time have had less and less say in two kinds of decisions: what policies will be decided at the national level versus the state level, and if they are decided at the national level, what those policies will be.

There are historical wrinkles having to do with subunits and their representation in the U.S. trajectory. The U.S. federation began with a Senate comprised of people appointed by state governments. Until the early twentieth century, this meant there was direct representation of state governments in one chamber in what was intended to be the most powerful branch (legislative) of that national government. This direct representation by state governments did not survive the Progressive Era. Owing largely to fatigue and exasperation at corruption in the awarding of those seats, through reform movements backed by popular demand, senators by 1917 became elected by popular vote in every state.

In response to that change, and because of changes in the nature of political parties toward more national organizations proposing national-policy goals, House and Senate representatives since the early twentieth century rarely consider themselves to be representing their states as units, but rather specific slices of popular constituencies within those states – constituencies who share the same partisan interests as those across the country. Senators today, then, are known partially by their ability to bring federal largesse to their home states, but even more by their ideological stances relative to the national distribution of ideological positions.[1] The end result is a national government with little voice for the states. State governments get their limited chances to voice state-level interests at governor's association meetings or when the president (or presidential candidate) comes to visit during reelection time and the state-level political machinery coordinates with the national campaign organizations.

To give the final indication that national politics has trumped state-level representation, governors often jostle to position themselves for a run at the presidency, and make policy decisions accordingly. State representatives and state senators largely position themselves for a run at Congress. Ambitious eyes point toward Washington, and political parties organize to capture control of the national government. As discussed in Chapter 3, all this resulting from ratchets of both representative and executive centralization, with the latter sealing the deal.

Examining the Church's trajectory requires less focus on expressed philosophies of governance and more on actual practice. The Church never claimed to be a federation, nor to be a separation of powers system, and certainly is not democratic in form or aspiration.[2] Nevertheless, the outlines are there from the beginning for federation and separation of powers. Governance at heart is about voice and decision-making processes. Over the years, most bishops were chosen by their local people or by their national governments up through the early modern period. The collection of bishops when gathered in Rome often pushed back against assertions of papal authority and on occasion proposed governing models that look much like separation of powers. The Church reformed multiple times, often to check the pope, and defined the appropriate decision-making procedures for choosing the pope, calling a council, and deciding on doctrine. Finally, the Church has always had, according to the definition from Chapter 2, a federated character. One can quibble with categorizations, but the universal problems of governing an enormous federated institution also apply to the Church.

In addition, the overall trajectory described in this book applies to the Church as well, especially if we examine the span of time since the mid-nineteenth century. Early on it was clear that Roman rule governs the operation of the Church everywhere. At times that rule looked mostly like representative centralization, but increasingly it looked like executive centralization. Although the bishops sometimes challenged papal authority, ultimately the papacy strengthened

---

[1] As noted in Chapter 3, there is a large literature on the nationalization of partisanship in the U.S. context. See Kawato (1987), Chhibber and Kollman (2004), Katz and Mair (1994), and Brady (1988).

[2] See Swindler (1996) for an interesting perspective on the possibilities for Church democracy. See also Collins (1997) and Penalver (2005). See de Thomasis (1984) for an entirely different view: run the Church like a business corporation.

relative to the collection of bishops. This change was solidified and codified in the two Vatican Councils, and it has meant a lock-in of strong centralization toward Rome. Wrapped around this centralization is the protective coating of the Curia and of a large majority of bishops who share the partisan goals of the pope. Moreover, cardinals from among those bishops will choose the next pope. All down the line to the subunit level, a partisanship oriented toward conservative religious principles and papal predominance pervades the modern Church because of codified changes wrought by the Vatican Councils and by the pope's powers of appointment won over the last few centuries.

As with our analysis of Church governance, we should pay less attention to the explicitly stated philosophies of GM's governance and more to the tectonic changes occurring within the organization that indicate recurring conflicts over separation of powers and federalism. After all, the debates within GM over the details of implementing the M-Form and the debates that played out in conflicts among various groups of players – Sloan, the primary owners led by DuPont, the subunit executives, and later, financially oriented executives and engineering-oriented executives – were often over the appropriate degree of autonomy for the subunits and the appropriate amount of voice the subunits ought to have in central management decisions. The series of organizational reforms at GM more often than not reflected victories by Sloan over the owners, and Sloan in general favored mild autonomy for subunits, and quite a bit of voice. On both dimensions he preferred more autonomy and more voice than the owners preferred. Yet over time, autonomy by subunits was reduced and voice was relegated to influencing relatively minor operational decisions, not the kinds of fundamental strategic decisions in which the subunit executives previously participated. Eventually, the GM central unit gained nearly complete authority over the company subunits, led by a strong president and central committees with little subunit representation.

Similar to the Church, executive centralization at GM was held in place by the ability of the central executive to hire and fire the executives of the subunits. This appointment authority was wielded quite early on by Sloan in the 1920s, but Sloan himself tolerated diversity of opinion among subunit executives, at least relative to later presidents. By the 1950s it was common for presidents to use that appointment authority to cement partisan consensus around common corporate goals, and more pointedly, for the central unit to make most policy decisions binding on all of them and to meddle in subunit affairs. One final piece of centralization was for the original subunits to cease being stand-alone automobile companies and become dependent on corporate units such as design, body, engine, and assembly to make their finished products. In the interest of what was seen as efficiency at the time, leaders instituted reorganizations that designed the corporation away from the federated model entirely, which may in the end be the most fundamental change that damaged the hallmark productivity of the GM of the past. It was once a corporation that arguably succeeded by virtue of its decentralized governance.

Our final case of the EU demonstrates an intriguing, ongoing trajectory. In a manner far different than our other cases, the EU has an identity problem. Citizens within the EU, the EU leaders, and leaders of member states are all internally divided over how to define the EU and what ought to be the aspirations of the union. The people who have the most at stake in EU governance disagree among themselves over precisely what it is that they have created. Partially because of this lack of consensus over ultimate institutional goals and partially because of worries over dominance by the strongest member states, the governments of the member states have collectively maintained a moderate to strong representative centralization and avoided intense executive centralization. European party politics at various levels, meanwhile, have slowly but steadily reorganized around policy questions made at the European level. This evolving partisan orientation toward European-level differences is both a consequence of the movement of authority toward the representative institutions in Brussels as well as an ingredient making it possible to strengthen the executive units and to find a glue to keep the executive-led centralization in place.

The EU member states collectively face a decision of monumental significance as they consider institutional change: to continue largely as they are, or to centralize along executive lines. They need to decide whether to permit a system based on representative centralization to function, with an executive highly constrained by representative institutions that include the interests of the member states, or to move toward a more presidential model with delegated authority to an executive having little direct accountability to the representative bodies in Brussels. It is not inevitable that they will decide on executive centralization, but the temptation is definitely there because of the nature of the crises facing the continent. The problems are perceived (not incorrectly) as ones of collective will, of pathologies caused by free-riding, and a lack of coordination among the subunits. In many quarters, there are calls for stronger executive actions to fix these problems, much as those calls occurred in the histories of our other three cases. The Europeans ought to recognize, however, that a representative model of centralized governance can work, can keep unity, and achieve collective goals. The key is that systems based on representative centralized governance are more flexible in being able to move back and forth between centralization and decentralization, a topic I return to shortly.

Let us now return to several of our familiar historical landmarks and concepts to hone the argument and to address some loose ends.

Within and Across Case Variation

For one thing, I ought to address variations within and across cases. The focus of attention in this book to this point has been on variation in the degree of centralization within each institution. Each analysis of the institutions explores changes occurring at key moments or over long time spans, and has made the claim that the trajectories share common features, especially in the overall direction (toward more centralization). One might ask: what about comparison in the levels of centralization across the institutions? Such comparison is not straightforward, although we can tentatively draw some conclusions.

For those who study nation-states, comparing the degree of centralization or decentralization across countries is fraught with methodological difficulties. Recently, however, scholars have made important progress. There are available datasets that create ordinal categories for countries, coding different kinds of authority, measuring for each of many countries the degree of political, economic, and legal centralization.[3] However, not everyone relies on these datasets. For example, it is common for economists or political scientists to avoid categories and to rely on spending data to gauge the degree of a country's decentralization.[4] The more subunit governments spend relative to a central government, the more decentralized that country is. Some scholars control for central government transfers in making these measurements, and others do not.[5] But even for those who do control for central government transfers, the degree to which money is transferred by the central government with specific instructions on how to spend it varies across countries, and this is notoriously difficult to measure in a consistent manner that allows for meaningful comparison either across countries or over time within a given country. Additionally, the clarity of the connection between spending and central government mandates will likely vary by the degree of "true" centralization that we cannot measure quantitatively. The unfortunate conclusion is that using spending, revenues, or tax collection as a measure of centralization introduces substantial measurement error of the worst kind: errors correlated with the concept we actually care about – autonomy by subunits to make policy decisions.

For our four institutions, using spending data is out of the question because of the lack of appropriate data over time within cases, and because of the lack of comparable data across the different institutions. Alas, systematic comparison using quantitative measures of any kind is not going to get us very far. All hope is not lost, however. We can evaluate the totality of our cases and make informed judgments about the relative degree of centralization, and feel quite comfortable with rankings at a minimum.

To make cross-case comparisons, we can attend to two dimensions of evaluation: first, the degree to which central-unit authorities – either executive or representational, but mostly the former – are empowered to make decisions for the whole system unchecked, and second, the day-to-day (i.e., regular) intrusions of the central unit on the policy decisions of the subunits. These two dimensions can fruitfully lead to more complicated rankings.[6] A given

[3] See Marks, Hooghe, and Shakel (2010); Triesman (2007); and Hix (2005).
[4] See Rodden (2004), Ebel and Yilmaz (2002), and Huther and Shah (1998) for overviews.
[5] Compare Brancati (2006 and 2007), Wibbels (2006, 2005a, 2005b), Treisman (2007), Huther and Shaw (1998), Ebel and Yilmaz (2002), and Mello and Barenstein (2001).
[6] Treisman (2007) has a helpful and related, although more detailed, categorization of different kinds of political authority across various units.

institution can be quite centralized on the first dimension but by all evidence, appears to leave the subunits alone for the most part. This can be misleading, however. The two dimensions might appear to be negatively correlated because if an executive has complete authority over subunits (for example, to hire and fire subunit leaders), the subunits on a daily basis may appear to be quite free from central meddling because the central unit does not have to meddle to get compliance. This is the opposite of de facto decentralized authority as discussed in Chapter 2. In that chapter, subunits might have authority because the central unit just cannot or chooses not to monitor for cost reasons. On the flip side, in the sense we mean here, the central unit does not need to be engaged day-to-day in the affairs of the subunits because, assuming an appropriate degree of monitoring by the central unit, the subunits comply out of knowledge that the central unit will act swiftly if subunits do not conform to their mandates. In sum, our cases turn out to be ranked quite differently depending on which dimension one wants to highlight.[7]

The Church offers our best example of the potential for negative correlation between the two dimensions of evaluating central authority. The Church sits atop our ranking of centralized systems in terms of unchecked central authority, and specifically executive central authority. As indicated clearly in modern canon law, popes over time successfully solidified all juridical, legislative, and executive final authority. A pope has complete meta-power, in the sense that he can interpret on his own the federal bargain among the parts of the Church. Moreover, with only a few exceptions, he chooses bishops and can remove them at will. Thus, not only is he not accountable to the bishops directly, but he controls the appointment of bishops and cardinals, and therefore can eliminate challenges to his authority. He can control the partisanship of the subunit leadership and thus fix inputs to achieve his goals. Talk about lock-in! He can virtually guarantee that the next pope will share not only his theological and political views, but also his views on hierarchical relationships within the Church. This is exactly what recent popes have done with their

---

[7] This discussion harkens back to an old debate between pluralists and critics of pluralism. Pluralists were at one time focused on evidence of who had power over whom politically (Dahl, 1961). The critics proposed second and third faces of power, which were respectively the power to control the agenda and the power to shape people's perceptions of their own interests (see Lukes 1974 for a full description). Pluralists argued in response to critics (Polsby, 1980) that separating out the different possibilities for the exercise of power was futile because of observational equivalence. As applied to one of the cases here (and amplified in the following two paragraphs), note that if the Vatican never interferes with the operation of a diocese, it could be because the Vatican is weak relative to the subunits in the Church or because the Vatican does not need to interfere, given that the diocese complies out of fear of encroachment by the Vatican. The fact of the lack of central meddling is the same in both scenarios. There is little to be done using systematic methods of data analysis to distinguish the scenarios. Thus, the idea that we might observe a negative correlation between actual authority by the central unit and the number of times it meddles in subunit business. See Moe (2005) for more on this general issue of observing power.

appointments: assigning conservative (in the sense that word is used in Church when interpreting the needed direction of the Church in the modern world) bishops everywhere.

Yet at the same time, the Church can seem highly decentralized if one focuses on the second dimension. Spending time in a diocese office, a religious order, or in a Catholic parish reveals that the interactions with the Vatican by these sub-units are extremely infrequent, and that these subunits are financially and in terms of personnel, boats on their own bottom (i.e., responsible for their own fiscal and legal affairs). Only the very top leader in a diocese – the bishop – is appointed by the Vatican. Leaders of religious orders as well are approved by the Vatican. Yet subsidiarity, on a daily basis, is alive and well in the Church. Leave the subunits alone to run their affairs unless it is necessary for the central unit to step in; the Vatican steps in, typically, only when it hears complaints from people within the subunits and investigates. Perhaps this daily hands-off approach is inevitable given the far-flung geography of the Church and its global reach. But it also seems to be a consequence of deliberate organizational choices by the Church over time – notions of the sanctity of the bishops' realms and of subsidiarity.

Compare this latter dimension of the Church to the current state of the U.S. government or GM. A state within the United States has at the very core of its budget large portions of federal funding. Within the states are federal government offices for social security, regulation of businesses through such organizations as the U.S. Department of Agriculture (USDA) and the Environmental Protection Agency (EPA), federal district courts, and national guard units that are sometimes federalized to fight wars or respond to emergencies. Federal regulations shape state-level lawmaking and regulation every day. States, in sum, interact concretely with the federal government constantly. Similarly, at GM the central corporate leadership is obviously "present" in the daily work of subunits, and the budgets and decision making by the subunits are not only overtly evaluated and made to conform to the goals of the central unit, but personnel flows between the central unit and subunits are heavy. They literally work together every day. On the second dimension, these seem more centralized than the Church.

On the first dimension, however, the autonomy of the central leadership, the U.S. case and the GM case surely rank as less centralized toward their executives than the Church. Focusing for the moment purely on the executives, the U.S. president shares authority with the other branches, and particularly needs the cooperation of Congress to get much done in certain policy areas. He has much independent, autonomous authority, certainly more than presidents in previous eras. He can use executive orders, for instance, which require two-thirds of both houses of Congress to undo. This is a tool presidents have used increasingly over time.[8] He influences the Supreme Court by having proposal

---

[8] See Howell (2003) for evidence.

power for new justices. As we have seen, this can shape the Court in terms of how it views the federal bargain. Generally, the Supreme Court has been deferential toward strong presidential power. He shapes the agenda on the national budget. He also has a vast bureaucracy at his disposal to interpret and implement laws in ways that can favorably redirect the meaning of congressionally approved statutes.[9] All of this together, however, does not add up to the awesome authority the pope has within his own institutional system.

Likewise, the president of GM is similar to corporate leaders in most other global companies – answerable to a board of directors and can be fired at any time. The president is not, however, directly answerable to a representative body, which includes the representatives of the subunit companies within GM. His authority is like that of other corporate presidents in that the relationship is hierarchical. He acts as a principal and the subunits are the agents. In his role as president, he can command conformity to central-unit dictates from subunits. At the same time, like the U.S. president but unlike the pope, he is subject to interpretations of the terms of governance (in anything resembling the federal bargain in the modern GM) by legal experts, and their decisions are binding on him.

To summarize the first dimension (power of the executive) to this point, the Church comes out clearly on top. On the second dimension (the central unit's involvement in the day-to-day affairs of subunits), the U.S. government and GM appear more centralized than the Church. To bring the EU into our discussion, we need to broaden the scope beyond executive centralization to centralization more generally, and centralization to the central unit en masse, relative to the subunits. How the EU stacks up relative to our other cases on that score raises interesting points of comparison.[10]

As discussed in Chapter 6, the executive authority in the EU is fragmented among several positions. None of the positions wields much authority over the others, or over the representative bodies, or over the member states (the relevant subunits). The president of the European Council, for instance, acts more as a convener than as an authoritative presence leading the EU. Moreover, the EU's fundamental model of federated governance is based mostly on a continental (i.e., German and French) model of bureaucracy. The French aspects have to do with the general use of detailed codified rules interpreted by panels of judges to settle regulatory disputes. This places the model more in line with a civil-law tradition than with a common-law tradition. Moreover, as mentioned in Chapter 6, the EU government can commandeer the bureaucracies of the member states to carry out centralized schemes, much like the German government can do with Lander-level bureaucracies (Lander are the "states" in Germany). This is why the EU bureaucracy is actually comparatively small,

---

[9] Posner and Vermeule (2011).

[10] See Donahue and Pollack (2001), Goldstein (2001), and Elazar (2001) for a discussion.

contrary to common impressions among Europeans.[11] To get something done, the EU can simply tell the government in, say, Italy, to do something using Italian-level government employees. Such a process is starkly at odds with the U.S. style of government, where such commandeering is not the norm. Instead, the national government in the United States has its own bureaucracy, which it can locate within the states. With the exception of the national guard, the U.S. government does not tell the government of Kansas to use its own employees to carry out federal policy; it does not commandeer subunit bureaucracies as a general rule. Thus, the U.S. national government (in budget and employees) is huge relative to that of the EU.

The ability to commandeer subunit bureaucracies has kept the EU bureaucracy small, but it has led to problems of accountability and legitimacy. Although the EU remains largely in a representative centralized mode, once the collective group makes central-policy decisions, individual countries can become deeply resentful. Often member-state governments experience the strangeness of having to implement policies unpopular within their own countries. If it were EU bureaucrats carrying out those unpopular policies, the member-state governments could complain and publicly take on the EU government in electoral policies. With commandeering, the member-state governments have to take on the mantle of enforcers of the EU policies, and incumbent governments bear the brunt of voters' frustrations with the EU.

The implications for federated governance in Europe, and for predicting the future trajectory of the EU, are complicated. On the one hand, to the extent that it is a model for the EU, Germany's experience is instructive. Germany as a federation is by some measures quite centralized (especially fiscally), but at the same time, it has a relatively small national bureaucracy. It is centralized because the Lander governments spend a good deal of their resources implementing national government policies. The national government is small because it can commandeer Lander bureaucracies. Increasingly within the EU, the member-state governments will be like German Lander governments, implementing central government policies and thus resembling a centralized state in some respects. On the other hand, Germany as a parliamentary system with an upper house having direct Lander representation maintains flexibility to devolve and even decentralize when necessary, and the ability to commandeer notwithstanding, the Lander can (in large enough groupings) resist central mandates. Additionally, the German party system is fragmented regionally in a manner reflecting suspicion among certain Lander subgroups of the national government. The lessons for the EU from the experience of Germany contrast, once again, with the lessons from our U.S. case (and from the Church and GM). A parliamentary model with direct representation of subunits in the representative institutions might lead to the maintenance of partisan groupings par-

---

[11] Halberstam (2001) makes this connection convincingly.

tially based on geography within the EU that can place a check on centralized authority (Spain offers a similar lesson as Germany in this regard).[12]

Inevitability

This discussion leads us to the second point of clarification. I should clarify whether my argument is, at heart, a description of an institutional equilibrium, where given a certain institutional design, a system will settle into a natural equilibrium.[13] More specifically, is the die cast for executive centralization when institutions become federated with separation of powers? What is the point of learning the history if we know how it ends up? If the die is cast, then the different histories do not really matter.[14]

---

[12] Halberstam, Reimann, Sanchez, and Cordero (2012) expand on this point.

[13] Many writers (see, for example, Diermeier and Krehbiel 2003, and Knight and Sened 1995) distinguish between an institutional equilibrium and an equilibrium of institutions. The former is an expected outcome or set of outcomes given an institutional form. The latter is an expected institutional form given a set of historical processes. Generally, social scientists in the rational choice tradition have tended to be more comfortable developing theories of institutional equilibrium as opposed to equilibrium of institutions (see Riker 1980). In contrast, scholars in the historical institutional tradition, especially those focusing on path dependence as a concept, have been comfortable with the latter (see, for example, Mahony and Thelen [2010]). See also Clemens and Cook (1999).

[14] The ideas proposed in this book can be fruitfully compared to the prominent notions of functionalism and neofunctionalism from the study of comparative politics and international organizations (Keohane 1984, Keohane and Martin 1995). As commonly formulated, functionalism refers to how centralized control over one area, such as transportation networks, spills over into centralized control over another area, such as energy regulation. Policy makers quickly recognize the inefficiencies in having one area centralized and another area decentralized. Neofunctionalism is a variant that deemphasizes the role of policy makers and emphasizes the autonomy of knowledgeable bureaucrats to make the linkages across policy areas. Bureaucrats with technical knowledge recognize the logical connections across policy areas and why it makes sense to have common standards and regulations for both policies X and Y, rather than centralized for X and decentralized for Y. Functionalism and neofunctionalism were proposed by international relations scholars to explain the rise of the European Community (and later the European Union) and the "mission-creep" of organizations such as the North Atlantic Trade Organization (NATO) or the World Trade Organization (WTO). Thus goes the argument: the European Community first centralized policies on coal and steel, and then it made sense to centralize policies on other industrial products and even to agriculture. The centralizing processes that are described by a functionalist or neofunctionalist account can be subsumed by the story I am pursuing here. To the functionalist, it is the logic of linkages across policy areas that explain the accretion of central power. Certainly, executives of federated institutions can use arguments along the lines of a functionalist to justify the actions taken. As a sample logic, it just makes sense to have centralized regulation of trucking if they are going to have centralized regulation of railroads. But functionalist justifications for centralization are just one of a number of rhetorical strategies to soften opposition among the subunits for assertions of centralized power. Alternatively, central executives might argue that they need more authority to protect the subunits from inside or outside threats, or to stave off an economic crisis, or to assure doctrinal or ideological purity. The point is that functionalism and neofunctionalism should be seen less as causal explanations and more as normative justifications for shifts in authority within federated systems.

Alternatively, and I think more accurately, "*how* it came to pass" does matter especially in light of the importance of partisanship and its relationship to
the nature of the executive authority. Social scientists constantly wrestle with
trying to understand the relationship between macro- and micro-level patterns
and the dynamics of both. For example, suppose a large entity such as an
organization, a government, or a corporation changes how it does business in
a fundamental way. How does that affect individual behavior and individual
attitudes and modes of thinking? When an organization alters its structure,
how does that affect the way people behave, perceive, and evaluate themselves
in relation to the organization? When policies change in Washington, D.C.,
how does that affect behavior and how people perceive and evaluate politicians at various levels of government?

The story told in this book hinges on establishing an account of how macro
change by organizations and governments affects micro behavior and micro
thinking about loyalty toward and support for leaders. In the political science
literature, attention goes toward partisanship – the loyalty of individuals to
political parties and their leaders. More generally, we can focus attention on
the manner in which individuals conceptualize and act in relation to a set of
leaders' expressed goals and plans.[15]

At a high level of abstraction, three of our four cases ended up in the same
place, with the fourth possibly going there. The U.S. government, the Church,
and GM ended up in a state of intensive, locked-in executive centralization
relative to where they were previously. Our fourth case, the EU, is poised to
follow, but can go in a different direction if the member states collectively
decide to maintain a more parliamentary model of governance as opposed
to a presidential model. What is common among all these cases is where they
ended up, and the fact that they ratcheted toward their current state in key
moments. They also share the fact that changing partisanship among leaders at
the subunit level and central representative-unit level was both a propeller of
increased centralization and the glue that enabled it to stick in place.

If we go below the high level of abstraction, however, and move beyond the
direction of trajectories, we do see differences across our cases. Details in the
paths are not the same and even the endpoints are not the same. The powers
of the pope, the president of GM, and the president of the United States dif-
fer in their respective systems. Their institutional relationships with subunits
and representative bodies are different, as are the resulting partisan divisions
existing among subunit leaders and representatives. The pope and president of
GM, by choosing subunit leaders themselves, can secure consensus on Church
or GM matters by stacking the deck. That comes with being hierarchical organizations, as opposed to governments based on ideas of democratic control. It
is important to note that the powers of appointment for the Church and GM
were essentially won over time in the processes described in this book. The

[15] For more on this, see Wendt (1999).

president of the United States, in contrast, cannot handpick governors of states nor the representatives in the Congress. His actions, and especially the success of those actions, influences who wins and loses in elections, but he does not have discretionary control over leadership personnel in the Congress or state governments.

Generalizability

A final point of clarification has to do with the vexing issue of whether these four cases stand as typical examples. Do these experiences generalize to other cases? For one crucial reason this is difficult to answer. Those federated systems that have failed – those that either began and broke apart or that never got started in the first place – do not show up as cases to be studied. Put another way, suppose we find that many federated systems with separation of powers have the same pattern as three of our four cases. Perhaps this is because the centralization is necessary for the federated systems to survive as federated and those that do not centralize in this manner end up falling apart or failing to be federated. If this is true, it would bolster my conclusions about the seeming inevitability of centralization.[16]

In spite of these difficulties in generalizing, we can once again make some headway. What might be counterexamples on the one hand or confirming examples on the other hand? Let me briefly summarize several interesting cases that deserve more scrutiny in light of the ideas presented in this book.

We can start with nation-states.[17] Countries can be divided into two general categories: parliamentary or separation of powers. With a research assistant, I conducted a systematic analysis of data on decentralized governance and institutional design among countries with available data.[18] Note that in the discussion that follows, I am blurring the lines between devolution and decentralization, a distinction made in Chapter 2. This blurring together is necessary because data sets on decentralization collected by other scholars do not maintain the distinction, labeling everything decentralization.

When we compare across countries, decentralized nations are more likely to have a separation of powers system than a parliamentary system.[19] That is, if we divide countries into separation of powers or parliamentary systems, the

---

[16] I thank Rob Franzese for making me think hard about this point. I cannot claim to have solved the problem.

[17] McKay (2001, 14–16) argues that three factors determine the mix of centralization and decentralization in a federation: 1) the institutional framework of constitutions, 2) the interaction of formal constitutional rules with other institutions and, in particular, political parties, and 3) political parties as agents of legitimization. These arguments are similar to my own, especially the first and third of his factors, but he does not offer precise mechanisms tying these factors together into a causal story.

[18] A summary of the quantitative analysis and all data sources can be supplied by the author (Kollman). Feel free to contact me and ask.

[19] See Tommasi (2006) for an illuminating case study on Argentina.

former group of countries – on average – has more decentralized governance by common measures. This may seem, at first glance, to challenge the underlying hypothesis of this book, that separation of powers is a component feature of institutional design that leads to executive centralization. But on closer examination, the data support the story told here. First, presidentialism is often chosen as an institutional design precisely because of concerns about maintaining unity among parts of the country. It therefore biases the data to appear as though presidentialism causes decentralization when the opposite causal effect is true: because of worries about too much decentralization, presidentialism is chosen as the constitutional design. Second, if we examine the trajectory of decentralization and centralization over time, we find that parliamentary systems exhibit two features in comparison with separation of powers systems: parliamentary systems vary more among themselves in terms of degrees of decentralization, and over time, individual countries vary more in their degrees of decentralization. Although the number of cases is not large among presidential systems, the tentative conclusion can be drawn that parliamentary systems experience more flexibility in terms of decentralization and centralization than do presidential systems.

Prominent examples of countries that have decentralized or devolved in recent decades highlight the general patterns. Canada and India, as mentioned in Chapter 1, have truly decentralized to their subunits (provinces and states, respectively) and are parliamentary. The U.K., Belgium, Italy, and Spain have also devolved authority, and in some instances it could be argued that the U.K. and Belgium have genuinely decentralized. In all these cases, and of direct relevance to the arguments here, it has mostly been pressure from the regions themselves and pressures that have been manifest through party politics within the national parliament and in the contest for control of the national parliament, that have led to these changes.[20] The parliamentary model of governance enables representation within representative institutions of subunit interests in regularized acts of policy making.[21]

The United Arab Emirates (UAE) is a telling case of a country that has always retained a highly decentralized political system. Comprised of seven monarchical states (emirates), the UAE is governed by a president who is elected from among the seven monarchs who themselves form the Federal Supreme Council. This Supreme Council makes all meaningful policy decisions for the country,

---

[20] Wibbels (2005a) disagrees with my depiction of the overall pattern: "even if we take a broad sweep of 200 years of history, most nations have seen a relatively small number of fundamental alterations in the relative balance of power between central and regional governments defined in Constitutions" (163). This may be true in terms of formalized constitutional provision.

[21] Switzerland is an interesting case. It has always been highly decentralized. Formally, according to its constitution, Switzerland is a presidential system, but any knowledgeable observer of Swiss government would indicate that the operation of Swiss democracy, although unusual because of its heavy reliance on direct democracy, is decidedly more like that of parliamentary systems as opposed to presidential systems. See Linder (2010).

although the general principle is that each emirate is its own absolute monarchy and has considerable autonomy. A separate Federal National Council consists of forty people from the emirates either appointed by the monarchs or indirectly elected. In practice and in constitutional form, the UAE is not a separation of powers system; the president is directly accountable to the Supreme Council and is in fact one of its constituent members. For its entire existence, the UAE has represented itself as a nation-state on the international stage, but in fact it is hardly that. Rather, it is a very loosely connected confederation of political subunits that prevent the tipping into more centralization by keeping a tight leash on executive authority. Any existing centralization of authority has been of the representative kind.

In contrast, many of the famous cases of centralization beyond the United States are presidential. The Latin American federations of Brazil and Mexico have become quite centralized fiscally and politically, which leads scholars to credit not only the existence of presidential systems, but also the presidentialized party systems that enabled the centralization to occur over time, much as I am arguing here. As for fiscal centralization, the fundamental problem is one of commitment: how can the local leaders be sure that the central unit will not exploit the financial dependence of the regions on the central unit?[22] Political parties enable the central unit to commit credibly to the subunits by limiting competition at the local level and ensuring that the local politicians can keep their careers. In return, the locals give votes and money to the central unit. The hegemonic party in Mexico for many decades allowed for true commitment by the central government that allowed for fiscal centralization. Earlier attempts in the 1920s and 1930s to establish national taxation schemes failed because there was no dominant party to bind the vertical coalitions. Later, centralization occurred as the regional politicians became more secure in their jobs largely through rock-solid party organization and discipline.[23]

Russia stands as a particularly poignant and stark example of executive centralization following crises.[24] After the break up of the Soviet Union, Russia slid into a highly decentralized political system. Regional and local governments had considerable autonomy for ten years after the break up in 1990. By the late 1990s, nearly two-thirds of all tax revenues in Russia were collected below the national level. The resulting decentralization had real downsides. The subunits were largely left to govern themselves, and there were elections held for offices at all levels, some more democratic in practice than others. But subnational authoritarian regimes emerged in regions and localities, and many

---

[22] Diaz-Cayeros (2006, 2) calls this problem of commitment the "fundamental dilemma of fiscal centralization." See also Seabright (1996) and Rodden (2006).

[23] Diaz-Cayeros (2006).

[24] Gel'man and various coauthors describe these events, and their effects on Russian federalism (Gel'man and Evans 2004, Gel'man and Marganiya 2010, and Gel'man and Cameron 2010). I rely on their accounts in what follows.

governments had strong links to organized crime. Russians suffered under the tight controls of local autocrats, who were left to oppress their populations without centralized rule of law or centralized control.

The financial crisis beginning in 1998 brought matters to a head. Regional governments reacted by closing their borders to trade and competition, even from other Russian regions. In the run-up to the 1999 (parliamentary) and 2000 (presidential) national elections, a coalition of regional leaders formed an electoral bloc to try to win the national Duma and presidency. They wanted to preserve the autonomy of regions. They were opposed by several Kremlin-based groups, and Vladimir Putin leading one of these Kremlin-based groups won the presidency, partially because of a widespread view that regional autonomy had led to lawlessness, ineffective responses to secessionist movements, violent insurgencies, and economic crisis. Opinion polls showed that many Russians wanted a stronger hand in Moscow.

Putin's centralization of Russia during his presidency is well known. With widespread support among the public, he and his partisans, under the banner United Russia, systematically took control over the governance of regions by eliminating elections for regional leaders, and then by installing regional leaders sympathetic to Putin and centralization (elections by 2013, however, were reinstated at the subnational level). Putin, and his successor as president, Dmitry Medvedev, successfully wrested authority away from regional leaders and brought it to Moscow. All but a few regional leaders quickly became members of United Russia and Putin loyalists. When asked in polls at the time, ordinary Russians tended to be supportive of Putin's centralization, expressing admiration for his improvements in law and order, controlling organized crime, and crushing secessionist movements. He easily won reelection in 2004.

Although not exactly Soviet style (there are differences in many particulars), Russia today is governed in a top-down style, with orders from Moscow followed assiduously by regional leaders. The governance occurs both by a party – United Russia – and by a government through ministries sympathetic to the party's goals. A nationwide political machine has replaced a set of local political machines, and the main mechanism bringing it about was the cooptation of local leaders through both carrots and sticks.[25] Leaders were fired if they did not conform to Putin's plans, and regional leaders were promoted to that position by toeing the Putin line.

The long-term implications for Russia are profound. The Kremlin has developed a new set of political institutions to control regional governments, to choose leaders for those governments first without resorting to elections (and now by tightly controlling elections), and to raise funds to build military and bureaucratic capacity. Additionally, it has glued it together by creating a party-

---

[25] This terminology, of political machine and cooptation, is used by Gel'man and others in the OpenDemocracy movement in Russia. From my own perspective, given the evidence I have seen, the language is apt.

based incentive system. The career fates of regional leaders rely on the success of the central leaders. Most of all, perhaps, the Kremlin has engendered a set of expectations among the population that a strong central hand is needed to solve collective problems among the regions and to protect people from lecherous local leaders. That population supports political parties oriented toward strong, centralized executive leadership.

Moving away from governments and into the realm of organizations, we can point to prominent examples that lend support to our arguments. In general, these examples are of highly decentralized institutions that do not have a separation of powers character to them. One example, the American Federation of Labor-Committee for Industrial Organization (AFL-CIO, discussed shortly), has developed into a strongly centralized, executive-led institution at the cost of maintaining organizational unity.

An interesting contrast to the Roman Catholic Church is the experience of the Eastern Orthodox Catholic Church. Far from having a pope-like leader at the top of an organizational hierarchy, the Eastern Church in general is quite decentralized. There are, in fact, multiple Orthodox Churches (either fourteen or fifteen, depending on which is officially recognized by others), each headed by a patriarch or supreme bishop. Like the Roman Church, the patriarchs are considered as descendent from Christ's Apostles. The Patriarch of Constantinople is generally recognized as above the others in prestige, although he has no formal authority over any of the other patriarchs. Within the patriarchies, matters are handled in a hierarchical fashion. The patriarchs meet together in synod.

It is worth pondering how the Orthodox churches have been largely successful at maintaining relative orthodoxy and uniformity of liturgy and theology without concrete organizational structure or codified hierarchical authoritative relations across the patriarchies. Moreover, there are various unresolved disputes across the various patriarchies over which calendars are appropriate, which patriarchies to recognize as officially part of the Eastern Church, and how relations with other Christian Churches, especially Roman Catholicism, should be handled. Similar kinds of disputes in the Roman Catholic Church have been resolved over the centuries, for better or worse, because of its centralized authority structure. In the Eastern Church, these disputes persist.[26]

Although the EU is unique in many respects, there are many examples of international organizations that claim to make rules, or even laws, that bind member nation-states. The International Red Cross is one of the oldest such entities and its origins and trajectory offer worthwhile opportunities for comparison. It began life highly decentralized, with national Red Cross organizations assisted only by guidelines from a central committee in Geneva. The central committee helped negotiate with national governments and beyond, insisting on a common emblem, a common purpose (to care for the sick and

---

[26] See McGucken (2011a and 2011b), Zernov (1961), and Meyendorff (1960) for historical summaries.

wounded), and neutrality in wars and partisan politics. The central committee, however, did not have any real authority over subunits. There were many disagreements among the various national-level organizations, but no central authority existed to resolve them with binding implementation of rules.

Throughout the late nineteenth and early twentieth centuries, there were repeated proposals to create a more centralized international organization, or to vest the International Committee with more authority to sanction or offer more concrete assistance to national units. The proposals were turned down repeatedly by the collection of national-unit leaders. Only after the First World War did momentum move toward some form of centralization. The heads of the national units agreed by 1919 to form a League of the Red Cross Societies, which would be independent of the International Committee of the Red Cross. By 1928, three separate bodies were formally recognized: the Committee, the League (eventually called the Federation, consisting of representatives of the National Societies), and then all the members of the National Societies altogether (a plenary group of everyone). In contrast to the Committee, the Federation represents all of the national units and in its Founding documents expressly describes the Red Cross movement as federated. The Committee has historically focused on zones of violent conflict whereas the Federation has had a universal mandate including disaster relief. They are legally separate entities. Every four years, the entire group of representatives and committee members across the different central units meet in Geneva as the International Red Cross to make joint decisions.[27]

Overall, the Red Cross conforms to our expectations. The organization, if we consider it all knit together as one, remains decentralized and lacks an executive separate from the representative bodies. It is federated but does not have separation of powers. The directorate of the Committee and the secretariat of the Federation are formally the executives of the two main central bodies, but they are more like bureaucracies reporting directly to those bodies than actual policy-making units.

A similar historical example is the League (or Confederacy) of Iroquois nations, which is still in existence after its founding in the sixteenth century. Each of six Native American tribes or nations sends representatives to the Grand Council, a body of fifty people that makes collective decisions for the entire group. An oral constitution – which in its entirety is verbally passed down from generation to generation (it reportedly takes days to recite and is only in abridged written form) – governs the decision-making processes of the federation. The basic principles of highly decentralized governance include representation of subunits with seats allocated according to traditional formulas (such as hereditary seats on the Council) and loosely on overall population numbers. Democracy is not the operating principle for choosing representatives to the

---

[27] Boissier (1963) and Durand (1978) have written the official histories of the Red Cross. See also Forsythe (2005).

council, but rather when a member of the council dies, he or she is replaced by a variety of "smoke-filled room" procedures within each tribe. In past centuries the council made weighty decisions of international significance, such as which side to support in the American Revolution. Nowadays it wrestles with other important issues, such as improving the health and education among Native Americans, strategies for lobbying the U.S. government, and whether to continue to pursue international passports for Iroquois. There is no separate executive, and enforcement of central decisions is weak. This is another federated organization without separation of powers that remains markedly decentralized, and always has been.[28]

The largest U.S.-based union organization, the AFL-CIO, has, in contrast, created over time a set of centralized governing institutions including large executive bureaucracies with unfortunate consequences for organizational unity. The AFL-CIO is an enormous federation of approximately sixty different unions. It holds a large meeting every four years, comprised of representatives from all the member unions (the "convention") to decide on matters of general policy, and most importantly, to elect the Executive Council that consists of forty-three vice presidents and three other executives: president, secretary/treasurer, and executive vice president. The AFL-CIO is not formally a separation of powers system because the executive body is elected by the representative body, but in practice it operates like one. This is because of the intermittent meetings of the representative body, which does not act like much of a legislative body by making policy decisions on a regular basis. In reality, in a pattern common among many federated organizations in the United States, the Executive Council led by the president makes most policy decisions and then is subject to reelection or removal by the convention every four years.[29] A sizable bureaucracy that manages the detailed governance of the federation surrounds the president and the Executive Council.

Commentators on the AFL-CIO typically bemoan the heavy, executive-led central governance of the federation as a direct consequence of the steady accretion of authority toward the president and his supporters.[30] Matters came to a head in 2005 when a group of dissident unions formed a rival, The Change to Win Federation, and seceded from the AFL-CIO. Representatives from this group of unions sought at the AFL-CIO convention to decentralize the federation by shrinking its bureaucracy, holding the president more regularly accountable to the convention, and leaving more policy decisions in the hands of locals and the specific member unions. They generally believed that

---

[28] For research on the Iroquois confederation and its constitution, see Crawford (1994), Fenton (1998), Hewitt (1920), Lutz (1998), Richter (1992), Parker (1991), and Tooker (2001). See also Carlson (1998) and Dowd (1991).

[29] Skocpol, Ganz, and Munson (2000).

[30] For discussions on this point, see Dunlop (1990); Dulles and Dubofsky (1984); Edelstein and Ruppel (1970); Ellis (1987); Galenson (1996); Gamm (1979); Jarley, Fiorito, and Dewey (1997); Schwartz and Hoyman (1984); and Zieger and Gall (2002).

centralization in the AFL-CIO had led it to be less aggressive than was required to revive the union movement. After their candidate for the presidency lost and they did not get their way on policy issues, these dissident unions left the AFL-CIO. This provides a revealing example of a federated organization that centralized over time toward executive authority because of the built-in weakness of the representative body, and operated in effect like a separation of powers system. When subunits pressed for decentralization and failed, the union federation broke apart. Secession threats (and then the ultimate secession in reality) did not work to decentralize a federated institution that had locked-in. The secession from the AFL-CIO of some of its members reflects the deep divisions within today's labor movement.[31]

Finally, a word about corporate governance and how GM, specifically, might compare to other organizations, and what lessons we can draw about generalizability. As discussed briefly in Chapter 5, large corporations constantly wrestle with questions of how much to devolve authority to subunits. We could call this a question of vertical-authority relations. A somewhat deeper and more abstract question has to do with a question of horizontal authority. To whom should corporate managers answer? This question can never be answered definitively because it is fundamentally normative. Most people in the business world answer, to shareholders and owners. Fair enough, but that begs the following questions: in serving the interests of shareholders, should corporate managers govern in a manner that vests some authority in subunits? In other words, is federated governance with representation of subunits one means to improving the interests of shareholders? Does it lead to better decision making? It is further complicated by the fact that in some corporations, a large portion of shareholders are employees who might have interests in one subunit at the expense of the good of the overall corporation. What conflicts of interest might arise when corporate subunits are given a voice in central-unit decision making or when they are given autonomy?

The academic literature on corporate governance focuses less today on such questions of centralization and decentralization and more on the relationships among shareholder boards, executive boards, managers, lending institutions, suppliers, and employees.[32] To the extent we can draw conclusions from comparative research on corporations, the experience of the contemporary GM does not appear to be all that different from that of other large corporations. The modern corporation typically does not operate on a federated model – one that gives subunits significant autonomy or voice in central governance institutions. This is partly because of the regulatory environment that requires substantial oversight of corporate subunits. The parent corporation is responsible

---

[31] See Greenhouse (2005).
[32] Mizruchi (1983); Becht, Bolton, and Roell (2002); Colley et al. (2003); Davis, Diekmann, and Tinsley (1994); Fligstein (1990); and Admati, Pfleiderer, and Zechner (1994). Dodd (1932) raised these points a long time ago.

for fiscal oversight and subunit labor relations. But more than this, few corporations are modeled like the original GM, with virtually stand-alone companies that can make and market their own products without much assistance from other units within the corporation. Rather, corporations have created functional, corporate units that are all needed to fund, create, and market any of the corporations' products. This result of repeated corporate reorganizations over decades in the name of efficiency has created the centralized, executive-led corporation of our times.

Known exceptions have included IBM, Google, and Cisco (some would also argue Apple). These companies were known or are known for permitting autonomous subunits much leeway to conduct research and seek innovation. However, we cannot base too much on such monumentally successful corporations. In reality, many relatively decentralized corporations have failed. More generally, we would benefit from research that includes a representative sample of corporations from across a range of organizational models and levels of success, and search for correlations. There simply is not much research on corporate organization that analyzes degrees of centralization.[33] The larger point, however, is that the experience of GM should not be dismissed as an interesting historical example, but one that is no longer relevant. In fact, corporations with ambitions to innovate and grow will never escape the fundamental tension between the efficiencies of centralized coordination and control and the potential payoffs from having subunits experiment with autonomy and lend their voices to corporate strategy.

What to Do?

Consider two pieces of common wisdom (or advice) about organizations, governments, and governance institutions in general. First, to avoid the problem of too much concentration of power in any one individual or unit, institutions should be designed to fragment authority, separate decision-making responsibility, and institute multiple checks or veto points. The belief that separating power prevents tyranny is, of course, an underlying premise behind the design of the U.S. system of government, and has been influential all over the world both in governments and in organizations. Many organizations divide authority to make decisions among multiple committees, and among executive and conciliar units. Theories about governance of large institutions with subunits – from the literature on federalism, corporate governance, and organizational

---

[33] For exceptions, see Hage and Aiken (1967), Hannaway (1993), Jennergren (1981), and Mileti, Timmer, and Gillespie (1982). One study of a single British insurance company showed that as the company decentralized, it become more formalized in its rules and more standardized in its practices across units. The conclusion of the authors was that "centralization and standardization are alternative ways of controlling an organization." The quote is from Jennergren (1981, 5).

design – are based on the idea that there ought to exist a balance between central authority over the subunits and subunit autonomy. The fragmentation of authority should be both vertical (between central unit and subunits) and horizontal (across units within the central unit); an institution out of balance risks spinning apart or becoming inefficient, leading to decline. Within the literature on political or fiscal federalism, these ideas about balance go back a long way to the Federalist Papers, through Bryce and to the contemporary legal and political economy literatures.

> The problem which all federalized nations have to solve is how to secure an efficient central government and preserve national unity, while allowing free scope for the diversities, and free play to the members of the federation. It is ... to keep the centrifugal and centripetal forces in equilibrium, so that neither the planet States shall fly off into space nor the sun of the Central government draw them into its consuming fires.[34]

Second, with all things being equal, decentralization of authority to subunits is desirable. Decentralization is widely promoted and is a popular theme of study in fields as diverse as corporate management, natural resources management, organizational design, constitutional law, economics, political science, sociology, and social psychology. Arguments for decentralization are usually made with reference to improved efficiency. Alternatively, people argue that decentralization promotes greater democracy, self-actualization, or well-being. If the standard proscriptions are to be followed, we should do these things: devolve authority to lower levels, relying on the principle of subsidiarity; empower small working groups to make decisions independent of central authority; let creativity blossom and information flow among local subunits; enable states, cities, and towns to tax and spend as they see fit; and also encourage local governments to become self-sustaining.[35]

The four prominent examples highlighted in this book suggest – to the extent that their experiences generalize – that taken together, the two pieces of common wisdom do not mesh together well in practice. That is, when the former (separate and fragmented decision-making authority) is instituted in certain, common ways, it undercuts the latter (decentralization). By "do not mesh well together," I mean that following the proscription to separate authority in a central, top-level unit of governance can make it difficult to sustain the proscription to decentralize authority to subunits. There are inherent tensions between the need for a strong executive to hold a federated institution together and the requirement that subunits retain both their status as the primary constituent units in the federated system and their power in central decision making. The

---

[34] This quote from Bryce is recounted in McKay (2001, 127).

[35] See, for example, Goldwin (1963) and Goldwin and Schambra (1987). For a generally pro-devolution view of social science research, see Azfar, Kahkonen, and Meagher (2001). See also Bardhan (2002); Cheema and Rondinelli (2007); Kollman, Miller, and Page (1997, 2000a, and 2000b); and De Vries (2000). For a counter argument, see Miller (1992).

roots of the problem in many cases are partially based on threats of secession.[36] However, threats of secession are used by those who argue for more decentralization and for more centralization. The former use it as a threat to get central governments to change behavior in the subunits' favor, and the latter use it to indicate that centralization is necessary to avoid secession. Secessionist threats can be, and have been repeatedly, mitigated by improved representational institutions that grant aggrieved subunits more voice. In other words, secessionist problems are strongly related to the issues of representation that lie at the center of this book.

During the arguments over the U.S. Constitution, the pseudonymous Brutus, representing the anti-Federalist position, wrote forcefully that the central government needed to be severely restricted in its scope. Giving the central government any room to override the states would open the door to ultimate dominance. Leaders in the central unit will exploit any weakness in the institutions to assert their dominance, resulting in the loss of the virtues of local governance by a small republic. This conclusion was based on assumptions about human nature that are perfectly in line with Brutus's opponents, the Federalists. These contend that ambitious people will pursue power until stopped by others. The Federalists and anti-Federalists differed not in their assumptions of human behavior, but in their predictions about the degree to which the Constitution would be constraining on the central unit.

If our ideas about governance rely on the notion that either centralization or decentralization might be necessary given certain circumstances, then these adjustments should be able to go in either direction. The institutions should be permitted to change flexibly. When necessary, institutions should be able to devolve to subunits for whatever reason(s) agreed to by subunits and their representatives among central authorities; alternatively, when called for, institutions should be able to centralize. But contrary to what we might consider to be the desired amount of flexibility for institutions, the flex is not symmetric. If anything, Brutus was right – not so much in his waxing over the virtues of local governance, but in his predictions about the future. Large institutions with multiple subunits and separation of powers tend to become more centralized over time. There is a ratcheting effect whereby authority migrates upward in large institutions at specific moments in time, and there are built-in barriers to prevent the commensurate migration of authority back to the subunits.

Brutus was concerned about the totality of the national government, including the Congress. He was also concerned about the presidency, but neither he nor anyone else could have foreseen the nature of the modern presidency.

---

[36] This is a theme in much writing on federalism. See Brancati (2006) for a valuable connection between partisanship and secessionist sentiments. See Rector (2009) for a theory of federation based on threats of secession. For a systematic analysis of the trade-off between central control and threats of secession, see Bolton and Roland (1997). See also Dion (1996) and Lakoff (1994).

More generally, however, focused authority is the problem, regardless of where it resides. This theme is prominent among certain political and intellectual groups. A central unit will be the ultimate leviathan if given the chance. The theme can be found among political conservatives in the United States, for instance, when they decry the increasing size of the national bureaucracy and the amount of taxes collected by the national government. It can also be found among liberal Catholics who complain about a papacy too overbearing, and it can be found among many European political parties and interest groups that fear a European Union sliding into a super-state status.

The notion that centralization proceeds apace and is the natural route for organizations or governments comes in various forms. Among those studying organizations and governments, some find a tendency for oligarchy to emerge over time, even if democracy is the underlying principle.[37] For both organizations and governments, it is argued that those achieving power make changes to the organization to cement that power. How? Leaders, once in charge, change the rules to make the organization or political system less democratic. They build around themselves a coterie of supporters who will fight any attempt to distribute benefits to those outside the small group identified with the current leadership. They build bureaucratic capacity that dwarfs even the collective capacity of all the subunits. They create interests outside of the organization or government that will pressure subunits to drop demands toward decentralization. To avoid the centralization trap, the solution is a specific form of governance in the spirit of Madison (checks on powers), but with a modern German model: checking executive authority or even fusing executive authority together with legislative authority. The subunits should be represented in the bodies that check executive authority.

[37] Michels [1911] 1962 and Ostrogorski (1902). See also Edelstein and Ruppel (1970) and Levi (1988). The work of Tilly (1990) bears resemblance to the overall arguments made in this book.

Bibliography

Abernathy, William. 1978. *The Productivity Dilemma: Roadblock to Innovation in the Automobile Industry*. Baltimore: Johns Hopkins University Press.

Admati, Anat R., Paul Pfleiderer, and Josef Zechner. 1994. "Large Shareholder Activism, Risk Sharing, and Financial Market Equilibrium." *Journal of Political Economy* 102: 1097–1130.

Aghion, Philippe and Jean Tirole. 1997. "Formal and Real Authority in Organizations." *Journal of Political Economy* 105(Feb): 1–29.

Aldrich, John. 1995. *Why Parties? The Origin and Transformation of Party Politics in America*. Chicago: University of Chicago Press.

Alesina, Alberto and Enrico Spolaore. 1997. "On the Number and Size of Nations." *Quarterly Journal of Economics* 112: 1027–56.

Alter, Karen. 2001. *Establishing the Supremacy of European Law: The Making of an International Rule of Law in Europe*. New York: Oxford University Press.

Ammon, Harry. 1990. *James Monroe: The Quest for National Identity*. 2nd ed. Charlotteville: University Press of Virginia.

Anton, Thomas. 1984. "Intergovernmental Change in the United States: An Assessment of the Literature." In *Public Sector Performance*, ed. Trudi Miller. Baltimore: Johns Hopkins University Press.

Arnold, Peri. 1998. *Making the Managerial Presidency*. 2nd ed. Lawrence: University Press of Kansas.

Associated Press. 2012. "Oregon: Vatican Is Not Employer of Abusive Priests, Judge Says," August 20. Available at: http://www.nytimes.com/2012/08/21/us/vatican-is-not-employer-of-abusive-priests-judge-says.html?_r=1&ref=europe

Austen-Smith, David and Jeffrey Banks. 1999. *Positive Political Theory I*. Ann Arbor: University of Michigan Press.

2005. *Positive Political Theory II*. Ann Arbor: University of Michigan Press.

Azfar, Omar, Satu Kähkönen, and Patrick Meagher. 2001. "Conditions for Effective Decentralized Governance: A Synthesis of Research Findings." IRIS Center, University of Maryland.

Azumi, Koya and Jerald Hage. 1972. *Organizational Systems*. Lexington, MA: DC Heath.

Baack, Bennett and Edward John Ray. 1985a. "Special Interests and the Adoption of the Income Tax in the United States." *Journal of Economic History* 45(3): 607–25.
   1985b. "The Political Economy of the Origins of the Military-Industrial Complex in the United States." *The Journal of Economic History* 45(2): 369–75.
Bachrach, Samuel and Edward Lawler. 1980. *Power and Politics in Organizations*. San Fransisco: Jossey-Bass.
Bardhan, Pranab. 2002. "Decentralization of Governance and Development." *Journal of Economic Perspectives* 16(4): 185–205.
Baron, David and John Ferejohn. 1989. "Bargaining in Legislatures." *American Political Science Review* 83: 1181–206.
Bartolini, Stefano. 2005. *Restructuring Europe*. Oxford: Oxford University Press.
Baumgartner, Frederic. 2003. *Behind Closed Doors: A History of the Papal Elections*. New York: Palgrave Macmillan.
Becht, Marco, Patrick Bolton, and Alisa Roell. 2002. "Corporate Governance and Control." Working paper 9371. National Bureau of Economic Research. Available at: http://www.nber.org/papers/w9371
Bednar, Jenna. 2008. *The Robust Federation*. New York: Cambridge University Press.
Bednar, Jenna, Scott Page, and Jameson Toole. 2012. "Revised Path Dependence." *Political Analysis* 20(2): 146–56.
Bednar, Jenna, William Eskridge, Jr., and John Ferejohn. 2001. "A Political Theory of Federalism." In *Constitutional Culture and Democratic Rule*, eds. John Ferejohn, Jonathan Riley, and Jack Rakove. New York: Cambridge University Press.
Beer, Samuel. 1977. "A Political Scientist's View of Fiscal Federalism." In *The Political Economy of Fiscal Federalism, ed.* Wallace Oates. Lexington, MA: Lexington Books.
   1993. *To Make a Nation: The Rediscovery of American Federalism*. Cambridge, MA: Belknap Press.
Bellitto, Christopher. 2002. *The General Councils: A History of the Twenty-One Church Councils from Nicaea to Vatican II*. Mahwah, NJ: Paulist Press.
Benoit, Kenneth and Michael Laver. 2006. *Party Policy in Modern Democracies*. London: Routledge.
Berle, A. A. 1931. "Corporate Powers as Powers in Trust." *Harvard Law Review* 44: 1049–1074.
Besley, Timothy and Stephen Coate. 2003. "Centralized versus Decentralized Provision of Local Public Goods: A Political Economy Approach." *Journal of Public Economics* 87(12): 2611–37.
Bibby, J. F. 1998. "Party Organization, 1946–1996." In *Partisan Approaches to Postwar American Politics*, ed. Bryon E. Shafer. New York: Chatham House, pp. 142–85.
Birch, A. H. 1955. *Federalism, Finance, and Social Legislation in Canada, Australia, and the United States*. Oxford: Clarendon Press.
Boadway, Robin and Anwar Shah. 2009. *Fiscal Federalism: Principles and Practice of Multiorder Government*. New York: Cambridge University Press.
Boissier, Peter. 1963. *History of the International Committee of the Red Cross: From Solferino to Tsushima*. Geneva: Henry Dunant Institute.
Bolton, Patrick and Gerard Roland. 1997. "The Break-Up of Nations: A Political Economy Analysis." *Quarterly Journal of Economics* 112:1057–90.
Bolton, Patrick and Joseph Farrell. 1990. "Decentralization, Duplication, and Delay." *Journal of Political Economy* 98(4): 803–26.

Book of the States. Various years from 1935 onward. Lexington, KY: Council of State Governments.

Brady, David. 1985. "A Reevaluation of Realignments in American Politics: Evidence from the House of Representatives." *The American Political Science Review* 79(Mar): 28–49.

1988. *Critical Elections and Public Policy Making*. Stanford, CA: Stanford University Press.

Brady, David and Bernard Grofman. 1991. "Sectional Differences in Partisan Bias and Electoral Responsiveness in US House Elections, 1850–1980." *British Journal of Political Science* 21(Apr): 247–56.

Brancati, Dawn. 2006. "Decentralization: Fueling the Fire or Dampening the Flames of Ethnic Conflict and Secessionism?" *International Organization* 60: 651–85.

2007. "The Origins and Strength of Regional Parties." *British Journal of Political Science* 38: 135–59.

Bromwich, Leo. 1959. *Union Constitutions*. New York: The Fund for the Republic.

Brown, F. Donaldson. 1927. "Centralized Control with Decentralized Responsibilities." *American Management Association, Annual Convention Series* 57: 3–24.

Brown, Norris. 1910. "*Shall the Income Tax Be Ratified.*" Document 705, 61st Congress, United States Senate, December 14.

Brownlee, Elliot W. 2000. "The Public Sector." In *The Cambridge Economic History of the United States Vol 3: The Twentieth Century*, eds. Stanley L. Engerman and Robert E. Gallman. New York: Cambridge University Press.

Brutus. [1787–88] (1981). *The Anti-Federalist Papers*. In *The Complete Anti-Federalist Papers*, 1–7, eds. Herbert Storing and Murray Dry. Chicago: University of Chicago Press.

Bryce, James. 1888. *The American Commonwealth*. New York: MacMillan.

Buenker, John. 1985. *The Income Tax and the Progressive Era*. New York: Garland.

Bueno de Mesquita, Bruce and Frans Stokman, eds. 1994. *European Community Decisionmaking*. New Haven, CT: Yale University Press.

Bulman, Raymond and Frederick Parrella, eds. 2006. *From Trent to Vatican II*. New York: Oxford University Press.

Burgess, Michael. 1993. "Federalism and Federation: A Reappraisal." In *Comparative Federalism and Federation: Competing Traditions and Future Directions,* eds. Michael Burgess and Alain-G. Gagnon. New York: Harvester Wheatsheaf.

Burke-Young, Francis A. 1999. *Passing the Keys: Modern Cardinals, Conclaves and the Election of the Next Pope*. Lanham, MD: Madison Books.

Burkhard, John. 1998. "The Interpretation and Application of Subsidiarity in Ecclesiology." *The Jurist* 58: 279–342.

Burnham, Walter Dean. 1970. *Critical Elections and the Mainsprings of American Politics*. New York: W. W. Norton.

Burns, Nancy and Gerald Gamm. 2000. "Creatures of the State: State Politics and Local Government, 1871–1921." *Urban Affairs Review* (September): 33: 59–96.

Burrows, Bernard and Geoffrey Denton. 1980. *Devolution or Federalism?* London: MacMillan Press.

Byrnes, Timothy. 1991. *Catholic Bishops in American Politics*. Princeton, NJ: Princeton University Press.

Campbell, Angus, Philip E. Converse, Warren E. Miller, and Donald E. Stokes. 1960. *The American Voter*. Chicago: University of Chicago Press.

Campbell, James. 1997. *The Presidential Pulse of Congressional Elections*. Lexington, University of Kentucky Press.

Canon Law: Letter & Spirit. 1995. Prepared by the Canon Law Society of Great Britain and Ireland. London: Geoffrey Chapman.

Caramani, Daniele. 2004. *The Nationalization of Politics*. New York: Cambridge University Press.

Carlson, Paul H. 1998. *The Plains Indians*. College Station: Texas A&M University Press.

Carmines, Edward and James Stimson. 1989. *Issue Evolution: Race and the Transformation of American Politics*. Princeton, NJ: Princeton University Press.

Carpenter, Daniel. 2001. *The Forging of Bureaucratic Autonomy*. Princeton, NJ: Princeton University Press.

Carubba, Clifford, Matthew Gabel, Lacey Murrah, Ryan Clough, Elizabeth Montgomery, and Rebecca Schambach. 2006. "Off the Record: Unrecorded Legislative Votes, Selection Bias, and Roll Call Votes Analysis," *British Journal of Political Science* 36(4): 691–704.

Casti Connubii. 1930. Encyclical from Pius XI, December 31. Available at: http://www.vatican.va/holy_father/pius_xi/encyclicals/documents/hf_p-xi_enc_31121930_casti-connubii_en.html

Cataldo, Anthony and Arline Savage. 2001. *U.S. Individual Federal Income Taxation: Historical, Contemporary, and Prospective Policy Issues*. Oxford: Emerald Group Publishers.

Catechism of the Catholic Church. 1995. New York: Doubleday.

Chambers, William Nisbett. 1974. "Party Development and Party Action." In *American Political Behavior: Historical Essays and Readings*, eds. Lee Benson, Allan Bogue, J. Rogers Hollingsworth, Thomas Pressly, and Joel Silbey. New York: Harper and Row.

Chandler, Alfred. 1977. *The Visible Hand*. Cambridge, MA: Harvard University Press.

Charles, Joseph. 1956. *The Origins of the American Party System*. New York: Harper & Row.

Cheema, Shabbir and Dennis A. Rondinelli, eds. 2007. *Decentralizing Governance: Emerging Concepts and Practices*. Washington, D.C.: Brookings Institutions Press.

Cheetham, Nicolas. 1982. *Keepers of the Keys: A History of the Popes from St. Peter to John Paul II*. London: MacDonald & Co.

Chhibber, Pradeep and Ken Kollman. 1998. "Party Aggregation and the Number of Parties in India and the United States." *The American Political Science Review* 92: 329–42.

2004. *The Formation of National Party Systems*. Princeton, NJ: Princeton University Press.

Schiltz, Patrick. 2003. "The Impact of Clergy Sexual Misconduct Litigation on Religious Liberty." *Boston College Law Review* 44: 949–75.

Claggett, William, William Flanigan, and Nancy Zingale. 1984. "Nationalization of the American Electorate." *The American Political Science Review* 78(Mar): 77–91.

Clemens, Elizabeth and James Cook. 1999. "Politics and Institutionalism: Explaining Durability and Change." *Annual Review of Sociology* 25: 441–66.

Cohen, William, ed. 1984. *The New Deal: Fifty Years After*. Austin, TX: Lyndon Baines Johnson Foundation.

Coleman, John J. 1996. *Party Decline in America: Policy, Politics, and the Fiscal State.* Princeton: Princeton University Press.

Colley, John L. Jr., Jacqueline L. Doyle, George W. Logan, and Wallace Stettinius. 2003. *Corporate Governance.* New York: McGraw-Hill.

Collins, Paul. 1997. *Papal Power: A Proposal for Change in Catholicism's Third Millennium.* London: Fount.

Collins, Roger. 2009. *Keeper of the Keys of Heaven.* London: Weidenfeld & Nicolson.

Coman, E. E. 2009. "Reassessing the Influence of Party Groups on Individual Members of the European Parliament." *West European Politics* 32(6): 1099–1117.

Comstock, Alzada. 1929. *Taxation in the Modern State.* New York: Longmans, Green, and Co.

Conable, Barber and A. L. Singleton. 1989. *Congress and the Income Tax.* Norman: University of Oklahoma Press.

Conglianese, Gary and Kalypso Nicolaidis. 2001. "Securing Subsidiarity: The Institutional Design of Federalism in the United States and Europe." In *The Federal Vision,* eds. Nicolaidis Kalypso and Robert Howse. New York: Oxford University Press.

Conlan, Timothy. 1998. *From New Federalism to Devolution: Twenty-Five Years of Intergovernmental Reform.* Washington, D.C.: Congressional Quarterly Press.

Converse, Philip E. 1964. "The Nature of Belief Systems in Mass Publics." In *Ideology and Discontent,* ed. David E. Apter. New York: Free Press.

Cooley, Alexander. 2005. *Logics of Hierarchy: The Organization of States, Empires, and Military Occupations.* Ithaca, NY: Cornell University Press.

Coppa, Frank J. 1998. *The Modern Papacy since 1789.* Singapore: Addison Welsley Longman.

Costigan, Richard. 2005. *The Consensus of the Church and Papal Infallibility: A Study in the Background of Vatican I.* Washington, D.C.: Catholic University of America Press.

Cotter, Cornelius P., James L. Gibson, John F. Bibby, and Robert J. Huckshorn. 1984. *Party Organizations in American Politics.* New York: Praeger.

Cotter, Cornelius P. and John F. Bibby. 1980. "Institutional Development of Parties and the Thesis of Party Decline." *Political Science Quarterly* **95**: 1–27.

Couch, Jim F. and William Shughart. 1998. *The Political Economy of the New Deal.* Cheltenham, U.K.: Edward Elgar.

Cox, Gary. 1987. *The Efficient Secret.* New York: Cambridge University Press.

Crawford, Neta. 1994. "A Security Regime among Democracies: Cooperation among Iroquois Nations." *International Organization* 48(3): 345–85.

Cray, Ed. 1980. *Chrome Colossus: General Motors and Its Times.* New York: McGraw-Hill.

Cremer, Jacques and Thomas Palfrey. 1996. "In or Out? Centralization by Majority Vote." *European Economic Review* 40: 43–60.

1999. "Political Confederation." *American Political Science Review* 93(1): 69–83.

Crombez, Christophe. 2001. "Institutional Reform and Co-Decision in the European Union." *Constitutional Political Economy* 11(1): 41–57.

Daft, Richard. 1992. *Organizational Design and Theory.* 4th ed. St. Paul, MN: West Publishing.

Dahl, Robert. 1961. *Who Governs?* New Haven, CT: Yale University Press.

"Federalism and the Democratic Process." In *Democracy, Identity, and Equality,* ed. Robert Dahl. Oslo: Norwegian University Press.

Dalton, Russell J. 1984. "Cognitive Mobilization and Partisan Dealignment in Advanced Industrial Democracies." *Journal of Politics* **46**: 264–84.

Dalton, Russell J. and Martin P. Wattenberg. 2000. *Parties without Partisans: Political Change in Advanced Industrial Societies.* Oxford: Oxford University Press.

Davis, Gerald, Kristina Diekmann, and Catherine Tinsley. 1994. "The Decline and Fall of the Conglomerate Firm in the 1980s." *American Sociological Review* **59**: 540–70.

Davis, Rufus. 1967. "The 'Federal Principle' Reconsidered." In *American Federalism in Perspective*, ed. Aaron Wildavsky. Boston: Little, Brown, and Company.

de Figueiredo, Rui and Barry Weingast. 2005. "Self-enforcing Federalism." *Journal of Law, Economics and Organization* **21**(1): 103–35.

de La Bedoyere, Quentin. 2002. *Autonomy and Obedience in the Catholic Church.* London: T&T Clark.

Democratic Party of the United States. 1956. *1956 Party Platform.* (http://www.presidency.ucsb.edu/ws/index.php?pid=29601)

Derthick, Martha, ed. 1999. *Dilemmas of Scale in America's Federal Democracy.* Washington, D.C.: Woodrow Wilson Center Press and Cambridge University Press.

De Thomasis, Louis. 1984. *My Father's Business.* Westminster, MD: Christian Classics.

De Vries, Michiel. 2000. "The Rise and Fall of Decentralization." *European Journal of Political Research* **38**: 193–224.

Diaz-Cayeros, Alberto. 2006. *Federalism, Fiscal Authority, and Centralization in Latin America.* New York: Cambridge University Press.

Diermeier, Daniel and Keith Krehbiel. 2003. "Institutionalism as a Methodology." *Journal of Theoretical Politics* **15**(2): 201–32.

DiIulio, John Jr. and Donald Kettl. 1995. *Fine Print: The Contract with America, Devolution, and the Administrative Realities of American Federalism.* Washington, D.C.: Brooking Institution's Center for Public Management.

DiMaggio, Paul. 1998. "The Relevance of Organizational Theory to the Study of Religion." In *Sacred Companies,* eds. Nicholas Demerath, Peter Hall, Rhys Williams, and Terry Schmidt. New York: Oxford University Press.

Dinan, Desmond. 2005. *Ever Closer Union.* 3rd ed. Boulder, CO: Lynne Rienner.
    2010. *Ever Closer Union.* 4th ed. Boulder, CO: Lynne Rienner.

Dinkin, Robert J. 1977. *Voting in Provincial America: A Study of Elections in the Thirteen Colonies, 1689–1776.* Westport, CT.: Greenwood Press.

Dinkin, Robert. 1982. *Voting in Revolutionary America.* Westport, CT.: Greenwood Press.

Dion, Stephen. 1996. "Why is Secession Difficult in Well-Established Democracies? Lessons from Quebec." *British Journal of Political Science* **26**: 269–83.

Dixit, Avinash and John Londregan. 1998. "Fiscal Federalism and Redistributive Politics." *Journal of Public Economics* **68**: 153–80.

Dodd, M. 1932. "For Whom are Corporate Managers Trustees?" *Harvard Law Review* **45**: 1145.

Donahue, John. 1997a. *Disunited States.* New York: Basic Books.
    1997b. "Tiebout? Or Not Tiebout? The Market Metaphor and America's Devolution Debate." *Journal of Economic Perspectives* **11**(4): 73–82.

Donahue, John and Mark Pollack. 2001. "Centralization and Its Discontents: The Rhythms of Federalism in the United States and the European Union." In *The*

Federal Vision, eds. Nicolaidis Kalypso and Robert Howse. New York: Oxford University Press.

Dowd, Gregory Evans. 1991. *A Spirited Resistance: The North American Struggle for Indian Unity 1745–1815*. Baltimore, MD: The Johns Hopkins University Press.

Drane, James. 1969. *Authority and Institution: A Study in Church Crisis*. Milwaukee, WI: Bruce Publishing.

Drucker, Peter. 1946. *The Concept of the Corporation*. New York: John Day.

    1972. *The Concept of the Corporation*. New York: John Day.

Duchacek, I. D. 1970. *Comparative Federalism*. New York: Holt, Rinehart, and Winston.

Duffy, Eamon. 2002. *Saints and Sinners: A History of the Popes*. 2nd ed. New Haven, CT: Yale University Press.

Dulles, Foster Rhea and Melvyn Dubofsky. 1984. *Labor in America: A History*. 4th ed. Arlington Heights, IL: Harlan Davidson.

Dunlop, John T. 1990. *The Management of Labor Unions: Decision Making with Historical Constraints*. Lexington, MA: Lexington Books.

Durand, Andre. [1978] 1984. *History of the International Committee of the Red Cross: From Sarajevo to Hiroshima*. Geneva: Henry Dunant Institute.

Duverger, Maurice. 1954. *Political Parties*. New York: John Wiley & Sons.

Ebel, Robert and Serdar Yilmaz. 2002. "On the Measurement and Impact of Fiscal Decentralization." World Bank Institute, Policy Research Working Paper No. 2809.

Edelstein, J. David and Howard J. Ruppel, Jr. 1970. "Convention Frequency and Oligarchic Degeneration in British and American Unions." *Administrative Science Quarterly* 15(1): 47–56.

Elazar, Daniel. 1972. *American Federalism: A View from the States*. New York: Crowell.

    1987. *Exploring Federalism*. Tuscaloosa: University of Alabama Press.

    2001. "The United States and the European Union: Models for their Epochs." In *The Federal Vision*, eds. Nicolaidis Kalypso and Robert Howse. New York: Oxford University Press.

Elazar, Daniel J. 1969. "The Meaning of American Federalism." In *The Politics of American Federalism*, ed. Daniel J. Elazar. Lexington, MA: Raytheon Education Company.

Eldersveld, Samuel J. 1964. *Political Parties: A Behavioral Analysis*. Chicago: Rand McNally.

    1982. *Political Parties in American Society*. New York: Basic Books.

Eldersveld, Samuel J. and Hanes Walton. 2000. *Political Parties in American Society*. 2nd. ed. New York: St. Martin's.

Ellis, Joseph. 2008. *American Creation*. New York: Vintage.

Ellis, Richard. 1987. *The Union at Risk*. New York: Oxford University Press.

Elster, Jon. 1995. "Equal of Proportional: Arguing and Bargaining over the Senate at the Federal Convention." In *Explaining Social Institutions*, eds. Jack Knight and Itai Sened. Ann Arbor: University of Michigan Press.

Engerman, Stanley L. 2000. "Introduction." In *The Cambridge Economic History of the United State Volume III: The Twentieth Century*, ed. Stanley L. Engerman and Robert Gallman. New York: Cambridge University Press, pp. 483–542.

Engstrom, Erik and Samuel Kernell. 2005. "Manufactured Responsiveness: State Electoral Laws and the Impact of Presidential Elections on Party Control of the

House of Representatives, 1840–1940." *American Journal of Political Science* 49(3): 531–49.

Epstein, L. 1986. *Political Parties in the American Mold.* Madison: University of Wisconsin Press.

Erie, Steven. 1988. *Rainbow's End.* Berkeley: University of California Press.

Eskridge, William and John Ferejohn. 1994. "The Elastic Commerce Clause: A Political Theory of American Federalism." *Vanderbilt Law Review* 47: 1355–1400.

Etzioni, A. 1965. *Political Unification.* New York: Holt, Rinehart, and Winston.

Europa.eu. 2012a. "On public opinion and enlargement." Available at: http://ec.europa. eu/public_opinion/topics/enlargement_en.htm

  2012b. Text of the Lisbon Treaty. Available at: http://europa.eu/lisbon_treaty/ index_en.htm

European Court of Justice 1964. *Costa v. ENEL.* Available at: http://eur-lex.europa.eu/ LexUriServ/LexUriServ.do?uri=CELEX:61964J0006:EN:NOT

Evans, R. and T. Thomas, eds. 1991. *Crown, Church, and Estates: Central European Politics in the Sixteenth Century.* New York: St. Martin's.

Fenton, William N. 1998. *The Great Law and the Longhouse: A Political History of the Iroquois Confederacy.* Norman: University of Oklahoma Press.

Ferejohn, John and Barry Weingast, eds. 1997. *The New Federalism: Can the States be Trusted?* Stanford, CA: Hoover Institution Press.

Ferrara, Christopher and Thomas Woods. 2002. *The Great Façade: Vatican II and the Regime of Novelty in the Roman Catholic Church.* Wyoming, MN: Remnant Press.

Filippov, Mikhail, Peter Ordershook, and Olga Shvetsova. 2004. *Designing Federalism: A Theory of Self-Sustainable Federal Institutions.* Cambridge: Cambridge University Press.

Finegold, Kenneth and Theda Skocpol. 1995. *State and Party in America's New Deal.* Madison: University of Wisconsin Press.

Fischer, David Hackett. 1974. "The Creation of the Federal Party." In *American Political Behavior: Historical Essays and Readings*, eds. Lee Benson, Allan Bogue, J. Rogers Hollingsworth, Thomas Pressly, and Joel Silbey. New York: Harper and Row.

Fligstein, Neil. 1990. *The Transformation of Corporate Control.* Cambridge, MA: Harvard University Press.

  1996. "Markets and Politics." *American Sociological Review* 61: 656–71.

Fogarty, Gerald. 2004. "Episcopal Governance in the American Church." In *Governance, Accountability, and the Future of the Catholic Church*, eds. Francis Oakley and Bruce Russett. New York: Continuum.

Foner, Eric. 2002. *Reconstruction: America's Unfinished Revolution, 1863–1877.* 1st Perennial Classics ed. New York: Perennial Press.

Forsyth, Murray. 1981. *Unions of States: The Theory and Practice of Confederation.* New York: Leicester University Press.

Forsythe, David. 2005. *The Humanitarians: The International Committee of the Red Cross.* New York: Cambridge University Press.

Fort, John Franklin. 1910. *Message of the Governor of New Jersey.* Document 365, 61st Congress, United States Senate. February 16.

Fowler, Linda and Robert McClure. 1989. *Political Ambition: Who Decides to Run for Congress.* New Haven, CT: Yale University Press.

Franchino, Fabio. 2007. *Powers of the Union: Delegation in the EU.* New York: Cambridge University Press.

Franzese, Robert and Jude Hays. 2006. "Strategic Interaction among EU Governments in Active Labor Market Policy-Making: Subsidiarity and Policy Coordination under European Employment Strategy." *European Union Politics* 7(2): 167–89.

Fraser, Steven. 1991. *Labor Will Rule: Sidney Hillman and the Rise of American Labor.* New York: The Free Press.

Freeland, Robert. 2001. *Struggle for Control of the Modern Corporation.* New York: Cambridge University Press.

Frendreis, John, James Gibson, and Laura Vertz. 1990. "Electoral Relevance of Local Party Organizations." *The American Political Science Review* 48(Mar): 225–35.

Freyer, Tony A. 2000. "Business Law and American Economic History." In *The Cambridge Economic History of the United States: Volume II: The Long Nineteenth Century*, eds. Stanley L. Engerman and Robert E Gallman. New York: Cambridge University Press.

Gabel, Matthew. 1998. *Interests and Integration.* Ann Arbor: University of Michigan Press.

Gagnon, Alain-G. 1993. "Political Uses of Federalism." In Michael Burgess, and Alain-G. Gagnon, eds. *Comparative Federalism and Federation: Competing Traditions and Future Directions.* New York: Harvester Wheatsheaf.

Galenson, Walter. 1996. *The American Labor Movement, 1955–1995.* Westport CN: Greenwood Press.

Gamm, Sara. 1979. "The Election Base of National Union Executive Boards." *Industrial and Labor Relations Review.* Vol. 32, No. 3. 295–311.

Gaudium et Spes. 1965. Document from the Second Vatican Council. Available at: http://www.vatican.va/archive/hist_councils/ii_vatican_council/documents/vat-ii_cons_19651207_gaudium-et-spes_en.html

Gel'man, Vladimir and A. Evans, eds. 2004. *The Politics of Local Government in Russia.* Lanham, MD: Rowman and Littlefield, 2004.

Gel'man, Vladimir and Cameron Ross, eds. 2010. *The Politics of Sub-National Authoritarianism in Russia.* London: Ashgate.

Gel'man, Vladimir and O. Marganiya, eds. 2010. *Resource Curse and Post-Soviet Eurasia: Oil, Gas, and Modernization.* Lanham, MD: Lexington Books.

General Motors Corporation. 1922, 1923, 1924, 1925, 1926, 1927, 1928, 1929, 1937, 1940, 1942, 1943, 1944, 1945, 1946, 1947, 1948, 1949, 1950, 1951, 1952, 1953, 1957, 1961, 1966, 1970, 1973, 1974, 1975, 1976, 1977, 1978, 1985, 1986, 1987. *Annual Report.* Detroit: Department of Public Relations.

    1949. *The Organization of General Motors.* Detroit: Department of Public Relations.

    1957. *Annual Meetings of the Stockholders.* Detroit: Department of Public Relations.

    1966. *Organizational Chart.* Detroit: Department of Public Relations.

    2000. *General Motors in the 20th Century.* Southfield, MI: Ward's Communications.

Gerber, Elisabeth and Ken Kollman. 2004. "Authority Migration." *PS: Political Science and Politics* 37(July): 397–401.

Gienapp, William E. 1987. *The Origins of the Republican Party, 1852–1856.* New York: Oxford University Press.

Gimpel, James. 1996. *National Elections and the Autonomy of American State Party Systems.* Pittsburgh, PA: University of Pittsburgh Press.

Goldstein, L. 2001. *Constituting Federal Sovereignty: The European Union in Comparative Context*. Baltimore: Johns Hopkins University Press.

Goldwin, Robert, ed. 1963. *A Nation of States*. Chicago: Rand McNally.

Goldwin, Robert and William Schambra, eds. 1987. *How Federal is the Constitution?* Washington, DC: American Enterprise Institute.

Gordon, Roger. 1983. "An Optimal Taxation Approach to Fiscal Federalism." *Quarterly Journal of Economics* 98(4): 567–86.

Greeley, Andrew. 2004. *The Catholic Revolution*. Berkeley: University of California Press.

Greenhouse, Steven. 2005. "Five Unions to Create a Coalition on Growth." *New York Times*. June 13.

Greenwood, J. and M. Aspinwall, eds. 1998. *Collective Action in the European Union*. New York: Routledge.

Greer, Scott. 2009. *The Politics of European Union Health Policy*. Philadelphia: Open University Press.

Greer, Scott and Simone Rauscher. "Destabilization Rights and Restabilization Politics: Policy and Political Reactions to European Union Health Care Services Law." *Journal of European Public Policy* 18(2011): 220–40.

Grodzins, Morton. 1961. "Centralization and Decentralization in the American Federal System." In *A Nation of States*, ed. Robert Goldwin. Chicago: Rand McNally & Co.

Gustin, Lawrence. 1973. *Billy Durant: Creator of General Motors*. Grand Rapids, MI: Eerdmans.

Hage, Jerald and Michael Aiken. 1967. "Relationship of Centralization to Other Structural Properties." *Administrative Science Quarterly* 12(1): 72–92.

Halberstam, Daniel. 2001. "Comparative Federalism and the Issue of Commandeering." In *The Federal Vision*, eds. Nicolaidis Kalypso and Robert Howse New York: Oxford University Press.

Halberstam, Daniel, Mathias Reimann, and Jorge Sanchez-Cordero. 2012. *Federalism and Legal Unification: A Comparative Empirical Investigation of Twenty Systems*. Paris: International Academy of Comparative Law.

Hannaway, Jane. 1993. "Political Pressure and Decentralization in Institutional Organizations: The Case of School Districts." *Sociology of Education* 66(3): 147–63.

Henn, William. 2000. *The Honor of My Brothers: A Brief History of the Relationship between the Pope and the Bishops*. New York: Crossroad Publishing.

Hewitt, J. N. B. [1920] 2001. "A Constitutional League of Peace in the Stone Age of America: The Language of the Iroquois and Its Constitution." In *An Iroquois Sourcebook*, eds. Nicolaidis Kalypso and Robert Howse. Vol. 1. New York: Garland Publishing.

Higgens-Evenson, Rudy. 2003. *The Price of Progress: Public Services, Taxation, and the American Corporate State*. Baltimore: Johns Hopkins University Press.

Higgs, Robert. 1987. *Crisis and Leviathan*. New York: Oxford University Press.

  2004. *Against Leviathan*. Oakland, CA: Independent Institute.

  2007. *Neither Liberty nor Safety*. Oakland, CA: Independent Institute.

Hirschman, Albert. 1970. *Exit, Voice, and Loyalty*. Cambridge, MA: Harvard University Press.

Hitchcock, William. 2002. *The Struggle for Europe*. New York: Doubleday.

Hix, Simon. 2005. *The Political System of the European Union.* 2nd ed. New York: Palgrave MacMillan.

    2008. *What's Wrong with the European Union and How to Fix It.* Cambridge: Polity.

Hix, Simon and Abdul Noury. 2009. "After Enlargement: Voting Patterns in the Sixth European Parliament." *Legislative Studies Quarterly* 32(2): 159–74.

Hix, Simon, Abdul G. Noury, and Gerard Roland. 2007. *Democratic Politics in the European Parliament.* New York: Cambridge University Press.

Holt, Michael. 1999. *The Rise and Decline of the American Whig Party: Jacksonian Politics and the Onset of the Civil War.* New York: Oxford University Press.

Hooghe, Liesbet. 2001. *The European Commission and the Integration of Europe.* Cambridge: Cambridge University Press.

Hooghe, Liesbet and Gary Marks. 2001. *Multi-level Governance and European Integration.* Lanham, MD: Rowman & Littlefield.

Hooghe, Liesbet, Gary Marks, and Arjan Schakel. 2010. *The Rise Of Regional Authority: A Comparative Study Of 42 Democracies.* New York: Routledge.

Howe, Daniel Walker. 2007. *What Hath God Wrought: The Transformation of America, 1815–1848.* New York: Oxford University Press.

Howell, William. 2003. *Power without Persuasion.* Princeton, NJ: Princeton University Press.

Hueglin, Thomas and Alan Fenna. 2006. *Comparative Federalism.* Petersborough, ON: Broadview Press.

Hug, Simon. 2002. *Voices of Europe.* Lanham, MD: Rowman and Littlefield.

Humanae Vitae. 1968. Encyclical from Paul VI, July 25. Available at: http://www.vatican.va/holy_father/paul_vi/encyclicals/documents/hf_p-vi_enc_25071968_humanae-vitae_en.html

Huther, J. and A. Shah. 1998. "Applying a Simple Measure of Good Governance to the Debate on Fiscal Decentralisation." World Bank Institute, Policy Research Working Paper No. 1894.

Ickes, Harold. 1941. "Who Killed the Progressive Party?" *The American Historical Review* 46: 306–37.

Inman, Robert. 2008. "Federalism's Values and the Value of Federalism." National Bureau of Economic Research, Working Paper 13735. Available at: http://www.nber.org/papers/w13735

Inman, Robert and Daniel Rubinfeld. 1997. "Rethinking Federalism." *Journal of Economic Perspectives* 11(4): 43–64.

Jaffee, David. 2001. *Organization Theory: Tension and Change.* New York: McGraw Hill.

James, Scott C. 2000. *Presidents, Parties, and the State: A Party System Perspective on Democratic Regulatory Choice, 1884–1936.* New York: Cambridge University Press.

Jarley, Paul, Jack Fiorito, and John Thomas Dewey. 1997. "A Structural Contingency Approach to Bureaucracy and Democracy in U.S. National Unions." *The Academy of Management Journal* 40(4): 831–61.

Jennergren, Peter. 1981. "Decentralization in Organizations." In *Handbook of Organizational Design,* eds. Paul Nystrom and William Starbuck. New York: Oxford University Press.

Jensen, Thomas and Thomas Winzen. 2012. "Legislative Negotiations in the European Parliament." *European Union Politics* 13(1): 118–49.

Johnson, John. 1990. "Subsidiarity and the Synod of Bishops." *The Jurist* 50: 488–523.

Joseph, Richard. 2004. *Origins of the American Income Tax: The Revenue Act of 1894 and Its Aftermath*. Syracuse, NY: Syracuse University Press.

Katz, Richard and Peter Mair. 1994. *How Parties Organize: Change and Adaptation in Party Organizations in Western Democracies*. London: Sage Publications.

Kaufman, Franz-Xavier. 1988. "The Principle of Subsidiarity Viewed by the Sociology of Organizations." *The Jurist* 48: 275–91.

Kawato, Sudafumi. 1987. "Nationalization and Partisan Realignment in Congressional Elections." *The American Political Science Review* 81(Dec): 1235–50.

Keller, Maryann. 1989. *Rude Awakening: The Rise, Fall, and Struggle for Recovery of General Motors*. New York: Morrow.

Keohane, Robert. 1984. *After Hegemony: Cooperation and Discord in the World Political Economy*. Princeton, NJ: Princeton University Press.

Keohane, Robert and L. L. Martin. 1995. "The Promise of Institutionalist Theory." *International Security* 20(1): 39–51.

Keohane, Robert and Stanley Hoffman, eds. 1991. *The New European Community*. Boulder, CO: Westview.

Key, V. O. 1949. *Southern Politics*. New York: Knopf.

Kim, Joon Suk. 2005. "Making States Federatively: Alternative Routes of State Formation in Late Medieval and Early Modern Europe." PhD Dissertation. Department of Political Science, University of Chicago.

King, Preston. 1982. *Federalism and Federation*. London and Canberra: Croom Helm.

Kleppner, Paul. 1987. *Continuity and Change in Electoral Politics, 1893–1928*. New York: Greenwood.

Knight, Jack and Itai Sened, eds. 1995. *Explaining Social Institutions*. Ann Arbor: University of Michigan Press.

Kollman, Ken. 2003. "The Rotating Presidency of the European Council as a Search for Good Policies." *European Union Politics* 4(Mar): 51–71.

2006. "Authority Migration in Federations." Working Paper Manuscript, Department of Political Science, University of Michigan.

2011. *The American Political System*. New York: Norton.

Kollman Ken, John H. Miller, and Scott E. Page. 1997. "Political Institutions and Sorting in a Tiebout Model." *American Economic Review* 87: 977–92.

2000a. "Decentralization and the Search for Policy Solutions." *Journal of Law, Economics, and Organizations* 16 (April):102–28.

2000b. "Consequences of Nonlinear Preferences in a Federal Political System." In *Political Complexity: Nonlinear Models of Politics*, ed. Diana Richards. Ann Arbor: University of Michigan Press.

Koremenos, Barbara, C. Lipson, and Duncan Snidal. 2001. "The Rational Design of International Institutions." *International Organization* 55(4): 761–99.

Kramer, Larry. 1994. "Understanding Federalism." *Vanderbilt Law Review* 47:1485–561.

Kreppel, Amie. 2002. *The European Parliament and Supranational Party System*. New York: Cambridge University Press.

Kulish, Nicholas and Jack Ewing. 2012. "Europe's Banking Chief Wields New Power in Crisis." *New York Times*. July 3. Available at: http://www.nytimes.com/2012/07/03/world/europe/european-central-bank-head-draghi-has-new-powers.html?_r=1&hp

Kung, Hans. 1981. *How the Pope Became Infallible*. Garden City, NY: Doubleday.

Lake, David. 2009. *Hierarchy in International Relations: Authority, Sovereignty, and the New Structure of World Politics*. Ithaca, NY: Cornell University Press.

Lakoff, Sanford. 1994. "Between Either/Or and More or Less: Sovereignty Versus Autonomy Under Federalism." *Publius* **24**(Winter): 63–78.

Lamberson, P. J. and Scott E. Page. 2012. "Tipping Points." *Quarterly Journal of Political Science* **7**(2): 175–208.

Levi, Margaret. 1988. *Of Rule and Revenue*. Berkeley: University of California Press.

Linder, Wolf. 1994. *Swiss Democracy: Possible Solutions to Conflict in Multicultural Societies*. New York: St. Martin's Press.

2010. *Swiss Democracy: Possible Solutions to Conflict in Multicultural Societies*. New York: Palgrave Macmillan.

Link, Arthur. 1959. "What Happened to the Progressive Movement in the 1920s?" *The American Historical Review* **64**: 833–51.

Lipset, Seymour M. and Stein Rokkan. 1967. "Cleavage Structures, Party Systems, and Voter Alignments: An Introduction." In *Party Systems and Voter Alignments*, eds. Seymour M. Lipset and Stein Rokkan. New York: Free Press.

Locke, John. [1690] 1952. *The Second Treatise of Government*. New York: Bobbs-Merrill.

Lockwood, Ben. 2002. "Distributive Politics and the Costs of Centralization." *Review of Economic Studies* **69**: 313–37.

Lukes, Stephen. 1974. *Power: A Radical View*. New York: Macmillan.

Lumen Gentium. 1964. Document from the Second Vatican Council. Available at: http://www.vatican.va/archive/hist_councils/ii_vatican_council/

Lutz, Donald S. 1998. "The Iroquois Constitution: An Analysis." *Publius*. **28**(2): 99–127.

Madison, James, Alexander Hamilton, and John Jay. [1887–88] 2003. *Federalist Papers*. New York: Bantam Classic.

Mahony, James and Kathleen Thelen. 2010. *Explaining Institutional Change*. New York: Cambridge University Press.

Main, Jackson T. 1973. *Political Parties before the Constitution*. Chapel Hill: University of North Carolina Press.

Majone, Giandomenico. 2002. "The European Commission: The Limits of Centralization and the Perils of Parliamentarization." *Governance* **15**(3): 375–92.

Maltzman, Forrest, Melissa Schwartzberg, and Lee Sigelman. 2006. "Vox Pouli, Vox Dei, Vox Sagittae." *PSOnline*. April. Available at: www.apsanet.org

March, James and Herbert Simon. 1993. *Organizations*. Oxford: Basil Blackwell.

Marks, Gary. 1989. *Unions in Politics*. Princeton, NJ: Princeton University Press.

Marks, Gary, Carole Wilson, and Leonard Ray. 2002. "National Political Parties and European Integration." *American Journal of Political Science* **30**(3): 433–59.

Martin, Andrew and Kevin Quinn. 2013. *Quinn-Martin Scores*. Available at: http://mqscores.wustl.edu/

Mattli, Walter. 1999. *The Logic of Regional Integration*. New York: Cambridge University Press.

McBrien, Richard. 1997. *Lives of the Popes*. New York: HarperCollins.

2008. *The Church: The Evolution of Catholicism*. New York: HarperOne.

McClory, Robert. 1995. *Turning Point: The Inside Story of the Papal Birth Control Commission, and How Humanae Vitae Changed the Life of Patty Crowley and the Future of the Church*. New York: Crossroad.

1997. *Power and the Papacy: The People and Politics behind the Doctrine of Infallibility*. Liguori, MO: Triumph.

McCormick, Richard P. 1975. "Political Development and the Second American party System." In *The American Party Systems*, 2nd ed., eds. William N. Chambers and Walter Dean Burnham. New York: Oxford University Press.

McElroy, Gail and Kenneth Benoit. 2012. "Policy Positioning in the European Parliament." *European Union Politics* 13(1): 150–67.

McGucken, John Anthony. 2011a. *Encyclopedia of Eastern Orthodox Christianity*. Vols. 1, 2. Malden, MA: Blackwell.

2011b. *The Orthodox Church*. Malden, MA: Blackwell.

McKay, David. 2001. *Designing Europe*. Oxford: Oxford University Press.

McPherson, James. 1988. *Battle Cry of Freedom*. New York: Oxford University Press.

Mello, L. and M. Barenstein. 2001. "Fiscal Decentralization and Governance: A Cross-Country Approach." International Monetary Fund, Working Paper 01/71.

Meyendorff, John. 1960. *The Orthodox Church*. New York: Pantheon.

Meyer, J. and B. Rowan. 1977. "Institutional Organizations." *American Journal of Sociology* 83: 340–63.

Michels, Roberto. [1911] 1962. *Political Parties*. New York: Free Press.

Mileti, Dennis S., Doug A. Timmer, and David F. Gillespie. 1982. "Intra and Interorganizational Determinants of Decentralization." *The Pacific Sociological Review* 25(2): 163–83.

Milkis, Sidney. 1993. *The President and the Parties: The Transformation of the American Party System since the New Deal*. New York: Oxford University Press.

Miller, Gary. 1992. *Managerial Dilemmas: The Political Economy of Hierarchy*. New York: Cambridge University Press.

Miller, Trudi, ed. 1984. *Public Sector Performance: A Conceptual Turning Point*. Baltimore: Johns Hopkins University Press.

Mizruchi, Mark. 1983. "Who Controls Whom? An Examination of the Relation between Management and Boards of Directors in Large American Corporations." *Academy of Management Review* 8: 426–35.

Moe, Terry. 2005. "Power and Political Institutions." *Perspectives on Politics* 3(2): 215–33.

Mohr, Lawrence. 1982. *Explaining Organizational Behavior*. San Francisco: Jossey-Bass.

Monks, Robert and Nell Minow. 2007. "GM Corporate Governance Case Study." *Corporate Governance*. 4th ed. New York: John Wiley & Sons.

Monnet, Jean. 1978. *Memoirs*. Garden City, NY: Doubleday.

Montinola, Gabriella, Qian Yingyi, and Barry R. Weingast. "Federalism, Chinese Style: The Political Basis for Economic Success in China." *World Politics* 48: 50–81.

Moravcsik, Andrew. 1998. *The Choice for Europe*. Ithaca, NY: Cornell University Press.

Morris, Edmund. 2001a. *Theodore Rex*. New York: Random House.

2001b. *The Rise of Theodore Roosevelt*. Rev. ed. New York: Modern Library.

Morrow, James. 1994. *Game Theory for Political Scientists*. Princeton, NJ: Princeton University Press.

Mott, Charles. 1924. "Organizing a Great Industrial Corporation: Tuning up General Motors – V." *Management and Administration* 7(5): 3–7.

Motu Proprio, Apostolica Sollicitudo. 1965. Papal encyclical issued September 15.

Mousley, Edward. 1940. "The Meaning of Federalism." In *Federal Union: A Symposium*, ed. M. Chaning-Pearce. London: Jonathan Cape Ltd.

Mueller, Dennis, ed. 1997. *Perspectives on Public Choice: A Handbook*. New York: Cambridge University Press.

Muller, Wolfgang. 1993. "The Relevance of the State for Party System Change." *Journal of Theoretical Politics* 5: 419–54.

Musgrave, Richard. 1997. "Devolution, Grants, and Fiscal Competition." *Journal of Economic Perspectives* 11: 65–72.

Myerson, Roger. 2006. "Federalism and Incentives for Success of Democracy." *Quarterly Journal of Political Science* 1(1): 3–23.

Nardulli, Peter. 1995. "The Concept of a Critical Realignment, Electoral Behavior, and Political Change." *The American Political Science Review* 89: 10–22.

Negandhi, Anant. 1972. *Conflict and Power in Complex Organizations*. Kent, OH: Kent State University, Comparative Administrative Research Institute, College of Business Administration.

Neudstadt, Richard. 1980. *Presidential Power*. New York: MacMillan.

Newsweek Magazine. 1963. "How 'The System' Works at GM." February 25.

New York (State of) Assembly. Various years since 1855. Albany: State of New York.

Nice, David and Patricia Fredericksen. 1995. *The Politics of Intergovernmental Relations*. 2nd ed. Chicago: Nelson-Hall.

Nicodemus, Donald. 1969. *The Democratic Church*. Milwaukee, WI: Bruce Publishing.

Nicolaidis, Kalypso and Robert Howse, eds. 2001. *The Federal Vision*. New York: Oxford University Press.

Nugent, Neill, ed. 2004. *European Union Enlargement*. Basingstoke: Palgrave MacMillan.

Nystrom, Paul and William Starbuck, eds. 1981. *Handbook of Organizational Design*. New York: Oxford University Press.

Oakley, Francis. 1969. *Council over Pope?* New York: Herder and Herder.

    2003. *The Conciliarist Tradition*. Oxford: Oxford University Press.

Oates, Wallace. 1972. *Fiscal Federalism*. New York: Harcourt Brace Jovanovich.

    1977. "An Economist's Perspective on Fiscal Federalism." In *The Political Economy of Fiscal Federalism, ed*. Wallace Oates. Lexington, MA: Lexington Books.

Oberholzer-Gee, Felix and Koleman S. Strumpf. 2002. "Endogeneous Policy Decentralization: Testing the Central Tenet of Economic Federalism." *Journal of Political Economy* 110: 1–36.

O'Malley, John. 2008. *What Happened at Vatican II*. Cambridge, MA: Harvard University Press.

    2010. *A History of the Popes*. Lanham, MD: Rowman and Littlefield.

Onuf, Peter. 1983. *The Origins of the Federal Republic*. Philadelphia: University of Pennsylvania Press.

Onuf, Peter and Cathy Matson. 1990. *A Union of Interests*. Lawrence: University Press of Kansas.

Onuf, Peter and Nicholas Onuf. 1994. *Federal Union, Modern World: The Law of Nations in an Age of Revolutions, 1776–1814*. Lanham, MD: Rowman and Littlefield.

Ordeshook, Peter and Emerson Niou. 1998. "Alliance versus Federations: An Extension of Riker's Analysis of Federal Formation." *Constitutional Political Economy* 9:271–88.

Osborne, David. 1988. *Laboratories of Democracy*. Boston, MA: Harvard Business School Press.

Ostrogorski, M. 1902. *Democracy and the Organization of Political Parties, Vol. 1*. London: Macmillan.

Ostrom, Vincent. 1991. *The Meaning of American Federalism: Constituting a Self-Governing Society*. San Francisco: Institute for Contemporary Studies.

Ottosen, Garry. 1992. *Making American Government Work: A Proposal to Reinvigorate Federalism*. Lanham, MD: University Press of America.

Pahre, Robert. 2005. "Formal Theory and Case Study Methods in EU Studies." *European Union Politics* 6: 113–45.

Panizza, Ugo. 1999. "On the Determinants of Fiscal Centralization: Theory and Evidence." *Journal of Public Economics* 74(1): 97–139.

Parker, Arthur C. [1916] 1991. "The Constitution of the Five Nations." *New York State Museum Bulletin* No. 184.

Paterson, T. T. 1969. *Management Theory*. London: Business Publications.

Patterson, James. 1967. *Congressional Conservatism and the New Deal*. Lexington: University of Kentucky Press.

  1969. *The New Deal and the States*. Princeton, NJ: Princeton University Press.

Paul VI. 1965. *Apostolic Letter for Establishing the Synod of Bishops for the Universal Church*. Delivered September 15. Available at: ⟨http://www.vatican.va/holy_father/paul_vi/motu_proprio/documents/hf_p-vi_motu-proprio_19650915_apostolica-sollicitudo_en.html

Pelfrey, William. 2006. *Billy, Alfred, and General Motors*. New York: Amacom.

Peltason, J. W. 1986. *Understanding the Constitution*. 12th ed. San Diego: Harcourt Brace Jovanovich.

Penalver, Eduardo. 2005. "Promoting Democracy in the Church." *National Catholic Reporter* May 27, p. 19.

Persson, Torsten and Guido Tabellini. 1994. "Does Centralization Increase the Size of Government?" *European Economic Review* 38: 765–73.

  2003. *Economic Effects of Constitutions*. Cambridge, MA: MIT Press.

Peters, Tom. 1988. *Thriving on Chaos: Handbook for the Management Revolution*. New York: Knopf.

Peterson, Paul. 1995. *The Price of Federalism*. Washington, DC: Brookings.

Peterson, Paul, Barry Rabe, and Kenneth Wong. 1986. *When Federalism Works*. Washington, DC: Brookings.

Petrocik, J. 1981. *Party Coalitions: Realignments and the Decline of the New Deal Party System*. Chicago: University of Chicago Press.

Pfeffer, Jeffery. 1997. *New Directions for Organization Theory: Problems and Prospects*. New York: Oxford University Press.

Pierson, Paul. 1996. "The Path to European Integration – A Historical Institutionalist Analysis." *Comparative Political Studies* 29(2): 123–63.

  2004. *Politics in Time*. Princeton, NJ: Princeton University Press.

Pius XI. 1931. *Quadragesimo Anno*. Delivered May 15. Available at: http://www.vatican.va/holy_father/pius_xi/encyclicals/documents/hf_p-xi_enc_19310515_quadragesimo-anno_en.html

Pollard, John F. 2005. *Money and the Rise of the Modern Papacy: Financing the Vatican, 1850–1950*. Cambridge: Cambridge University Press.

Polsby, Nelson. 1968. "The Institutionalization of the U.S. House of Representatives." *American Political Science Review.* 62(1): 144–68.

1980. *Community Power and Political Theory.* 2nd ed. New Haven, CT: Yale University Press.

Posner, Eric and Adrian Vermeule. 2011. *The Executive Unbound.* New York: Oxford University Press.

Potter, David and Don Fehrenbacher. 1976. *The Impending Crisis, 1848–1861.* New York: HarperCollins.

Pound, Arthur. 1934. *Turning the Wheel: The Story of General Motors through Twenty-Five Years, 1908–1933.* Garden City, NY: Doubleday, Doran.

Qian, Yingyi and Barry Weingast. 1997. "Federalism as a Commitment to Preserving Market Incentives." *Journal of Economic Perspectives* 11(4): 83–92.

Rakove, Jack. 1997. *Original Meanings.* New York: Knopf.

Ratner, Sidney. 1942. *American Taxation: Its History as a Social Force in Democracy.* New York: W. W. Norton & Co.

Rauch, Basil. 1963. *History of the New Deal, 1933–1938.* New York: Capricorn Books.

Rector, Chad. 2009. *Federations: The Political Dynamics of Cooperation.* Ithaca, NY: Cornell University Press.

Reese, Thomas. 1989. *Archbishop.* New York: Harper and Row.

Reese, Thomas, S. J. 1996. *Inside the Vatican: The Politics and Organization of the Catholic Church.* Cambridge, MA: Harvard University Press.

Remini, Robert. 1988. *The Life of Andrew Jackson.* New York: Harper and Row.

Republican Party of the United States. *1956 Party Platform.*

Rhode Island Manual. Various editions starting in 1889. Providence, RI: E. L. Freeman.

Richter, Daniel K. 1992. *The Ordeal of the Longhouse: The People of the Iroquois League in the Era of European Colonization.* Chapel Hill: University of North Carolina Press.

Riker, William. 1964. *Federalism.* Boston, MA: Little and Brown.

1980. "Implications from the Disequilibrium of Majority Rule for the Study of Institutions." *American Political Science Review.* 74: 432–46.

Riker, William H. 1987. *The Development of American Federalism.* Boston, MA: Kluwer Academic Publishers.

Robbins, Stephen P. 1990. *Organization Theory: Structure, Design and Applications.* Englewood Cliffs, NJ: Prentice-Hall.

Rodden, Jonathan. 2004. "Comparative Federalism and Decentralization: On Meaning and Measurement." *Comparative Politics.* July: 481–500.

2006. *Hamilton's Paradox: The Promise and Peril of Fiscal Federalism.* New York: Cambridge Press.

Roland, Gerard and Y. Qian. 1998. "Federalism and the Soft Budget Constraint." *American Economic Review* 88(5): 1143–62.

Root, Elihu. 1910. Letter to the Editor of the *New York Times.* March 1.

Rosen, Frederick. 1992. *The Great Depression and the New Deal.* Jefferson, NC: McFarland & Co.

Rosenstone, Steven J., Edward H. Lazarus, and Roy L. Behr. 1994. *Third Parties in America: Citizen Response to Major Party Failure.* Princeton, NJ: Princeton University Press.

Rousseau, Jean-Jacques. [1762] 1978. *On the Social Contract.* New York: St. Martin's.

Rubin, Edward and Malcolm Feeley. 1994. "Federalism: Some Notes on a National Neurosis." *UCLA Law Review* 41: 903–52.

Rubinstein, Saul and Thomas Kochan. 2001. *Learning from Saturn*. Ithaca, NY: Cornell University Press.

Russell, Peter, Rainer Knopff, and Ted Morton. 1989. *Federalism and the Charter*. Ottawa: Carleton University Press.

Safire, William, 2000. "Federalism: The Political Word that Means Its Opposite." *New York Times Magazine*. January 30, p. 20.

Samuels, David. 2002. "Presidentialized Parties: The Separation of Powers and Party Organization and Behavior." *Comparative Political Studies* 35: 461–83.

Samuels, David and Matthew Shugart. 2010. *Parties, Presidents, and Prime Ministers: How Separation of Powers Affects Party Organization and Behavior*. New York: Cambridge University Press.

Sawer, Geoffrey. 1969. *Modern Federalism*. London: C. A. Watts & Co. Ltd.

Scharfstein, David. 1988. "The Disciplinary Role of Takeovers." *Review of Economic Studies* 55: 185–99.

Scharpf, Fritz. 1999. *Governing in Europe*. Oxford: Oxford University Press.

Schattschneider, E. E. [1960] 1975. *The Semisovereign People*. Hinsdale, IL: Dryden Press.

Scheiber, Harry. 1980. "Federalism and Legal Process." *Law & Society Review* 14: 663–722.

    1989. "Constitutional Structure and the Protection of Rights: Federalism and the Separation of Powers." In *Power Divided: Essays in the History and Practice of Federalism*, eds. Harry Scheiber and Malcolm Feeley. Berkeley, CA: Institute for Governmental Studies.

Schelling, Thomas. 1978. *Micromotives and Macrobehavior*. New York: Norton

Schlesinger, Joseph. 1991. *Political Parties and the Winning of Office*. Ann Arbor: University of Michigan Press.

Schmidt, Susanne. 2000. "Only an Agenda Setter? The European Commission's Power over the Council of Ministers." *European Union Politics* 1(1): 37–61.

Schwartz, Arthur R. and Michele M. Hoyman. 1984 "The Changing of the Guard: The New American Labor Leader." *Annals of the American Academy of Political and Social Science* 1(473): 64–75.

Seabright, Paul. 1996. "Accountability and Decentralization in Government: An Incomplete Contracts Model." *European Economic Review* 40:1161–89.

Searle, G. W. 1974. *The Counter Reformation*. London: University of London Press.

Sewell, William H. Jr. 1996. "Three Temporalities: Toward an 'Eventful' Sociology." In *The Historical Turn in the Human Sciences*, ed. Terrence J. McDonald. Ann Arbor: University of Michigan Press.

    Jr. 2005. *Logics of History: Social Theory and Social Transformation*. Chicago: University of Chicago Press.

Shafer, Byron and Anthony Badger, eds. 2001. *Contesting Democracy: Substance and Structure in American Political History, 1775–2000*. Lawrence: University Press of Kansas.

Shafritz, Jay M. and J. Steven Ott. 2001. *Classics of Organization Theory*. Orlando, FL: Harcourt Publishers.

Shapiro, David. 1995. *Federalism: A Dialogue*. Evanston, IL: Northwestern University Press.

Sheehan, Robert. 1958. "G. M.'s Remodeled Management." *Fortune*. November.

Shefter, Martin. 1994. *Political Parties and the State: The American Historical Experience*. Princeton, NJ: Princeton University Press.

Shipan. Charles and Craig Volden. 2006. "Bottom-up Federalism: The Diffusion of Antismoking Policies from U.S. Cities to States." *American Journal of Political Science* 50(4): 825–43.

2008. "The Mechanisms of Policy Diffusion." *American Journal of Political Science* 52(4): 840–57.

Shugart, Matthew and John Carey. 1992. *Presidents and Assemblies: Constitutional Design and Electoral Dynamics*. New York: Cambridge University Press.

Siedentop, Larry. 2001. *Democracy in Europe*. New York: Columbia University Press.

Simon, Herbert. 1960. *The New Science of Management Decision-Making*. New York: Harper.

Skocpol, Theda. 1992. *Protecting Soldiers and Mothers*. Cambridge, MA: Harvard University Press.

1995. *Social Policy in the United States: Future Possibilities in Historical Perspective*. Princeton, NJ: Princeton University Press.

Skocpol, Theda, Marshall Ganz, and Ziad Munson. 2000. "A Nation of Organizations." *The American Political Science Review* 94(3): 527–46.

Skowronek, Stephen. 1982. *Building a New American State: The Expansion of National Administrative Capacities*. New York: Cambridge University Press.

1997. *Politics Presidents Make*. Cambridge, MA: Harvard University Press.

Sloan, Alfred. 1964. *My Years with General Motors*. New York: Doubleday.

Smiley, Donald V. 1988. "Public Sector Politics, Modernization and Federalism: The Canadian and American Experiences." In *Canadian Federalism: From Crisis to Constitution*, eds. Harold Waller, Filippo Sabetti, and Daniel Elazar. Lanham, MD: University Press of America.

Smith, Graham. 1995. "Mapping the Federal Condition: Ideology, Political Practice and Social Justice." In *Federalism: The Multiethnic Challenge*, ed. Graham Smith. London and New York: Longman Group Limited.

Spruyt, H. 1994. *The Sovereign State and Its Competitors*. Princeton, NJ: Princeton University Press.

Stanley, Robert. 1993. *Dimensions of Law in the Service of Order: Origins of the Federal Income Tax*. New York: Oxford University Press.

Steinfels, Peter. 2003. *A People Adrift: The Crisis of the Roman Catholic Church in America*. New York: Simon & Schuster.

Stepan, A. 1999. "Federalism and Democracy: Beyond the U.S. Model." *Journal of Democracy* 10(4): 19–34.

Stepan, Alfred. 2001. "A New Comparative Politics of Federalism." In *Arguing Comparative Politics, ed*. Alfred Stepan. New York: Oxford University Press.

Stiglitz, Joseph E. and Raaj K. Sah. 1991. "The Quality of Managers in Centralized vs. Decentralized Organizations." *Quarterly Journal of Economics* 106(1): 289–95.

Stone-Sweet, Alex and W. Sandholtz. 1997. "European Integration and Supranational Governance." *Journal of European Public Policy* 4(3): 297–317.

Storey. R. 1959. "Diocesan Administration in the Fifteenth Century." In *Borthwick Papers 1959–62*. London: St. Anthony's Press, 16: 3–26.

Strumpf, Koleman and Felix Oberholzer-Gee. 2002. "Endogenous Policy Decentralization: Testing the Central Tenet of Economic Federalism." *Journal of Political Economy* 110: 1–36.

Sundquist, James. 1973. *Dynamics of The Party System: Alignment and Realignment of Political Parties in the United States*. Washington, DC: The Brookings Institution.

   1983. *Dynamics of the Party System: Alignment and Realignment of Political Parties in the United States*, rev. ed. Washington, DC: The Brookings Institution.

Swindler, Leonard. 1996. *Toward a Catholic Constitution*. New York: Crossroad Publishing.

Sylla, Richard. 2000. "Experimental Federalism: The Economics of American Government, 1789–1914." In *The Cambridge Economic History of the United States: Volume II The Long Nineteenth Century*, eds. Stanley L. Engerman and Robert E Gallman. New York: Cambridge University Press.

Taylor, Alex, Andrew Erdman, Justin Martin, and Tricia Welsh. 1992. "U.S. Cars Come Back." *Fortune*, November 16.

Teaford, Jon C. 2002. The *Rise of the States: Evolution of American State Government*. Baltimore, MD: Johns Hopkins University Press.

Thelen, Kathleen. 2004. *How Institutions Evolve: The Political Economy of Skills in Germany, Britain, the United States, and Japan*. New York: Cambridge University Press.

Thatcher, Margaret. 1993. *The Downing Street Years*. New York: HarperCollins.

Tierney, Brian. 1955. *Foundations of the Conciliar Theory*. Cambridge: Cambridge University Press.

Tillman, Erik. 2012. "Support for the Euro, Political Knowledge, and Voting Behavior in the 2001 and 2005 UK General Elections." *European Union Politics* 13: 367–89.

Tilly, Charles. 1990. *Coercion, Capital, and European States, AD 990–1990*. Cambridge, MA: Blackwell.

Tobin, Greg. 2003. *Selecting the Pope*. New York: Sterling.

Tommasi, Mariano. 2006. "Federalism in Argentina and the Reforms of the 1990s." In *Federalism and Economic Reform: International Perspectives*, eds. T.N. Srinivasan and Jessica Wallak. Cambridge: Cambridge University Press.

Tooker, Elisabeth, ed. 2001. *An Iroquois Sourcebook*. Vol 1. New York: Garland Publishing.

Triesman, Daniel. 1999. "Political Decentralization and Economic Reform: A Game Theoretic Analysis." *American Journal of Political Science* 43(2): 488–517.

   2006. "Explaining Fiscal Decentralization: Geography, Colonial History, Economic Development, and Political Institutions." *Journal of Commonwealth and Comparative Politics* 44(3): 289–325.

   2007. *The Architecture of Government: Rethinking Political Decentralization*. New York: Cambridge University Press.

Tsebelis, George. 2002. *Veto Players*. Princeton, NJ: Princeton University Press.

Tsebelis, George and Geoffrey Garrett. 2001. "The Institutional Foundations of Intergovernmentalism and Supranationalism in the European Union." *International Organization* 55: 357–90.

Tsebelis, George and Jeanette Money. 1997. *Bicameralism*. Cambridge: Cambridge University Press.

Tullock, Gordon. 1994. *The New Federalist*. Vancouver: Fraser Institute.

United States Department of Labor. 1965. *Union Constitutions and the Elections of Local Union Officers*. Washington, DC: U.S. Department of Labor.

United States Senate. 1913. "*The Income Tax: Opinions of Hon. John K. Shields, Hon. Cordell Hull, and Thurlow Gordon.*" Document 171, 63rd Congress, United States Senate. August 26.

Van Kersberen, K. and B. Verbeek. 2004. "Subsidiarity as a Principle of Governance in the European Union." *Comparative European Politics* 2(2): 142.

   2007. "The Politics of International Norms: Subsidiarity and the Imperfect Competence Regime of the European Union." *European Journal of International Relations* 13(2): 217–38.

Verdun, Amy. 2000. *European Responses to Globalization and Financial Market Integration*. London: Macmillan.

Vietor, Richard. H. K. 2000. "Government Regulation of Business." *In The Cambridge Economic History of the United States: Volume III The Twentieth Century*, eds. Stanley L. Engerman and Robert E Gallman. New York: Cambridge University Press.

Votewatch.eu. 2012. Publicly available European Parliament and European Council of Minister roll calls. Available at: http://www.votewatch.eu/

Wagner, A. 1958. "Three Extracts on Public Finance." In *Classics in the Theory of Public Finance*, eds. R. A. Musgrave and A. P. Peacock. London: MacMillan.

Wallace, Helen and William Wallace. 2000. *Policy-Making in the European Union*. Oxford: Oxford University Press.

Wallis, John. 1991. "The Political Economy of New Deal Fiscal Federalism." *Economic Inquiry* 29 (July): 510–24.

Waltman, Jerold. 1985. *Political Origins of the U.S. Income Tax*. Jackson: University Press of Mississippi.

Ware, Alan. 1987. *Citizens, Parties and the State*. Oxford: Polity Press.

   1996. *Political Parties and Party Systems*. New York: Oxford University Press.

Wattenberg, M. P. 1991. *The Rise of Candidate-Centered Politics*. Cambridge, MA: Harvard University Press.

Weingast, Barry. 1995. "The Economic Role of Political Institutions: Market-Preserving Federalism and Economic Growth. " *Journal of Law, Economics, and Organization* 11: 1–31.

   1998. "Political Stability and Civil War." In *Analytical Narratives*, eds. Robert Bates, Avner Greif, Margaret Levi, Jean-Laurent Rosenthal, and Barry Weingast, eds. Princeton, NJ: Princeton University Press.

Weisman, Steven. 2002. *The Great Tax Wars: Lincoln to Wilson*. New York : Simon & Schuster.

Wendt, Alex. 1999. *Social Theory of International Politics*. New York: Cambridge University Press.

Wheare, K. C. 1964. *Federal Government*. 4th ed. New York: Oxford University Press.

Whitaker, R. 1992. *A Sovereign Idea: Essays on Canada as a Democratic Community*. Montreal and Kingston: McGill-Queen's University Press.

White, G. Edward. 2000. *The Constitution and the New Deal*. Cambridge, MA: Harvard University Press.

Whitman, Marina. 1999. *New World, New Rules*. Boston, MA: Harvard Business School Press.

Wibbels, Erik. 2005a. "Decentralized Governance, Constitution Formation, and Redistribution." *Constitutional Political Economy* 16: 161–88.

2005b. *Federalism and the Market*. New York: Cambridge University Press.

2006. "Madison in Baghdad? Decentralization and Federalism in Comparative Politics." *Annual Review of Political Science* 9: 165–88.

Wilbourn, Beth. 1996. "Suffer the Children: Catholic Church Liability for the Sexual Abuse Acts of Priests." *The Review of Litigation* 15: 251.

Wilde, Melissa. 2007. *Vatican II: A Sociological Analysis of Religious Change*. Princeton, NJ: Princeton University Press.

Williamson, Oliver. 1985. *The Economic Institutions of Capitalism*. New York: Free Press.

Williamson, Richard. 1990. *Reagan's Federalism: His Efforts to Decentralize Government*. Lanham, MD: University Press of America.

Witte, John. 1985. *The Politics and Development of the Federal Income Tax*. Madison: University of Wisconsin Press.

Wittman, Donald. 1991. "Nations and States – Mergers and Acquisitions – Dissolutions and Divorce." *American Economic Review* 81(2): 126–29.

Wood, Gordon. 1969. *Creation of the American Republic*. Chapel Hill: University of North Carolina Press.

Yanik, Anthony. 2009. *Maxwell Motor and the Making of the Chrysler Corporation*. Detroit, MI: Wayne State University Press.

Zald, Mayer, ed. 1970. *Power in Organizations*. Nashville, TN: Vanderbilt University Press.

Zernov, Nicolas. 1961. *Eastern Christendom*. London: Weidenfeld and Nicolson.

Ziblatt, Daniel. 2006. *Structuring the State: The Formation of Germany and Italy and the Puzzle of Federalism*. Princeton, NJ: Princeton University Press.

Zieger, Robert H. and Gilbert J. Gall. 2002. *American Workers, American Unions: The Twentieth Century*. Baltimore: The Johns Hopkins University Press.

Index

Karen E. Ferree, *Framing the Race in South Africa: The Political Origins of Racial Census Elections*

M. Steven Fish, *Democracy Derailed in Russia: The Failure of Open Politics*

Robert F. Franzese, *Macroeconomic Policies of Developed Democracies*

Roberto Franzosi, *The Puzzle of Strikes: Class and State Strategies in Postwar Italy*

Timothy Frye, *Building States and Markets after Communism: The Perils of Polarized Democracy*

Geoffrey Garrett, *Partisan Politics in the Global Economy*

Scott Gehlbach, *Representation through Taxation: Revenue, Politics, and Development in Postcommunist States*

Jane R. Gingrich, *Making Markets in the Welfare State: The Politics of Varying Market Reforms*

Miriam Golden, *Heroic Defeats: The Politics of Job Loss*

Jeff Goodwin, *No Other Way Out: States and Revolutionary Movements*

Merilee Serrill Grindle, *Changing the State*

Anna Grzymala-Busse, *Rebuilding Leviathan: Party Competition and State Exploitation in Post-Communist Democracies*

Anna Grzymala-Busse, *Redeeming the Communist Past: The Regeneration of Communist Parties in East Central Europe*

Frances Hagopian, *Traditional Politics and Regime Change in Brazil*

Henry E. Hale, *The Foundations of Ethnic Politics: Separatism of States and Nations in Eurasia and the World*

Mark Hallerberg, Rolf Ranier Strauch, and Jürgen von Hagen, *Fiscal Governance in Europe*

Stephen E. Hanson, *Post-Imperial Democracies: Ideology and Party Formation in Third Republic France, Weimar Germany, and Post-Soviet Russia*

Silja Häusermann, *The Politics of Welfare State Reform in Continental Europe: Modernization in Hard Times*

Gretchen Helmke, *Courts Under Constraints: Judges, Generals, and Presidents in Argentina*

Yoshiko Herrera, *Imagined Economies: The Sources of Russian Regionalism*

J. Rogers Hollingsworth and Robert Boyer, eds., *Contemporary Capitalism: The Embeddedness of Institutions*

John D. Huber and Charles R. Shipan, *Deliberate Discretion? The Institutional Foundations of Bureaucratic Autonomy*

Ellen Immergut, *Health Politics: Interests and Institutions in Western Europe*

Torben Iversen, *Capitalism, Democracy, and Welfare*

Torben Iversen, *Contested Economic Institutions*

Torben Iversen, Jonas Pontussen, and David Soskice, eds., *Unions, Employers, and Central Banks: Macroeconomic Coordination and Institutional Change in Social Market Economies*

Thomas Janoski and Alexander M. Hicks, eds., *The Comparative Political Economy of the Welfare State*

Joseph Jupille, *Procedural Politics: Issues, Influence, and Institutional Choice in the European Union*

Stathis Kalyvas, *The Logic of Violence in Civil War*

David C. Kang, *Crony Capitalism: Corruption and Capitalism in South Korea and the Philippines*

Junko Kato, *Regressive Taxation and the Welfare State*

Orit Kedar, *Voting for Policy, Not Parties: How Voters Compensate for Power Sharing*

Robert O. Keohane and Helen B. Milner, eds., *Internationalization and Domestic Politics*

Herbert Kitschelt, *The Transformation of European Social Democracy*

Herbert Kitschelt, Kirk A. Hawkins, Juan Pablo Luna, Guillermo Rosas, and Elizabeth J. Zechmeister, *Latin American Party Systems*

Herbert Kitschelt, Peter Lange, Gary Marks, and John D. Stephens, eds., *Continuity and Change in Contemporary Capitalism*

Herbert Kitschelt, Zdenka Mansfeldova, Radek Markowski, and Gabor Toka, *Post-Communist Party Systems*

David Knoke, Franz Urban Pappi, Jeffrey Broadbent, and Yutaka Tsujinaka, eds., *Comparing Policy Networks*

Allan Kornberg and Harold D. Clarke, *Citizens and Community: Political Support in a Representative Democracy*

Amie Kreppel, *The European Parliament and the Supranational Party System*

David D. Laitin, *Language Repertoires and State Construction in Africa*

Fabrice E. Lehoucq and Ivan Molina, *Stuffing the Ballot Box: Fraud, Electoral Reform, and Democratization in Costa Rica*

Mark Irving Lichbach and Alan S. Zuckerman, eds., *Comparative Politics: Rationality, Culture, and Structure, 2nd Edition*

Evan Lieberman, *Race and Regionalism in the Politics of Taxation in Brazil and South Africa*

Pauline Jones Luong, *Institutional Change and Political Continuity in Post-Soviet Central Asia*

Pauline Jones Luong and Erika Weinthal, *Oil Is Not a Curse: Ownership Structure and Institutions in Soviet Successor States*

Julia Lynch, *Age in the Welfare State: The Origins of Social Spending on Pensioners, Workers, and Children*

Doug McAdam, John McCarthy, and Mayer Zald, eds., *Comparative Perspectives on Social Movements*

Lauren M. MacLean, *Informal Institutions and Citizenship in Rural Africa: Risk and Reciprocity in Ghana and Côte d'Ivoire*

Beatriz Magaloni, *Voting for Autocracy: Hegemonic Party Survival and Its Demise in Mexico*

James Mahoney, *Colonialism and Postcolonial Development: Spanish America in Comparative Perspective*

James Mahoney and Dietrich Rueschemeyer, eds., *Historical Analysis and the Social Sciences*

Scott Mainwaring and Matthew Soberg Shugart, eds., *Presidentialism and Democracy in Latin America*

Isabela Mares, *The Politics of Social Risk: Business and Welfare State Development*